OPENI

DUNCAN   C.BELL   MOTHELL   McCALL   DRAKE   SWEATT   WILKINSON   DR.SMITH SPEDDEN   POMPEZ

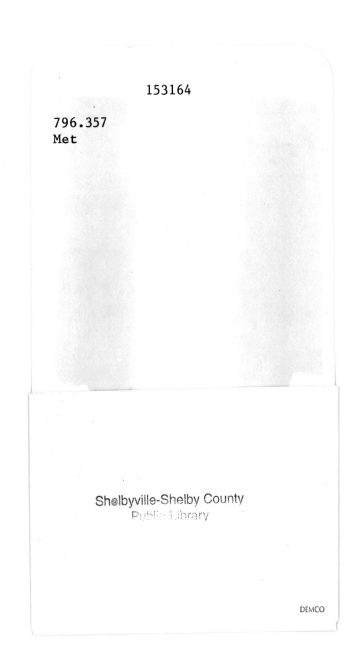

A Game
for All Races

A Game
for All Races

Henry Metcalfe

MetroBooks

MetroBooks

An Imprint of Friedman/Fairfax Publishers

Library of Congress Cataloging-in-Publication data

Metcalfe, Henry
    A game for all races / Henry Metcalfe.
        p.   cm.
    Includes bibliographical references (p.) and index.
    ISBN 1-56799-419-9
    1. Negro leagues—History. 2. Baseball—United
States—History. 3. Discrimination in sports—United
States. I. Title.
    GV863.A1M48 1999
    796.357′1089′96073—dc21   99-29245
                                                    CIP

Editor: Nathaniel Marunas
Art Director: Kevin Ullrich
Designer: Charles Donahue
Photography Editors: Jennifer Bove, Chris Toliver
Production Manager: Camille Lee

Color separations by Bright Arts Graphics
Printed in China by Leefung-Asco Printers Ltd.

1 3 5 7 9 10 8 6 4 2

For bulk purchases and special sales, please contact:
Friedman/Fairfax Publishers
Attention: Sales Department
15 West 26th Street
New York, NY 10010
212/685-6610 FAX 212/685-1307

Visit our website:
www.metrobooks.com

Acknowledgments

This book would never have come to be without the hard work of the good people at the Michael Friedman Publishing Group—thank you for never giving up on the project. Likewise, professional baseball wouldn't be the dynamic, riveting, colorful game it is today had it not been for the courage and determination of the Negro league players and personnel—all sports fans are eternally indebted to these heroes of an earlier age.

PAGE 2: *The Atlanta Black Crackers were one of the teams of the Negro Southern League, one of several leagues formed in the wake of Rube Foster's creation of the Negro National League in 1920.*

PAGES 6–7: *New York Giants catcher Roy Campanella watches as a ball goes into the stands during the 1955 World Series. The future Hall of Famer got his training in the Negro leagues playing for the Baltimore Elite Giants from 1938 to 1945 (except for a stint in Mexico during 1943).*

CONTENTS

A Game for All Races

From 1887 to 1946, an unofficial but nonetheless effective "gentlemen's agreement" between the owners of white-run professional baseball teams excluded African-Americans from both the minor and major leagues. In the wake of this segregationist policy, black ballplayers and entrepreneurs organized their own teams, and soon a nationwide baseball subculture of black professionals evolved.

In 1920, Andrew "Rube" Foster organized the Negro National League (NNL). Foster was already the biggest celebrity in "blackball": his spectacular pitching performances in the 1903 and 1904 Colored World Series made him a legend throughout black America, and since 1910 he had owned and managed the Chicago American Giants, the nation's most prestigious black professional team. Foster's NNL was composed of the top black franchises in the Midwest and became the first successful black major league.

Three years later, a second black major league, the Eastern Colored League (ECL), began play. There were also two black minor leagues (in the deep South and Texas), and countless all-black semipro and industrial teams flourished throughout the land. Organized black baseball flourished in

* * * *

OPPOSITE: *First baseman John Jordan "Buck" O'Neil as seen sometime in the 1940s playing for the Kansas City Monarchs. O'Neil's Negro league career began in 1937 with the Memphis Red Sox, but from 1938 until 1950 he was a Monarch (except for two years, 1944 and 1945, spent with the U.S. Navy), managing the team from 1948 to 1950.* **ABOVE:** *The first major league team to sign African-Americans was the Brooklyn Dodgers, and the courage of the team's management had netted them an impressive sampling of Negro league talent by 1951, including (from left) second baseman Jackie Robinson, catcher Roy Campanella, and pitchers Dan Bankhead and Don Newcombe.*

9

the early to mid-twenties, survived the Great Depression years, and rebounded to boom in the early to mid-forties. However, after Jackie Robinson broke the color barrier, paving the way to the majors for other black stars, the Negro leagues fell into rapid decline as black fans across the country turned their attention to the white-run major leagues.

The story of black baseball in segregated America has two equally compelling dimensions—on the field and off. The game of baseball as played by black professionals in the first half of the century was fast and exciting, with a greater emphasis on speed, both afoot and off the mound, than in "white-ball." Just like major league baseball, the history of black professional baseball is rife with legendary pitching duels, dramatic showdowns between top teams, and unbelievable feats of athleticism.

Of special note were the games that pitted the top black teams against major league players. Early in the century, the elite black teams were occasionally granted an exhibition showdown against an actual major league team; but in 1923, Baseball Commissioner Keenesaw Mountain Landis, a renowned racist, ruled that major league teams could no longer appear in unsanctioned exhibition matches (thus ending what had become an increasingly embarrassing situation for the major leagues, as the black teams had started to win the majority of the contests). After Landis's ruling, Negro leaguers could no longer play against the Cleveland Indians, but they could (and did) face Indian ace Bob Feller in off-season exhibition games between black teams and barnstorming major league "all-star" teams. Existing records show that black teams won approximately sixty-five percent of the showdowns with teams composed of major league talent.

Indeed, in every era the top black teams were loaded with brilliant players who collectively excelled at every aspect of the game: there were sluggers, line drive hitters, slap hitters, base stealers, great infielders, fleet outfielders, outfielders with

cannons for arms, power pitchers, finesse pitchers, and, a specialty of the times, spitballers. The very best Negro leaguers—such as shortstop John Henry "Pop" Lloyd, pitching ace "Smokey" Joe Williams, outfielder Oscar Charleston, slugging catcher Josh Gibson, and legendary hurler Leroy "Satchel" Paige—rightfully belong in the pantheon of baseball immortals alongside their white contemporaries Wagner, Mathewson, Ruth, Gehrig, and Grove.

Away from the diamond, the history of black baseball tells a tale of how successive generations of talented young men learned to survive, and prosper, in a racist society. Like much of black America, the players spoke and behaved very differently when among themselves than they did when interacting with white people. Together they shared a language that in no way compromised their dignity; while

among whites, even the proudest black players understood it was necessary to watch what was said in order to avoid conflict, since the society's unjust rules were stacked against blacks. Veteran players provided guidance for the "youngbloods" and taught them to conduct themselves in a manner appropriate for "representatives of the race." Failure to behave appropriately in the eyes of one's peers could prove as damaging to a blackball player's career as failure to perform on the field. Not surprisingly, teammates formed deep bonds as they crisscrossed the country on seemingly interminable road trips throughout the long season. But despite the brutal travel schedule and the hostile environment of white America, most Negro leaguers managed to have the time of their lives.

Make no mistake about it: black professional baseball was more than a popular spectator sport. It was a project intended to empower an oppressed people and was recognized as such. After all, one question dominated African-American discourse during the one hundred years between the end of slavery and the triumph of the civil rights movement: how can racial equality be achieved in the United States? By the 1890s, the brutal reality of Jim Crow convinced most African-Americans that direct attacks on white racism were more dangerous than fruitful. Thus, black America pursued more subtle, long-term strategies to combat its subjugation. Booker T. Washington called on blacks to build strong institutions that actively benefited the race and also showed white America that black people merited treatment as equals. Rube Foster heeded the call, saying he wanted to "do something concrete for the loyalty of the race." His Negro leagues fit Washington's prescription to a T.

From the early 1920s through the mid-1940s, the Negro leagues represented one of the largest black-owned and black-operated industries in America. Yet all the while, the leagues' owners, players, and fans overwhelmingly supported (and petitioned for) the integration of professional baseball. In baseball-crazed America, no single issue generated more debate about racial integration than whether contemporary black stars belonged in the majors. It was a question that could not have been raised without the existence of black professional circuits.

Thus, the Negro leagues' greatest triumph came when Jackie Robinson, a former Negro American League shortstop, not only broke the national pastime's color barrier but won Rookie of the Year honors and led his team to the World Series in 1947. Robinson's brilliant play and his stoic courage in the face of tremendous adversity dealt a major blow to American racism. In a bittersweet irony, the Negro leagues, which had laid the groundwork for Robinson's breakthrough, would soon fade away, destroyed by having achieved their goal: integrated baseball.

But the fact that the Negro Leagues were designed, in effect, to help bring about the conditions of their demise only adds to their mystique. Black professional baseball had been building momentum, gaining popularity right up until the major leagues were integrated. Soon thereafter,

✳ ✳ ✳ ✳

OPPOSITE: *Perhaps the most famous of all the Negro league players was pitcher Leroy Robert "Satchel" Paige, whose longevity, awesome athletic skills, and showmanship made him a legend. His importance in the history of the Negro leagues is immeasurable.* **RIGHT:** *After Paige, the most famous Negro leaguer was slugger Josh Gibson, whose prowess with the bat was the stuff of legend; it was said that he once hit a ball so high in one game that it didn't return to earth until the following day during another game. Here he is tagged out at home by Ted "Double Duty" Radcliffe during the annual East-West All-Star Game.*

blackball was gone, existing only on the margins of history, rumored to have produced some of the greatest baseball ever played, the telling of its history a project for archivists.

Beginning with Robert Peterson's groundbreaking *Only the Ball was White* (1971), the researchers have been busy unearthing the details of Negro league baseball. And as this swell of literature has increased, many baseball fans have encountered the fascinating history of the Negro leagues for the first time. It's safe to say that today more white fans know more about the Negro leagues than when the leagues existed. Most white Americans, even diehard baseball fans, were completely oblivious to Negro league baseball during its heyday, even though it was home to some of the best baseball in the world and was among the most prominent institutions in black America.

The world of black professional baseball offers a unique window on America in the era of institutionalized racial segregation. After all, the Negro leagues were an attempt to mirror major league baseball, which was one of the most—if not *the* most—popular spectacles of white culture. Thus, every facet of the Negro league experience—from the players' lives on the road, to the economics of running a team, to the fans' relationship to the game, and so on—begs comparison with its parallel in the white major leagues, a process that reveals

with tremendous clarity the vast, often unjust differences between white and black America at the time. There is, however, one shared constant—the game of baseball itself, which is the same for all players, regardless of race.

A Game For All Races is structured chronologically, beginning with the early history of the Negro leagues and concluding with the signing of Jackie Robinson to a major league contract with the Brooklyn Dodgers in 1947. The hope is that the photographs will fill in the gaps—and there are many, for a variety of reasons, not the least of which is limited space—in the history. Finally, the period of integration is addressed because it represents the succesful conclusion of the project set in motion by the formation of the Negro leagues. In the opinion of countless lovers of the game (this writer included), many of the Negro league stars discussed in the following brief essays were as great as any who ever played the game of baseball.

POST–CIVIL WAR COLORED BASEBALL

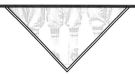

If, as has been claimed, the Negro leagues represent the last frontier of baseball research, then it would follow that the early years of black baseball (during the second half of the nineteenth century) would be virtually uncharted territory. Little is known about how baseball initially took root in the black community other than that black America was swept up in the "baseball mania" that spread across the nation following the Civil War. Nor does much data exist about the all-black teams and leagues (for boys and for men) that existed in the black community. But it is evident that such teams and leagues did flourish on the local level, and that they provided fertile ground for the development of top-flight ballplayers. For in the 1880s, a generation of black ballplayers emerged that included numerous stars who were easily on par with white major leaguers. And when, by 1887, these black players began to dominate the upper rungs of the minor leagues, it proved so threatening to the world of organized white baseball

✻ ✻ ✻ ✻

OPPOSITE: *Utilityman Josh Johnson, whose short career in the Negro leagues included stints with the Cincinnati Tigers, Homestead Grays, and New York Black Yankees.* **ABOVE:** *The long career of Bud Fowler (born John Jackson) included time with numerous teams, including this integrated Keokuk squad of 1885. The early 1880s saw many integrated minor league teams such as this.*

that the team owners agreed (in a backroom, "gentlemanly" sort of way) not to hire any more black players, regardless of skill.

However, the history of professional black baseball is well documented from the mid-1880s on, thanks to Sol White's marvelous *History of Colored Base Ball*, published in 1907. White was a great second baseman who played on some of the best all-black pro teams of the 1890s, but who gained even greater renown as the player-manager of the dynastic Philadelphia Giants, blackball's greatest franchise during the first decade of the new century. White's *History* tells the story of the black professional teams that came to represent the pinnacle of black baseball following the "gentlemen's agreement." During this era there were only a few successful, independent black clubs at any one time; consequently, these squads were veritable all-star teams that consistently overwhelmed the amateur, semipro, and low minor league opponents against whom they earned their keep. The real excitement took place when two of these elite black teams met in a showdown, or when one of them squared off against major leaguers.

OPPOSITE: *The Oberlin, Ohio, varsity team included brothers Moses Fleetwood Walker (middle row, left) and Weldy Walker (back row, third from left). Moses was the first African-American to play for the major leagues.*

✳ ✳ ✳ ✳

These teams became a familiar feature of the black American landscape and carried blackball into the twentieth century with a full head of steam. But the defining feature of these teams—namely, that they were all-black—was an outgrowth of the sociopolitical context of late nineteenth-century America. To understand the world of Rube Foster, Satchel Paige, and Jackie Robinson, and the uphill struggle they fought for the racial integration of the national pastime, it is necessary to look at the legacy they inherited from their equally heroic nineteenth-century progenitors.

Of course, organized baseball's policy of segregation merely reflected the racism of American society. American history is in many ways a glorious story; the descendants of European settlers rapidly transformed a land with unparalleled natural resources into a great economic, military, and political power. But the tale is also a story of brutality and exploitation. Two grievous sins stand out from the rest: the white man's use of deception, warfare, and systematic genocide to force Native Americans off their land; and, of course, the terrible institution of chattel slavery that is the historical backdrop to this book and any subject that deals with American race relations. The European colonists solved their manpower shortage by enslaving West African men, women, and children who had been kidnaped by mercenaries and brought in chains to America, where they were sold to the highest bidder and forced to work for nothing, all the while under the constant threat of torture or death. The color of a person's skin betrayed (with very few exceptions) whether he or she was a citizen or mere property.

While the European-Americans' treatment of the Native Americans and the black slaves was motivated by economic self-interest and was the byproduct of prevailing social power relations, it was also informed by the belief, widely held among American whites, that Caucasian people were simply superior to the other races. This belief, whether cloaked in the rhetoric of Christianity or science, justified the brutal oppression of Native Americans and black people in the minds of most white Americans.

However, various regions of the newly settled continent evolved differently, and by the mid-nineteenth century, the United States of America was divided over the issue of slavery. While the northern states outlawed slavery at the time of the revolution, slave labor remained the backbone of the southern plantation economy. As the North began to evolve into a modern industrial society during the mid-nineteenth century, the southern economy remained unchanged, and the political interests of the two regions became so dissimilar that the southern states seceded from the Union. The Civil War ensued, and when the northern states won, slavery was outlawed throughout the whole country.

It was during the Civil War (in fact, because of the war), that baseball's popularity spread like wildfire across the country. The roots of the sport are not known for certain, but it is widely believed to be an ancestor of various bat and ball games from the British Isles, of which cricket is another modern descendant. Since people of British ancestry lived throughout the United States, variations of the game were actually played in all regions of the country before the war. Indeed, historians have documented that plantation slaves played "towne ball" (a common name for baseball-type games before the war) with makeshift equipment.

However, it was in the antebellum Northeast that baseball became so popular that top amateur teams from neighboring cities would compete on weekends in front of sizable audiences. In this era, most of the sport's players and enthusiasts were socially well-positioned young men; it was more of a gentleman's diversion than the hard-nosed competition it was destined to become. Records from the 1850s reveal that a few black players participated in these inter-town showdowns (there was a small "free" black population in the North) and that, on occasion, some rival white players would object to their presence. Nevertheless, when the National Association of Baseball Players (NABBP) was founded in 1858, black players were included on the roster of a few clubs, including some of the elite teams of the day.

Before the war, base, bat, and ball games were played in a number of different ways throughout America, varying by region. However, during the war, as the sport became a favorite form of recreation for troops across the land, the New York game's basic framework and rules became accepted as the standard guidelines for the game of baseball. The sport was still a far cry from modern baseball: the pitcher threw underhanded from forty-five feet (13.7m), a foul ball caught on one bounce was an out, it was four strikes before the batter was out, and games were decided not after nine innings but by which team was the first to tally twenty-one "aces" (runs). But many familiar parameters—nine players to a side, three outs per team per inning, the general dimensions of the diamond, and most of the regulations for advancing around the bases or registering an out—were established by this time. The national pastime was forming in the womb.

As peace settled in across the land, baseball teams sprang up in virtually every town. Most of these teams were all white even though black America was also swept up in the baseball craze. African-Americans quickly realized, after their initial euphoria over emancipation, that they still lived in a stringently racist society in which the vast majority of whites (even in the North) believed that the races should not intermingle freely because they

felt blacks were inferior to whites. It could be very dangerous for a black person to protest this order of things. In postbellum America, white-on-black violence went largely unpunished.

Against this backdrop, black baseball players began to form all-black teams, especially in the northeastern population centers, where sizable black communities were emerging. Only one year after the war, all-black clubs existed in Philadelphia and Harrisburg, Pennsylvania; Camden, New Jersey; Albany and Jamaica, New York; and Chicago, Illinois. A few times a year, these teams would travel to square off against one of the other all-black teams. These inter-city showdowns were huge events in black society. The games would be scheduled in advance, and the home team would cover the visiting team's expenses. Many of the players were from relatively well-to-do black families, since only the black "upper class" had the means to afford intercity transportation. Indeed, black Union Army officers, heroes in the African-American community, were well represented: Major Charles R. Douglass, son of the great orator Frederick Douglass, played for the Washington, D.C., Mutuals; and the top black team of the postwar years, the Philadelphia Pythians, was organized by former U.S. Army Major Octavius V. Catto.

An outspoken advocate of racial equality, Catto broached the race issue at the NABBP convention held in Philadelphia in 1867. The NABBP, which had its roots in the New York

City area, had grown to include more than two hundred teams from around the country and was the closest thing to a national umbrella organization for the young sport. Catto sent a liaison across town who eloquently petitioned the convention to grant the Pythians membership in the NABBP. Apparently, the issue was dealt with politely and Catto's messenger was treated with respect, but the end result was an official resolution that excluded "any club which may be composed of one or more colored persons." (But the NABBP had limited authority, and over the next two decades some talented black players landed jobs on predominantly white professional teams. Of course, these players were few in number and often encountered resistance.)

Nevertheless, a vital culture of all-black teams continued to flourish in the northern population centers. And Catto's Pythians were the undisputed champions of black baseball. The Pythians won all of their games in 1869, including a victory in the World's Colored Championship over the Uniques of Chicago. The Pythians even played a number of well-attended contests against all-white squads from around Philadelphia, which, according to the press accounts of the time, were great successes in terms of both fan interest and racial harmony.

Then tragedy struck. The Pythians' success had made Octavius Catto one of the preeminent figures in the Philadelphia black community, and the outspoken promoter soon became a leader in the struggle for black voting rights in the city. On October 10, 1871, a white man opposed to letting blacks vote approached Catto on the street. An argument ensued. Then, in clear view of many onlookers, the man pulled a gun and shot the thirty-one-year-old Catto to death. The man was detained by the police but was let go shortly thereafter.

In the wake of Catto's death, the Pythians lasted only one more season and the first era of intercity black baseball came to an abrupt end. Black baseball continued to exist in the major population centers, but black teams competed only on the local level until the mid-1880s.

Meanwhile, the year 1877 represented a significant turning point in the history of American race relations, as Congress passed, and President Ulysses S. Grant signed into law, the Compromise of 1877, ending the postwar period of Reconstruction and initiating a new, government-sanctioned era of segregation in the American South. "Reconstruction" had been the name given to the United States (i.e., northern) government's post-Civil War policies, which were intended to reintegrate the defeated Confederacy into the fabric of the national union. After the war, many Southern states had balked at outlawing slavery; when the federal government proved inflexible with regard to the ban, southerners tried to institute "black codes," which denied basic legal and economic rights to the former slaves. These were outlawed by Congress, which had granted African-Americans equal rights throughout the nation.

Perhaps the most intense political struggle in American history took place in Washington, D.C., over which policies to adopt in order to best reintegrate the South into the Union. The plan that was eventually adopted was sponsored by progressive Republicans (Lincoln's party), widely supported by blacks, and vehemently opposed by most southern whites. Although it's arguable whether any strategy could have worked given the almost total devastation of the South's prewar economic infrastructure, white southerners widely blamed Reconstruction and

* * * *

OPPOSITE: *Cap Anson, seen here circa 1880, was one of major league baseball's earliest stars, but his outstanding record with the Chicago White Stockings is marred by his history of racism, which may have led to the ban on African-Americans in major league baseball in the late 1880s.*

its perceived beneficiaries (blacks and Northern carpetbaggers) as the cause of the continued crisis in Dixie. The early 1870s saw the rise of the vigilante Ku Klux Klan, an organization that imposed a reign of terror on black southerners.

Still, Reconstruction was a period of relative hope for black America, hope that was dashed when the elections of 1876 made the supporters of Reconstruction a minority in Congress. Conservative whites reestablished political control in the South, and throughout the region drew up laws that segregated the races, and, for all intents and purposes, allowed for unequal treatment before the law. In that more than 90 percent of African-Americans still lived below the Mason-Dixon line, the passage and implementation of these Jim Crow laws, as they came to be known, represented more than just a step back; it snuffed out the slight glimmer of hope that black Americans could lead lives free of subjugation and fear.

Meanwhile, baseball was booming in America, and the game was evolving rapidly into its modern form. Nine-inning games and three strikes per batter were soon the standards of the sport, though it would take until 1893, when the pitcher's mound was moved back ten feet (3m)—to sixty feet, six inches (18.4m)—for the rules of baseball (give or take a few minor adjustments) to be set in place.

So many people proved willing to pay to watch the top white clubs compete in the years after the war that the players on these teams became professional, career baseball players. Thus, in 1870, the NABBP evolved into the National Association of Professional Baseball Players (NAPBBP). Black teams did not make a parallel jump to professionalism, no doubt due to the lack of necessary resources in the impoverished black communities. However, over the next decade and a half, a few of the top black players were recruited by all-white professional teams. By this time, the "gentlemen's agreement" of 1867 was either forgotten about, routinely

disregarded, or, perhaps, viewed as obsolete since it stemmed from before the advent of pro ball.

The first black professional player on record was John "Bud" Fowler, a pitcher and infielder from Cooperstown, New York (which would soon become mythologized—incorrectly—as the birthplace of baseball and thus be chosen as the site for the Baseball Hall of Fame in 1939). Fowler's first documented appearance was as a pitcher for the Chelsea, Massachusetts, professional team in 1878. Over the next decade, Fowler jumped around the minor leagues, evolving into an everyday player by the mid-1880s. *The Sporting Life*, a weekly publication from Philadelphia that featured coverage of professional baseball, made numerous references to Fowler as a top-flight player. Yet Fowler frequently changed teams, no doubt on account of racism. Though there was only one case, when he was playing for a team from Guelph, Ontario, in which Fowler was asked to leave a team explicitly because enough white players found it objectionable to play alongside him, Fowler kept losing his job to the next capable, if frequently inferior, white player who happened to come along.

Fowler may have been one of the best players of his day, but he never played on a major league team, a feat that was accomplished by two African-American brothers, Moses and Wedley Walker, in 1884. The distinction between the major and minor leagues came into existence with the founding of the National League in 1876. By 1884, there were two other major leagues, the American Association and the Union Association (which lasted only one year). Moses "Fleetwood" Walker had played on the school baseball team while at Oberlin College in Ohio in 1881. He then starred for the University of Michigan team in 1882 and 1883. During the 1883 season, he joined the minor league Toledo Blue Stockings. When the franchise joined the American Association for the 1884 season, Walker became the first black major leaguer. And when the Blue Stockings found themselves depleted due to injuries during the season, they signed up Moses' younger brother, Wedley, who had also played ball at Oberlin. Basically a fill-in, Wedley appeared in just five games, hitting .222. Moses, on the other hand, had a solid season, batting .263 in forty-two games.

Apparently, having a black man on the team did not cause any outcry among Toledo's players or fans. The only time the Walkers' presence led to racial tension was when the Blue Stockings traveled to the South. In Richmond, Baltimore, and Louisville the fans jeered Moses Walker, and he even received death threats. The young catcher returned to Toledo the following season, but he suffered a cracked rib in July and the club released him. No African-American would play in the majors again until Jackie Robinson took the field for the Brooklyn Dodgers on April 15, 1947.

Walker returned to minor leagues, where he joined a number of other black standouts including pitcher George Stovey (who won thirty-four games for Newark in 1887, an International League record that still stands), second baseman Frank Grant (who batted .340 for Buffalo in 1886, third best in the International League, and won the batting title with a .366 clip the next season), and Sol White (an infielder who batted .371 in the Ohio State League in 1887, but nowadays is best remembered as the author of *History of Colored Base Ball*).

While there were no black players in the majors in 1887, no fewer than twelve African-Americans populated the minors, and seven of these men played in the prestigious International League, which was only one rung below the majors. The presence of so many black players was cause for considerable consternation in the white baseball community. On June 1, the *Sporting News* begged the question: "How far will this mania for engaging colored players go? At the present rate of progress the International League may ere many moons change its name to 'Colored League.'" A few days

earlier, a Toronto paper, under a headline reading "The Colored Ball Players Disgraceful," noted that "to put it mildly [the black players'] presence [in the International League] is distasteful to the other players." Indeed, though most white players voiced no objection to interracial baseball, many did. Some white players even refused to sit for team pictures alongside a black teammate, and there were tales of white players who intentionally played poor defense when a black teammate pitched.

The situation came to a head on July 14, 1887, with the convergence of two significant events. In Newark, New Jersey, the Chicago White Stockings, the defending National League Champions, were scheduled to square off against the International League's Newark club in an exhibition game. Before the game, Chicago's player-manager Cap Anson, a confirmed racist, demanded that Newark's black pitching ace George Stovey and its starting catcher, none other than Moses "Fleetwood" Walker, be barred from the game. Anson was a living legend. His brilliant play led the White Stockings to five pennants in the 1880s, and in the process he became baseball's first nationally revered superstar. The Newark team obliged Anson and the game was played without Stovey and Walker.

In Buffalo, New York, the directors of the International League met on the very same day and reached another "gentlemen's agreement" that league teams would no longer sign black players. Whether Anson's actions significantly influenced the league's decision is debatable; nonetheless, at the end of the day African-Americans were once again (un)officially banned, an accomplishment that Anson, no doubt, would have been proud of. By the end of the season, the rest of organized baseball had endorsed the International League's new race policy.

Sure enough, African-Americans began to drop out of the ranks of the minor leagues. Walker, Grant, and pitcher Robert Higgins were the only three black players left in the International League in 1888, and

only Walker played in the league in 1889; the next black to play in the IL would be Jackie Robinson in 1946. A smattering of black players remained throughout the lower minor leagues, but the die had been cast. Occasionally, one of the great black players would sign on with a minor league team—for instance, Frank Grant played in both the Middle States League and the Atlantic Association in 1890, while the peripatetic Bud Fowler's last documented stint in the minors was with the Adrian team of the Michigan State League in 1895. A few more black men played in the lower minors from 1896 through 1900, but there are no records of any black players in the minors from 1901 until 1946.

However, blacks did not disappear from the baseball landscape in the face of exclusion from white organized ball. In fact, an independent barnstorming club known as the Cuban Giants, the prototype for the professional black baseball teams of the next three decades, began play in 1885. The team was originally composed of waiters and porters at the Argyle Hotel in Babylon, New York, on Long Island, who would play games against local competition for the entertainment of the hotel's summer guests. However, the squad was so good that they attracted the attention of a white promoter, Jack Lang, who brought in stronger competition and, offering them salaries, took the team, known as the Athletics in their first season, on the road after the hotel closed. In Philadelphia, they defeated the top local black team, the Orions, and after the

* * * *

OPPOSITE: *The Cuban Giants of 1888 included (back row, from left) Abe Harrison, George Stovey, Ben Holmes, Shep Trusty, Arthur Thomas, Ben Boyd; (middle row, from left) William T. Whyte, George Williams, George Parago, Clarence Williams; (front row, from left) Jack Frye, unknown (possibly Frank Grant), and another unknown.*

game Lang signed three of the previously amateur Orions to contracts. By the end of the season, which included a 5–4 victory over Bridgeport, the newly crowned champion of the Eastern League (an official minor league), the legend of a brilliant, black barnstorming team had spread throughout the eastern seaboard.

Walter Cook, a wealthy entrepreneur from Trenton, New Jersey, was impressed by the team's success and bought them in the off-season. He gave the team a new home, further upgraded the talent, paid healthy salaries, and rechristened the team the Cuban Giants. Cook believed that if the players masqueraded as Cubans, they would be more appealing to white audiences, so part of being a Cuban Giant meant speaking gibberish with a Spanish accent and mimicking stereotypical Latin behavior. The team was a huge success, both on the field and in the stands, in 1886. Sol White wrote of the team, "With the exception of F. Grant, Walker, and Fowler, they had the best the colored base ball world could produce." Only two former employees of the Argyle Hotel remained on the team. Cook had assembled a black dynamo, led by pitching ace Shep Trusty, catcher Clarence Williams, and team captain and second baseman George Williams (unrelated to Clarence); on occasion the brilliant southpaw hurler George Stovey took the mound for the Cubans. The ambitious Cook scheduled exhibition games against top-rung minor league teams and a few against major league squads. The results of these exhibitions astonished the baseball world. The Giants won the balance of the games

against minor league foes and proved competitive against the major leaguers, even defeating the National League's Cincinnati Reds in one game. Of course, the Giants spent most of the season overwhelming small-town opponents as they barnstormed through the Northeast, entertaining the large crowds with their Cuban shtick. Although anyone with any degree of sophistication could see through the Latin charade, the act did not seem to diminish the respect accorded to the

★ ★ ★ ★

ABOVE: *The Argyle Hotel in Babylon, New York, first home to the barnstorming Cuban Giants of the 1880s.*
OPPOSITE: *The Cuban Giants of 1887 featured (back row, from left) George Parago, Ben Holmes, Shep Trusty, Arthur Thomas, George Williams, Miller; (front row, from left) William T. Whyte, Clarence Williams, Abe Harrison, S.K. Govern, Ben Boyd, Jack Frye, and Frank Allen.*

team in the baseball world, or make Cook's club any less popular in black America, where, after only one season, the Cuban Giants had become heroes.

But the Giants were not the only story in black baseball in 1886, for that was also the year of the Southern League of Base Ballists, the first intercity league of black teams. The league was organized by the editors of a black newspaper from Jacksonville, Florida, *The Leader*, which put out the call for established black teams to join up. The response was tremendous, reflecting the incredible popularity of baseball in the black South. Ten teams, all amateur, started the season: three from Jacksonville, two each from Memphis and Savannah, and one each from Atlanta, Charleston, and New Orleans; three more (Jacksonville again, Savannah again, and Montgomery) came aboard soon thereafter. Visiting teams were put up by the host teams, and the league's organizers hoped that the money from the gate would cover expenses. The league began play in early June, one month after the originally scheduled opening day, and games were played throughout the summer. The Fultons of Charleston, led by star pitcher B.B.H. "Babe" Smith, were a strong unit, but the Memphis Eclipse captured the pennant. However, all the teams lost money and the league disbanded after the season.

The year 1887 saw an even more ambitious project undertaken by Walter Brown, a black businessman from Pittsburgh: the National Colored Base Ball League (NCL). Brown, who modeled the NCL after its major league namesake, envisioned a league

of professional teams from large northern cities. He succeeded in recruiting eight strong clubs from New York, Boston, Philadelphia, Pittsburgh, Cincinnati, Louisville, Baltimore, and Washington, D.C., all of which were previously amateur but ready and willing to make the leap to professionalism given Brown's assurance that players would earn good money in the NCL. But the one team Brown wanted most, the Cuban Giants, declined the invitation. Giants owner Walter Cook had no desire to bog down his marquee team with league obligaions. And anyway, the Giants were head and shoulders above other black clubs; the previous season they had annihilated the New York Gorhams (charter members of the National Colored League) 24–6 in a game that was hyped as the Colored World Championship. Similarly, the top black stars would be absent from the NCL (with the exception of Bud Fowler, who had signed on to manage the Cincinnati team) since they were still playing in the minor leagues in 1887.

Prospects for the league looked good as opening day approached. Brown, legitimately worried that minor league teams would raid the NCL's talent pool, petitioned the National League to sanction it as an official minor league (thereby guaranteeing that its players would be protected under the reserve clause). Amazingly, the request was granted. And though the NL's motivation was probably to insure against further integration of the minors, the sanction added considerable prestige to Brown's league. Nevertheless, the NCL was a catastrophe. Without sufficient financial backing, teams could not afford the costly long-distance train fares. The Boston franchise got stranded in Louisville after the opening weekend and the players had to make their way back home on their own. Only thirteen league games were ever played.

There was, however, a silver lining: the quality of play had been high. Thus, once the teams made it back home, they proudly advertised themselves as having been in the NCL, which elevated them above other black teams in the minds of baseball fans and made them a premier drawing card in their respective regions. In fact, later in 1887, two of the NCL's charter teams, the New York Gorhams and the Pittsburgh Keystones, greatly enhanced their reputations by upsetting the Cuban Giants.

Despite those two setbacks, which they later revenged, the Cuban Giants enjoyed another watershed year in 1887. On a western road trip, they defeated major league teams in Cincinnati and Indianapolis, but the highlight of their season was a late-season showdown against the recently crowned National League champions, the Detroit Wolverines. Accounts of the game vary, but they all concur that behind the superb pitching of Bill Whyte, the Giants held a slight lead after seven innings, and that Detroit managed to forge a victory only because of a series of fielding errors committed by the Cubans in the eighth and ninth innings. At season's end, the Giants were rightly hailed as one of the best teams in the world. Thus, as the dust settled after a tumultuous 1887—in which the likes of Cap Anson and the overlords of white baseball declared their intent to keep the game segregated and the first effort to organize an all-black professional league failed miserably—the Cuban Giants stood alone as a positive model for black professional baseball, which began remaking itself in the team's image.

By 1888, the New York Gorhams, who remained professional after their stint in the NCL, had greatly improved their roster. Guided by their new player-manager, Bud Fowler, they established themselves as the Cuban Giants' eastern rivals. Accepting the challenge, the Giants' new owner, J.M. Bright (Walter Cook had died in 1887), organized a four-team tournament between the Giants, the Gorhams, the Pittsburgh Keystones, and the Norfolk, Virginia, Red Stockings. The Giants swept the tournament, but the surprise was the strong play of the still-amateur Keystones, who finished second.

After the tournament, Bright signed the Keystones' top player, second baseman Sol White (who had been brought in as a ringer), to play for the Cubans.

However, White ended up on the Gorhams in 1889, when the Cubans signed another second baseman, Frank Grant, the greatest everyday black ballplayer of the era. With the likes of Grant and ace hurler Stovey, who had returned to the Giants in 1888, added to their already lethal nucleus, the 1889 Cuban Giants were probably the greatest black team of the nineteenth century. In an unprecedented move, Bright had arranged for his team to compete in an official minor league, the Middle States League, as the Trenton Cuban Giants, making them the first all-black team in the minor leagues. The Gorhams followed suit. The Cubans tore through the league, with only a strong team from Harrisburg keeping pace; the Gorhams started slow and dropped out. The Giants finished first with a .780 winning percentage but played eight fewer games than Harrisburg, so the league declared that the team had forfeited some of these games and speciously awarded the title to Harrisburg.

The following season, the story line gets difficult to follow in a manner that would recur throughout the history of black baseball. Basically, J. Monroe Kreiter of York, Pennsylvania, successfully lured five of the Cuban Giants stars onto a new team dubbed the Colored Monarchs of the Diamond, slated to play in the new Eastern Interstate League. Meanwhile, Harrisburg, which also jumped to the new league, signed Grant and catcher Clarence Williams away

* * * *

OPPOSITE: *Second baseman Charlie Grant was a standout for the Page Fence Giants and went on to star for several teams, including Page Fence's next incarnation, the Chicago Columbia Giants, as well as the Philadelphia Giants and the New York Black Sox.*

from Bright's Giants, who were reduced to a shadow of their former selves. Once the season began, the Monarchs of York swept through the league, moving ahead of the field. Meanwhile, Frank Grant's return to an integrated team proved disastrous: taunted by both fans and opposing players to a degree he hadn't experienced in the International League, he left the team by July. Without Grant, Harrisburg fell further behind the Monarchs and, rather than allow their black rivals the satisfaction of defeating them, they jumped to the Atlantic Association, and the Interstate League abruptly folded.

By the spring of 1891, Bright had managed to reassemble his mighty Giants, who were to play in the Connecticut State League. But as the previous season had shown, Bright could be outbid for his talented players. This time, the raid was made by an old nemesis, the New York Gorhams. After the Giants devastated the struggling Gorhams in two contests in May, Gorhams

owner Ambrose Davis offered big money to the Giants' best players. Stovey and Grant were the first to switch teams, and soon the balance of the Giants were playing for the Gorhams. Bright had to close up shop for the season, abruptly ending what turned out to be the final appearance of an all-black team in a minor league. Davis renamed his squad the Big Gorhams, and much like previous constellations of this core group of players, they ran roughshod over the competition, reportedly winning forty-one games straight during one stretch (though their opposition was rarely top-flight). However, the Big Gorhams

did not have the reputation, or the burlesque appeal, of the Cuban Giants, and did not attract sizable crowds. Davis lost money on his investment and the Gorhams were no more.

In 1892, Bright once again reformed the Cuban Giants, and for the next three seasons they were the only black professional baseball team in operation. This era was a downtime not only for black baseball, but for the American economy in general. The country was immersed in a depression and jobs were scarce, especially for African-Americans. Few people, and almost no African-

Americans, had disposable income to spend on baseball games.

Nevertheless, baseball was so popular and there were so many good black players that by the middle of the 1890s, the second era of black professional baseball had dawned. The first new team on the scene recalled the Cuban Giants in that they mixed excellent baseball with an element of the absurd. The Page Fence Giants were a team without a home, but they had a sponsor, whose name—the Page Woven Wire Fence Company of Adrian, Michigan—was emblazoned on the side of the opulent sixty-foot (18.3m) railroad coach where the players lived during their never-ending road trip. When the team arrived in a town for a game, the players disembarked with bicycles (donated by their other sponsor, the Monarch Bicycle Company) on which they went door-to-door selling tickets to the day's game before reconvening on the main street for a pregame parade. The Giants also hammed it up on the field to the delight of the crowd, and they usually breezed to a victory.

That the Page Fence Giants were a superb squad was no accident, since they were the brainchild of Bud Fowler. In 1894, the legendary infielder was playing for a team in Findley, Ohio, when he and his sole black teammate, a powerful young shortstop named Grant Johnson, decided to try to organize an all-black team. The two wanted to base the team in Findley, Johnson's hometown, but they weren't able to find a sponsor there. They found one in Adrian, Michigan, and the West's first successful pro black franchise was born. (The Lincoln Giants of Lincoln, Nebraska, were actually the first black pro team in the West; they barnstormed across the Plains states in 1890 but lasted only part of one season.) By the spring of 1895, Fowler had assembled some of the top black players in the country, including Sol White. The ever-restless Fowler abandoned his creation in midseason for a final stint in the minors, but the Giants had a strong inaugural campaign nonetheless, winning 118 of 156 games.

The team was even stronger the following year. Grant "Home Run" Johnson was a budding superstar; the team featured two brilliant young hurlers, Billy Holland and George Wilson; and with the departure of Sol White, they added a rookie second baseman, Charlie Grant (unrelated to Frank), who would become a legend in his own right. Representing a new generation of blackball stars, the Page Fence nine, who won more than 80 percent of their games in 1896, challenged the previous generation's great-est black team, the Cuban Giants, to a fifteen-game Colored Championship in September. Bright's Cubans were still strong; their veteran stars included Frank Grant and stalwart shortstop Abe Harrison,

* * * *

ABOVE: *Frank Leland was a player as well as the first black owner of a successful black ball club. His career lasted a quarter of a century and included stints with the Washington Capital Citys, Chicago Unions, Chicago Union Giants, Leland Giants, and Chicago Giants.*
OPPOSITE: *A full-time barnstorming team, the Page Fence Giants were accustomed to traveling in style in this large and comfortable railway car, which provided accommodations that were far better and more reliable than those offered in segregated America. Few black teams of any generation would have it so easy.*

but they were nothing like the Giants teams of the late 1880s. The easterners shelled Billy Holland in game one, but the Page Fence Giants bounced back to trounce the Cubans 20–6 in game two and took control after that. At the end of the series, the Page Fence Giants had captured ten of the fifteen games. The balance of power had shifted west, and to a new generation.

The 1896 season was also a watershed for black baseball because two more professional clubs appeared on the scene, one in the West and the other in the East. The western club, the Chicago Unions, grew out of a successful amateur team that had earned a showdown with the Cuban Giants in 1894, when they claimed the western championship (Bright's Cubans won handily). Beginning in 1894, the Unions played their home games in a five thousand-seat stadium that had once been home to the major league White Stockings. Owner Frank Leland took note of the Page Fence Giants, who signed the Unions' best pitcher, Billy Holland, in 1895. And by the next spring, the Unions were professional; they would tour the Midwest six days a week and play in their spacious stadium every Sunday. The Unions were not on par with the Page Fence Giants in 1896, but Leland, the first black owner of a successful pro franchise, would soon correct that.

The new professional team back East had one of the strangest names in sports history, the Cuban X-Giants. If losing to Page Fence was not enough humiliation, J.M. Bright had to deal with a new rival on his turf with (almost) the same name. The new franchise, with its home base in New York City, was funded by a white businessman, E.B. Lamar. The team's moniker was chosen not merely to capitalize on the popularity of blackball's most storied team, but because the initial group of Cuban X-Giants were "ex-Cuban Giants" lured away from Bright's team by higher salaries, just as had happened with the Monarchs of York in 1890, and the Big Gorhams of 1891. Former Cuban Giant Sol White, who

played on the Cuban X-Giants from 1896 to 1899 (as well as for the Monarchs of 1890 and the Big Gorhams of 1891), said that Bright was "a lover of the game and a money-getting man...extremely selfish in his financial dealings and naturally shrewd." Lamar, by contrast, "spent his time and mind making the game a lucrative calling for his ball players." In 1897, the two Cuban Giants teams played a

three-game series on successive Sundays, and Bright's Cubans went down to ignominious defeat, as Lamar's X-Giants won two of three to capture the Colored Championship of the East. Bright's troops, officially renamed the Genuine Cuban Giants in 1898, remained a quality team through 1899 but were always a step behind the X-Giants, the East's top black team into the next century.

Out west, the balance of power was shifting as well. Actually, the Page Fence Giants, the Colored Champions of 1896, played even more brilliantly the next season, but they were less successful at the gate. Rural America was still suffering through a severe economic slump, and small towns had been the Giants' bread and butter. Page Fence was in the midst of an eighty-two-game winning streak when a lack of funds ended their 1897 season prematurely. They regrouped for 1898, were only slightly less dominant on the field, and managed to finish the season; but they again failed to turn a profit. In the off-season, the sponsors lowered the curtain on the short, spectacular history of the Page Fence Giants.

Meanwhile, Leland's Chicago Unions were raking in the dough and becoming a formidable team in the process. Leland stole back pitching ace Billy Holland from Page Fence when the Giants shut down early in 1897 and he signed a brilliant young

lefthanded hurler late in the 1898 season. Leland must have licked his chops at the demise of his midwestern rivals, the Page Fence Giants, but before he could raid the team's corpse, an organization of black Chicago businessmen called the Columbia Club, who had no doubt marveled at Leland's profits, decided to invest in black baseball. This cadre of investors signed up virtually the entire Page Fence team, rechristened them the Columbia Giants, and relocated them to Chicago, in a park only a few blocks away from the Unions' home. If that wasn't

enough, Columbia wooed one of Leland's brightest young stars, pitcher Harry Buckner, to the Giants. Infuriated but virtually powerless, all Leland could do was refuse to play his new intercity enemy.

There had been no colored championship series pitting East against West since the Page Fence Giants' 1896 triumph over the Cuban Giants. However, 1899 was a banner year for championship series. The Cuban X-Giants were the undisputed powerhouse of the East, having established their superiority over Bright's Genuine Cubans every

year since 1897 and consistently beaten the Norfolk Red Stockings, who became the South's first pro franchise early in 1899. The X-Giants of 1899 were a team of solid, professional players led by two of black baseball's transcendent veteran stars, Sol White and Frank Grant. During the season, Lamar's New York franchise ventured west for a fourteen-game showdown against the Chicago Unions. Leland's troops were perhaps still green, but pitching ace Billy Holland was at the top of his game and the franchise's three jewels—pitcher Bert Jones, outfielder Mike Moore, and shortstop Bill Monroe—were just reaching their prime. The teams played fourteen games "in and around Chicago, the crowds on several occasions being enormous," according to Sol White. The games were tight, but the more experienced X-Giants won the series nine to five.

Before and during the series, the Columbia Giants, who had already impressed Chicago with a substantial midseason winning streak, issued numerous challenges to both teams, and finally, even the reluctant Leland acquiesced. A five-game city championship followed. Public interest, spurred by heavy betting, was tremendous in both white and black Chicago. The series, however, was lopsided: the Unions were sloppy in the field, making numerous costly errors, and the Giants of "Home Run" Johnson, Charlie Grant, and pitchers George Wilson

* * * *

OPPOSITE: *The short-lived (1895 to 1898) Page Fence Giants were the creation of the ageless Bud Fowler. Pictured here are (left to right) Walker, Charlie Grant, George Wilson, John W. Patterson, Pete Burns, Augustus Parsons, unknown, Grant "Home Run" Johnson, unknown, Billy Holland, and unknown. Sol White played with the team for one season, 1895.*

and Harry Buckner swept all five games to claim the Chicago and Western Colored Championships. Finally, the Cuban X-Giants faced the Columbia Giants in September in an eleven-game series played in Chicago and Michigan to determine the undisputed colored champion of the world. The Columbia (né Page Fence) Giants had once again had an amazing season, winning an astonishing percentage of their games, but they had yet to face the likes of the wily X-Giants. The New Yorkers won seven of the eleven games. E.B. Lamar's Cuban X-Giants reigned supreme over colored baseball at the close of the 1890s.

It would be a long time before a colored championship would be decided as clearly as it had been in 1899. Over the next decade, there was a proliferation of pro teams, especially in the East. While the top eastern team would readily pronounce itself the colored champion, it was usually unproven against the West's dominant team.

In 1900, Leland's Unions faced the X-Giants in a fourteen-game rematch. However, the X-Giants were weaker than they had been the previous season, as both Frank Grant and Sol White had departed; and not only were the maturing Unions a year older, but Leland had lured the great "Home Run" Johnson away from the Columbia Giants. Leland's squad got their revenge, taking nine of the games. Meanwhile, the Columbia Giants were still formidable, having added Sol White to compensate for the loss of Johnson; they trounced the Genuine Cuban Giants in a series. Another intracity showdown, this time for all the marbles, would have made sense, but the rival teams proved too obstinate and the season ended without a city, western, or world colored champion when one game could have settled all three.

And so it was that blackball entered the twentieth century with the momentum built up by a handful of brilliant African-American stars. This core group—which roughly numbered enough to

fill the rosters of one and a half to two excellent squads, and over time had included such legends as Bud Fowler, Fleetwood Walker, Frank Grant, George Stovey, "Home Run" Johnson, and Sol White—began its playing days at a time when there remained an opening, ever so slight, for blacks to play in organized white professional baseball. But this group had to persevere, as that opportunity dissipated in the face of white America's staunch racism. And they met the challenge, shifting gears, joining forces on barnstorming teams, and, in the process, establishing the foundation for black professional ball. The legendary teams, such as the Cuban Giants, the Monarchs of York, and the Page Fence Giants, proved to black America that black professional baseball could succeed, often with brilliant results, both on the field and in the accounting coffers, though the latter remained a constant struggle.

The true heroism of this generation of black-ball stars cannot really be appreciated outside of its historical context, for the post-Reconstruction era, roughly from 1877 to 1901, was in many ways the nadir for black America in terms of its hope of attaining equality. The vast majority of American blacks still lived in the Jim Crow South at the turn of the century, and, conspicuously, the prospects for professional blackball were in the North, where the economic and social outlook was still bleak, though nowhere near as harsh as in the South. Over the next two decades, a great migration of American blacks would begin, up from Jim Crow Dixie to the burgeoning cities of the industrial North. And as the country lifted itself out of the economic depression of the 1890s, fans once again had more money to spe\nd on the national pastime, whether played by white or black Americans. And with that, black teams based in the great northern cities would expand dramatically upon the foundation laid by the likes of Fowler, Grant, Walker, and White.

Blackball Takes Hold

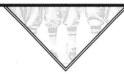

Whereas the last two decades of the nineteenth century had been a particularly bleak time for black Americans, when the hopes generated by the end of slavery were squelched in a racist backlash personified by Jim Crow, the first two decades of the twentieth century represented a marked, though still qualified, improvement for African-Americans. As the American economy recovered from the depressions and recessions of the 1890s, more blacks migrated to the booming industrial North. And though the balance of the new factory jobs were filled by poor immigrants who came to the United States in unprecedented numbers from southern and eastern Europe (who, while they were routinely mistreated and condescended to by "American" racists, were clearly above blacks in the American racist hierarchy), enough blacks found employment in the North that African-American neighborhoods became an established part of every sizable northern city. Even though these communities were far from prosperous and remained thoroughly segregated, the people who lived there were functioning in a bustling (and increasingly impersonal) society, and inevitably they earned more money and had more varied contact with white society than was

* * * *

OPPOSITE: *The great Oscar Charleston, who broke in with the Indianapolis ABCs in 1915 and was known as the Hoosier Comet, had a career that spanned thirty-five years.*

ABOVE: *The 1909 Leland Giants included (back row, from left) Pete Hill, Andrew Payne, Pete Booker, Walter Ball, Pat Dougherty, Bill Gatewood, and Rube Foster; (front row, from left) Danger Talbert, Mike Moore, Frank C. Leland, Bobby Winston, Sam Strothers, and Nate Harris.*

possible below the Mason-Dixon Line, where the vast majority of American blacks still resided.

By the onset of the twentieth century, prominent leaders in the struggle for racial equality such as Booker T. Washington and W.E.B. DuBois were calling on blacks to build strong institutions themselves, such as all-black universities and black-owned businesses. The collapse of Reconstruction, which had been followed by the advent of Jim Crow, had shown African-Americans that even well-intentioned assistance from whites was unreliable, and that the onus was on them to find means to alleviate poverty and insulate themselves from racist oppression. Thus, new connections were forged, these networks were expanded, and a nationwide infrastructure began to emerge, which evolved into an entire subsociety, Black America, that existed within the United States but outside the influence of white paternalism.

Black professional baseball flourished during the early years of the twentieth century, albeit in much less spectacular fashion than "organized" white baseball. However, most of the top all-black teams were still owned by white men. This fact troubled the greatest black pitcher of the century's first decade, a rotund, hard-throwing righthander from Texas named Rube Foster. Rube decided it was incumbent upon him to put blackball in the hands of blacks—and he did just that.

The two most intriguing events of 1901 in black baseball occurred before the season began. First, to the delight of Frank Leland, the Columbia Giants were maneuvered out of existence, abruptly ending the great Chicago rivalry. What happened was that both teams lost their stadiums when Chicago's new white professional team, the White Sox of the new American League, needed a stadium to play in and chose to renovate the Unions' home park. The Giants also had to move from their home field because it was deemed too close to the White Sox' park. So suddenly, both the Giants and Unions were uprooted. Leland, however, had connections at city

hall and he landed a cozy park in the same general region of Chicago. The Columbia club had no such connections; the former Page Fence Giants were homeless once again, but this time without a luxury railroad coach at their disposal. The team was forced to disband. Leland rechristened his team the Chicago Union Giants, implying that he would

* * * *

ABOVE: *Booker T. Washington was the preeminent African-American educator in the post–Civil War United States and as an early proponent of self-sufficiency for blacks in America was an inspiration to men like Rube Foster.* **OPPOSITE:** *Like Washington, W.E.B. DuBois was an accomplished author and thinker who urged African-Americans to build economic and social institutions for themselves.*

merge the two teams together, though the only Columbia player he signed in 1901 was pitching ace George Wilson. At any rate, in the world of black baseball, Chicago was once again a one-team town, and Leland's Union Giants were unrivaled throughout the West. The Cuban X-Giants continued their reign as the class of the East in 1901, but unlike the previous two seasons, they did not travel west to face Leland's squad.

The other significant event of 1901 involved legendary coach John McGraw's underhanded attempt to sneak Charlie Grant into the majors. McGraw, skipper of the American League's Baltimore Orioles at the time, supported the integration of organized baseball throughout his career, but knowing the inflexibility of the color barrier, he resorted to chicanery in this instance. Grant, a brilliant second baseman who starred for the Page Fence and Columbia Giants, was a very light-skinned black man, and McGraw was so covetous of his skills that he conspired with Grant to pass him off as an American Indian known as Chief Tokahoma. Grant, aka Tokahoma, showed up at the Orioles' spring training camp, but Chicago's owner, Charlie Comiskey, was tipped off by the enthusiasm of Chicago's black community and the ruse was exposed. Sadly, Grant was forced to return to Chicago, where, upon arrival, he learned that he was without a job because of the demise of the Columbia Giants.

The most important events of the 1902 season were the arrival of a new pro franchise in the East, the Philadelphia Giants, and of a young pitcher who would become the single most important figure in black baseball history, Andrew "Rube" Foster. Much as the appearance of the Columbia Giants in Chicago had been an infringement upon Frank Leland's turf, the Philadelphia Giants represented a direct challenge to E.B. Lamar's Cuban X-Giants, who had moved from New York City to Philadelphia. The new team in Philly was founded by wealthy white sports journalist H. Walter Schlichter, who knew enough about black baseball to bring in Sol White to organize his team. To anchor his first team, White brought in two veterans from the Cuban Giants heyday, Frank Grant and catcher Clarence Williams. To this nucleus, White added promising rookie outfielder Andrew "Jap" Payne and star infielder Bill Monroe, the former Leland protégé (who had played for the Cuban X-Giants in 1901) White's Giants posted an 81–43 record, including two competitive losses to Connie Mack's Philadelphia Athletics, who had captured the American League pennant that year. They laid claim to the Eastern Colored Championship, but so did the still-powerful X-Giants, and the two did not settle the issue on the field.

Out west, Leland's Union Giants remained unchallenged and their future looked bright, as they added two former Columbia Giants, infielder William Binga and outfielder John Patterson, and signed pitcher Andrew "Rube" Foster, from Calvert, Texas, who at age twenty-two was already a folk hero. Legend has it that this son of a country minister was organizing baseball teams in grade school. After the eighth grade, he ran away from home to pursue his dream of playing baseball. By the time he was seventeen, he was the ace hurler of the Waco Yellow Jackets, an all-black amateur team, and was known by the northern black teams who toured the South during the winter.

In the spring of 1901, Foster was pitching for a hotel team in Hot Springs, Arkansas, where Connie Mack's Athletics happened to be training. Mack invited Foster "to fling 'em over" to the Athletics. In the contest that ensued, Foster outdueled legendary hurler Rube Waddell, earning him the nickname Rube Beater, which soon became just Rube. The following season, Leland got personally involved in luring the massively broad six-foot-two-inch (188cm) Foster up north to join his Union Giants. Foster was in the throes of another brilliant year, but he would be a bust in his first few appearances

in big-time black baseball. He stayed on the Union Giants only a couple of weeks before he jumped to a white semipro club in Otsego, Michigan, where he regained his form.

Foster's departure from Leland's team presaged the disastrous exodus that devastated the Union Giants in 1903. Perhaps it was the result of bad karma from Leland's squeeze-out of the Columbia Giants, but he lost almost all of his quality players in one spring. Leland's roster was raided from two directions. Philadelphia Giants GM Walter Schlichter was offering top dollar to build up his already strong team, and what better place to find premier talent than the best black team in the West? Meanwhile, a biracial semipro team in Algona, Iowa, the Brownies, had provided a home for some of the former Columbia Giants, and decided to field an all-black team for 1903. A feeding frenzy took place, in which four of the leading Union Giants went to Algona (joining pitcher Billy Holland): pitcher Walter Ball, catcher George Johnson, infielder Harry Moore, and former pitcher Bert Jones, who had

moved to the outfield. And four more of Leland's stars were signed by Schlichter: outfielder John Patterson, third bagger William Binga, catcher Robert Footes, and hurler Harry Buckner. Algona then succeeded in signing most of the remainder of the Union Giants roster from the previous season. The Algona Brownies added to the humiliation by coaxing Leland's new, second-rate squad into a Western Championship series, which the Brownies won handily.

Back in the City of Brotherly Love, Schlichter's signings put pressure on the Cuban X-Giants to improve their team. E.B. Lamar managed to secure two of the nation's best black players, Charlie Grant and "Home Run" Johnson, both of whom hadn't played for a pro black team since 1900, but by the end of the season it would become apparent that Lamar's most important acquisition was a young pitcher known as Rube. With their freshly charged lineups, both of the eastern black powers swept to impressive records in 1903; their fans waited in anticipation for a grudge match, and this time they were not disappointed. Schlichter and Lamar billed the showdown, which called for eight games, as the Colored World Series, disregarding, perhaps appropriately, western black baseball. Meanwhile, Foster once again struggled in his initial appearances, but he settled down over the course of the season and established himself as the ace of the X-Giants' staff. The young Texan was a power pitcher who complemented his fastball with a full repertoire of pitches, most notably a fadeaway, or screwball, which, legend has it, New York Giant manager John McGraw convinced Foster to teach to Christy Mathewson before the 1903 season (when Mathewson won thirty-four games, up from fourteen the previous year).

Foster was tapped to start game one of the much-anticipated series, and he was also slated to bat cleanup for the X-Giants. Foster pitched a three-hitter as the Cubans triumphed, 3–1. Sol White's Giants evened the series at a game apiece, but then

Foster returned to the mound in game three to lead the X-Giants to a 12–3 victory, in which Foster contributed three hits. By the end of the series, Foster had four victories to his credit, as the X-Giants won five of the seven games played. It was the single most dominant performance to date in the history of black baseball. Foster, after all, was not mowing down semipro talent but a lineup loaded with black legends like Frank Grant and Sol White, and stars like Bill Monroe, John Patterson, and William Binga, and his brilliant showing laid the foundation for the larger-than-life stature he would attain in the world of black baseball over the next two decades.

In 1904, the Philadelphia rivalry remained center stage. Out west, Frank Leland failed to bring back any of his wayward stars, though his outfit was the only pro black team in the region (the Algona Brownies had proven to be a one-season wonder). Of the top Algona stars, pitcher Walter Ball and outfielder Harry Moore landed on the Cuban X-Giants, while catcher George Johnson moved to the Philadelphia Giants. But the most notable off-season move was across town, by Rube Foster. Schlichter was intent on defeating Lamar's X-Giants and was willing to up the ante; along with Foster, he bought two other X-Giant stars, Charlie Grant and starting center fielder Andrew Payne. Still, the X-Giants had a formidable team that featured "Home Run" Johnson, John Patterson, star pitchers Harry Buckner and Dan McClellan, and first baseman Robert Jordan, who batted a remarkable .560 in the 1903 series.

As the two teams roared through the balance of the season, the debate over which was superior raged not only in Philadelphia but in black communities up and down the eastern seaboard. Finally, September arrived and the teams decided on a three-game series in Atlantic City for the Colored Championship. As the first game approached, Foster fell ill with a fever and was rumored to be too sick to pitch. The X-Giants declared that he wasn't sick at all, but frightened. Of course, Foster had to respond

to the challenge. In the most dramatically charged environment in black baseball history, Foster took the mound and proceeded to strike out a record eighteen X-Giants en route to an 8–4 victory. Overall it wasn't Foster's best performance, but given the circumstances, it was his most spectacular. Led by John Patterson's four stolen bases, the Cubans fought back to take game two, setting up a decisive final game. The environment was electric. According to Sol White, still the player-manager of Philadelphia, "both players and spectators were worked to the highest pitch of excitement. Never in the annals of colored baseball did two nines fight for supremacy as these teams fought."

In the end, one man made the difference. Foster pitched a two-hitter and the Philadelphia Giants

* * * *

Pitcher, manager, visionary, Rube Foster is one of the central figures in Negro league history. He is seen here in the uniform of his Chicago American Giants.

won 4-2, capturing the Colored Championship. The leading hitter in the series was none other than Rube Foster, with a .400 average. The young Texan had somehow managed to outdo his performance of the previous year, and in only two years' time, he had proceeded first to shut down a lineup with virtually half the black superstars of the day, and then turn around and conquer the other half. As the 1904 season closed, Foster was the undisputed champion of black baseball.

Black baseball had its first superstar. Foster's exploits not only became legend throughout black America, but even penetrated white America—and Rube was a demigod in Cuba. E.B. Lamar had taken his champion Cuban X-Giants on tour to Cuba following their 1903 season, and Foster's brilliant performance made him a legend on the baseball-crazed island. A baseball boom swept black America on the heels of the excitement generated by Foster and the 1903 and 1904 championship showdowns. As for Foster himself, he would soon become less concerned with his own on-field performance than with the state of black baseball in general.

In 1905, however, Foster's pitching remained brilliant. He won fifty-one of fifty-five decisions for the Philadelphia Giants, including a no-hitter versus Camden, New Jersey's minor league team. The defending colored champions were even stronger than the previous year, with the addition of three top stars from the ranks of the Cuban X-Giants: shortstop "Home Run" Johnson, outfielder Harry Moore, and lefthanded ace Dan McClellan, who in 1903 tossed the first recorded perfect game by a black pitcher. Giants manager Sol White was not merely boasting in his 1907 *History of Colored Base Ball* when he chose his 1905 Giants as the greatest team of their era. E.B. Lamar must have realized that his depleted X-Giants were no match for the mighty Giants and the indomitable Foster; the teams could not agree on an arrangement for a series, and the season ended anticlimactically.

The next season offered more drama, both on and off the field. By spring 1906, the Rube Foster–inspired baseball mania in black America was reflected in a proliferation of teams in the Northeast. The most significant of these was the Brooklyn Royal Giants, owned by John W. Connors, the black proprietor of a restaurant/nightclub called the Royal Cafe. The club began play in 1905, and after only one season Connors showed the other teams in the East that he intended to "play hardball" when he raided the dynastic Philadelphia Giants to sign "Home Run" Johnson as his player-manager. Among the lesser black clubs that made the jump to professionalism in 1906 were the Quaker Giants of New York, the Keystone Giants of Philadelphia, and the Baltimore Giants of, strangely, Newark (note the ubiquity of the Giants moniker, as clubs tried to cash in on black fans' association of the name with excellence). And in 1906, two teams made up of actual Cuban players, the Cuban Stars and the Havana Stars, toured the Northeast for the first time.

In this environment, Cuban X-Giant owner E.B. Lamar forged a new league, the International League of Independent Professional Base Ball Clubs, which consisted of two marginal white teams; the Cuban clubs; the Genuine Cuban Giants, the Royal Giants, the X-Giants; and a handful of weaker black clubs. Conspicuously absent from this confederation were the Philadelphia Giants. Lamar's motivation was obvious: he was organizing the league in the hopes of revitalizing his struggling franchise with a championship pennant. Not a single one of the 1904 X-Giants' plethora of stars remained at the start of the 1906 season. Nevertheless, Lamar managed to field a decent team, bringing back Charlie Grant to play alongside, and tutor, the sensational John Henry Lloyd, a young shortstop destined for greatness. However, Lamar's scheme backfired when the Havana Stars and Quaker Giants ran out of money by July, and prospects for the league looked bleak. Facing a debacle of the first order, Lamar appealed

to Walter Schlichter for help. The mighty Giants came aboard and righted the ship.

Actually, Sol White's juggernaut was experiencing some hitches. First, "Home Run" Johnson split to manage Brooklyn, and then the team experienced a rash of injuries, mostly minor, that kept many of its stars, including the great Foster, on the sidelines for long stretches. The players' persistent grumblings about the tightfisted Schlichter raised suspicion that the petty injuries were more a form of protest than anything else. However, the opportunity to vanquish their foes and once again assert their dominance over black baseball awoke the slumbering Giants.

The International League season came down to a four-team round-robin playoff among the Philadelphia Giants, the Brooklyn Royal Giants, Lamar's Cuban X-Giants, and the good old Genuine Cuban Giants, to be followed by a championship game between the top two teams. Philadelphia won all three of its preliminary series, taking eleven of seventeen contests from the Royal Giants, ten of fifteen from the X-men, and four of four (with a tie) against the Genuines. Lamar's X-Giants took second in the tournament, earning a shot at the title.

The championship game was played at the Baker Bowl, the home field of the National League's Philadelphia Phillies, making it the first black baseball game in a major league park. And the Labor Day contest drew more than ten thousand fans, the largest crowd in black baseball history to date. The contest itself offered little in the way of drama, as the heavily favored Giants trounced the X-Giants and were crowned International League Champions. In fact, by virtue of their successful western swing, in which they bettered both of the black professional teams in Chicago, the 1906 Philadelphia Giants could rightfully claim to be the first undisputed champions of "colored" baseball since the Cuban X-Giants of 1899.

Basking in the glory of the moment, Schlichter made a proposal to the teams in the 1906 World

Series, Connie Mack's Philadelphia Athletics and John McGraw's New York Giants, for a best-of-three or best-of-five series between his black Giants and the winner of the World Series to determine unequivocally the best baseball team in America. He received no replies.

In the off-season, Rube Foster and a few other black ballplayers spent the winter playing baseball in Cuba, inaugurating a black baseball tradition. The island's winter league had racially integrated teams, which, within a few years, would begin to attract major leaguers. Before Cuba became an option, the only black ballplayers who found steady work on the diamond during the off-season were the members of teams like the Cuban X-Giants and the Cuban Giants before them, which had contracts with large Florida hotels to play exhibition games for the entertainment of their guests. Baseball did flourish throughout the South all year long, but there were few black semipro teams in Dixie and fewer integrated teams of any variety. So the Cuban league was a boon for black players in terms of providing both employment and a less racist environment. The sport had been popular on the island since the 1880s, and white professional teams had made winter tours as early as the 1890s. As mentioned earlier, Foster and the Cuban X-Giants had dazzled Cuban audiences in 1903. And four years later, Foster landed a winter job during the winter league's inaugural season. Foster pitched for the Havana Fe's, starting almost half their games and collecting nine victories in the short season.

Back in the United States, black baseball's reigning dynasty, Walter Schlichter's Philadelphia Giants, was dealt a major blow when Rube Foster and a number of other Giants stars left the team following a dispute over salaries and headed west to join Frank Leland's Giants in Chicago for the 1907 season. Foster had been in negotiation with Leland during the off-season, but he wanted to manage Leland's club and the owner was reluctant to hand over the reins of his team. But when Foster promised to bring a number of other Philly Giants along with him, Leland gave in. Foster was true to his word, delivering catcher James Booker, second baseman Nate Harris, and line-drive-hitting outfielder Pete Hill to the revitalized Chicago team. With this coup, Leland's club figured to end the eastern domination of black baseball.

Following the Algona Brownies' improbable 1903 season, midwestern blackball had lost most of its stable of stars to the East. Frank Leland's Union Giants stayed afloat as a mediocre team, and then Leland reorganized his team prior to the 1905 season, rechristening them the Leland Giants, returning to the role of field skipper. Pitcher Billy Holland came back to Leland's fold, and the team once again became a midwestern power. In 1906, Leland incorporated his franchise, getting more substantial financial backing in the process. And after another strong season on the field (mediocre, however, at the gate), in which the Leland Giants beat back the challenge of the Chicago Unions, the city's new black professional team, Leland was poised to raid the rosters of the elite eastern teams.

With Foster he landed a gold mine. Black Chicago was abuzz over the legend in their midst. Leland needn't have worried about empty stands. With Foster managing, fans filled the sizable grandstand at Auburn Ball Park on the south side for every weekend contest, even when their hero wasn't on the mound. At twenty-seven, Foster already had a superlative baseball mind. Under his tutelage, the 1907 Leland Giants swept to the Chicago City League title over inferior white semipro competition, won forty-eight straight games during one stretch, and posted a 110–10 record.

Back east, Walter Schlichter did not stand idly by after the departure of Foster and three other Philly stars. The wily owner, in the best tradition of blackball, proceeded to raid the rosters of other black teams and landed two gems in the process: the

Brooklyn Royal Giants' star catcher Bruce Petway and the Cuban X-Giants' brilliant young shortstop John Henry Lloyd (whose on-field education continued under the watchful eye of brilliant veteran infielder and manager Sol White). The International League of Colored Base Ball Teams still existed, at least in name, and under this heading the X-Giants, Royal Giants, Cuban Stars (the real Cubans), and Philly Giants all played five-game series against each other. Again, Schlichter and White's team proved their dominance, winning all three of their series and claiming the championship. However, the Philly Giants did not tour the West and the Leland Giants did not travel east, so neither could claim, in good conscience, the title of Colored World Champion.

The long-awaited showdown between Foster's Leland Giants, the West's top black team, and blackball's eastern dynasty, the Philadelphia Giants (which Foster had left on bad terms), took place the following season. The series called for four games in Detroit, followed by three in Chicago.

Sol White's Giants still featured a powerful lineup, with White at first, Nux James, a top-flight player, at second, the already brilliant and still maturing Lloyd at short, another young first-rate talent, Billy Francis, at third, Petway at catcher, and the ever-dependable southpaw ace Dan McClellan as the cornerstone of a solid staff. Rube Foster, whom many considered, regardless of race, baseball's leading authority on pitching (he wrote a brilliant essay on pitching for White's *History of Colored Base Ball*), had, not surprisingly, built his team around an excellent pitching staff. Foster, of course, remained the ace, though he pitched less and less frequently after his stint in Philadelphia, and under his tutelage quality hurlers Walter Ball, Arthur Hardy, and Bill Gatewood became even more formidable.

Alongside the three Philly Giant defectors—Hill (of), Booker (c), and Harris (2b)—Foster's starting lineup included two more former Philly Giants, star outfielder Mike Moore and the versatile Emmett

Bowman, as well as Jap Payne, another top-flight outfielder formerly with the Brooklyn Royal Giants. Given the air of invincibility surrounding Foster, his team was favored in the series, but events turned out differently. The Philly Giants took three of four from the Lelands in Detroit, and perhaps because he didn't want to face losing to another black team in front of his home fans, Foster then called off the remainder of the series—a remarkable move considering the sizable loss of revenue involved. Sol White's team returned back east triumphant.

At the end of the season, the reigning champs of blackball, the Philadelphia Giants, faced Connie Mack's Philadelphia Athletics for the second straight year in a City of Brotherly Love grudge match. Following the 1907 season, the major leaguers shut out Schlichter's club 3–0 behind the four-hit pitching of Rube Vickers, negating a fine effort by Giant hurler Harry Buckner. In 1908, the A's, coming off a second-place finish in the American League, again prevailed, 5–2, with pitcher Cy Morgan getting the win, despite two hits by the great Lloyd.

The 1909 season signaled the beginning of another of black baseball's tempestuous times. The trouble began with a mismatch of wills between the amiable Frank Leland and the irrepressible Rube Foster. Both men had been involved in negotiating business deals for their team, and Foster wanted complete control over the organization's finances because he consistently secured a higher percentage of a game's gate than did Leland.

* * * *

OPPOSITE: *The World Champion Philadelphia Giants of 1905–1906 included (back row, from left) H. Smith, Mike Moore, Emmett Bowman, Sol White, Tom Washington, Dan McClellan; (middle row, from left) Grant Johnson, Charlie Grant, Walter Schlichter, Rube Foster, Pete Hill; (front row, from left) William Monroe and Pete Booker.*

Leland, of course, demurred and the result was a regretful season. Foster supposedly broke his leg in July (though some doubt was raised as to the legitimacy of the injury), making the team less of an attraction to fans.

After the injury the club played poorly. In fact, late in the season, one of the recently formed black professional touring teams in the region, the St. Paul (Minnesota) Colored Gophers, defeated the Leland

Giants in a series to claim the Western Colored Championship.

Nevertheless, the season could still be salvaged, since the Giants were slated to play a three-game series with the Chicago Cubs, the Windy City's better major league team. The Cubs were a perennial National League power in the first decade of the century, led by their legendary "Tinker to Evers to Chance" double-play combination. The Cubs won

the NL pennant from 1906 to 1908 and again in 1910, taking the World Series in 1907 and 1908. In 1909, however, they finished second to Honus Wagner's Pittsburgh Pirates, in spite of an astonishing 104–49 record. Of their celebrated infield trio, only shortstop Joe Tinker agreed to play against black players. But player-manager Frank Chance and second bagger Johnny Evers were the only Cubs not to play (and Chance was present as the man-

himself out of the game for a relief pitcher. But the umpire didn't call time-out and Schulte raced home from third with the winning run. Foster argued vehemently, but to no avail. The Cubs were declared the winners, 6–5.

In the final game of the series, Brown pitched again for the Cubs and hurled a gem, stymieing the Giants 1–0. In the years that followed, Foster would try to arrange a similar series with the Cubs (or White Sox), but he was never granted an opportunity for revenge. The Cubs had won all three games, but by a mere four runs cumulatively, and one of the victories was controversial (and if Foster had possessed the requisite humility and replaced himself with a rested pitcher, game two would probably have been a Giants victory). Foster's team had proven to all of Chicago that a black team could compete with major leaguers.

Before the next season began, Rube Foster and Frank Leland's partnership dissolved. In a somewhat preposterous maneuver, Foster told Leland to get out of the operation or he would sue for control of the "Leland Giants." The reality of the situation was that Foster had already won the loyalty of the club's two key financial backers, Major R.R. Jackson and lawyer Beauregard Mosely, both prominent members of Chicago's black community. Leland, however, called Foster's bluff, and the issue went to court, where both sides lost. Foster, believe it or not, won the rights to the name "Leland Giants," while Leland won exclusive rights to the team's home field, Auburn Park, as well as players on the team (if one of the Giants did jump teams, the judge declared that he would be breaking the law if he signed on with Foster).

Oddly, the next casualty of the Foster-Leland war was the greatest black baseball franchise of the century's first decade, the Philadelphia Giants. Sol White's nine had cruised through another excellent campaign in 1909, claiming another Eastern Colored title. However, in the off-season, Foster, in need of players, and with considerable financial backing, raided Walter Schlichter's club, taking

ager). Evers' absence was quite ironic, as he was among the Cubs players who would frequently earn extra cash as a ringer for white semipro teams in City League games, and he had faced the Leland Giants before in that capacity. (It is possible that manager Chance didn't know of Evers' extracurricular activities and the star infielder feared being exposed.) At any rate, the Cubs didn't pull any punches in game one, throwing their ace Mordecai "Three Finger" Brown, who had just finished a brilliant 27–9 campaign with a record 1.31 ERA. Brown allowed only five hits, but the Giants' aggressive base running translated this into two runs. The Cubs, however, tallied four to win the first game.

One of the most controversial moments of Foster's career occurred during the second game of the series. The Giants great manager-pitcher had not played since midseason, when he had broken his leg, but he could not resist the challenge of facing the great Cubs. So Rube declared himself fit to pitch

and, to the delight of the huge audience, took the mound for game two. The Giants quickly scored five runs on the Cub's starter, Orval Overall (20–11). The Cubs got one back in the fourth, and another in the eighth. Foster was tiring; severely out of shape from the long layoff, he was even more obese than usual. But Rube Foster wasn't a man who readily backed down, and he returned to the hill for the ninth. After retiring Tinker, the Cubs got three straight hits followed by a walk, to make the score 5–3 with the bases loaded. Still Rube labored on. He got Frank Schulte to ground into a force play at home. Two outs, bases loaded, 5–3, and the weak-hitting Del Howard, Frank Chance's replacement at first, was up to bat. By this point, Foster had nothing left and Howard drilled the ball off the right field fence, scoring two. It was a tie game, with Schulte on third, when Foster walked into the dugout. Foster claimed that he called time-out on the way past the umpire, that he was merely taking away star catcher Bruce Petway and the franchise's jewel, John Henry Lloyd. Foster's pillaging led to a disagreement between White and Schlichter, and the long-term manager moved on to the Brooklyn Royal Giants. Philadelphia fielded a decent team in 1910 that featured two young talents who had been recruited by White, outfielder Spottswood Poles and catcher Louis Santop. But by the next season, even these two had moved on and Schlichter's club was a mere shadow of its former self. The Philadelphia Giants persevered until 1916, but as a great club they ceased to exist once White left.

Back in Chicago, Frank Leland proved no match for Rube Foster. Leland's newly rechristened Chicago Giants were a strong team in 1910; the problem was that Foster's Leland Giants were a great team. Defying the judge's ruling (and getting away with it), Foster pilfered three players from Leland's club: catcher-first-baseman Pete Booker and outfielders Jap Payne and Pete Hill. He pried "Home Run" Johnson away from his managerial post with the Brooklyn Royal Giants to go along with Petway and Lloyd, who came from Philly, and Rube filled out his starting eight with talented rookies like outfielder Frank Duncan and third baseman Wes Pryor. Joining Foster on the pitching staff were talented youngbloods Frank Wickware, Bill Lindsay, and lefthanded Pat Dougherty.

* * * *

OPPOSITE: *Jack Johnson became the first black heavyweight champion of the world on December 26, 1908. With his success and his defiance of the status quo, Johnson (seen here behind the wheel of an early sports car) paved the way for such men as Rube Foster. In addition, his flashy lifestyle—of "fast women, fast cars, and sloe gin"—was a cautionary example. In the wake of his victories (and of his marriages to three white women), the U.S. government enacted legislation banning interracial prize fights as well as interracial marriages.*

At the start of the season, Foster took his team down to his home state of Texas for spring training (Foster's Leland Giants were the first black team to have spring training, beginning in 1908). The response in Texas' black communities was overwhelming—it was the glorious return of a prodigal son. Foster was received like a king, his players like princes. At the end of spring, Foster's Giants boarded their luxurious Pullman railroad coach, a poignant symbol of power for impoverished American blacks, and headed north prepared to annihilate all comers.

Back in Chicago, Foster's skills as a backroom dealer were in full evidence as he swung a stadium deal with Chicago White Sox owner Charlie Comiskey. As it happened, the White Sox were moving from their old home, South Side Park, the very park out of which Frank Leland had been pushed a decade earlier. The only way it made sense for Comiskey not to level the stadium would be if a popular tenant were moving in, and any Rube Foster enterprise fit that description. The problem was that Foster and his club were black, and there was no way a major league owner could enter into a business deal with a black team. So a front was set up through the auspices of Comiskey's brother-in-law, John Schorling. Thus, Foster purchased the stadium from Schorling, while the land remained in Schorling's name—though Comiskey really owned both—and the stadium was even renamed Schorling Park for good measure. And in a backroom deal, Foster agreed to pay out a percentage of the concession and gate earnings to Schorling-Comiskey. Thus, the pair made a bundle off a lucrative tenant, while Foster not only shared in the sizable profits but also enjoyed the prestige of owning his own ballpark.

Actually, Foster's team rarely played in Chicago during 1910; their stadium was undergoing renovations for much of the season, the city's semipro teams offered little in the way of competition, and Foster wanted to avoid Frank Leland's team, which

was stocked with his former players. Thus, Foster's Giants took their show on the road, playing throughout the land and, in the process, reaching a large portion of the nation's black fans, further cementing Foster's reputation as the biggest name in black baseball. African-Americans were impressed not only with the Giants' brilliant play and their manager's regal bearing, but also with the organization's unwavering professionalism, signified in everything from their splendid white and red uniforms to their state-of-the-art equipment to their composed and dignified manner on the field, all of which were trademarks of Rube Foster teams. One of Foster's prime motivations for having his own team was to build an organization that was a role model for black America.

But the Leland Giants' demanding travel schedule betrayed two ulterior motives. Foster realized that by touring the country—and he ended the season with the first-ever West Coast swing by a professional black team—he could scout the nation's black talent and sign up the best of the lot. (What young black ballplayer could turn down a spot on Rube Foster's team?) His commitment to recruiting was a main reason he was able to build such a powerful team so quickly. Also, Foster, who had learned about baseball booking in Chicago, got to learn the setup in the rest of the country. Significantly, Foster managed to snub the man who dominated independent bookings in the East, Nat C. Strong, when his club made its eastern swing. Foster perceived that Strong, a white New Yorker, was the single most powerful force in eastern black baseball. The two would soon clash. For the time being, however, Foster could not challenge Strong's grip on eastern booking; Foster was able to capitalize on his own renown to avoid dealing with Strong as the Leland Giants passed through the eastern booker's "territory."

Foster's Giants also happened to be the best team in black baseball in 1910, posting an amazing 123–6 record. Shortstop John Henry Lloyd led the way; his .417 average and brilliant performance in all facets of the game cemented his reputation as the best all-around player in black baseball. Lloyd soon parted ways with Foster, however, and joined the Lincoln Giants for the 1911 season.

Not to be confused with the early (1890) Nebraska touring team, these new Lincoln Giants were from New York City, and they would fill a power void in eastern blackball. With the sudden collapse of the Philadelphia Giants in 1909, eastern blackball was without a first-rate power in 1910. Ironically, the Brooklyn Royal Giants claimed their first Eastern Colored title in 1910, their first season without their longtime captain and best player, "Home Run" Johnson, and their final full season under owner John Connors. By 1911, Connors gave up trying to fight Nat C. Strong's stranglehold on New York baseball and sold him the team.

Strong's initial significant holdings, in the 1890s, had been the top two independent baseball venues in Brooklyn, the Brighton Oval and Dexter Park. Strong took a percentage out of the gate and concessions for every game played on his property. Soon he was buying up small-to-medium-sized venues throughout the East Coast, which greatly increased his influence in the region because he could deny teams lucrative dates against the top semipro, amateur, and black teams in his fold if they didn't play at his ballparks against less competitive teams. Schlichter allied himself closely with Strong during the Philadelphia Giants' heyday; meanwhile John Connors, a black man, was squeezed out by Strong.

Historians are split as to whether Strong had a positive or negative effect on blackball, and whether or not he was a racist. On the one hand, Strong certainly sponsored more blackball and interracial baseball games than any other promoter before the advent of the Negro leagues. Many black baseball men felt that Strong was an equal opportunity businessman who recognized blackball as the profit-making machine that it was fast becoming. On the

* * * *

ABOVE: *Smokey Joe Williams was one of blackball's greatest pitchers, admired by the likes of Rube Foster and Satchel Paige.*
OPPOSITE: *Rube Foster (in the suit) poses in the midst of his team, the Chicago American Giants.*

other hand, to the likes of Rube Foster he was still a white man who was skimming a considerable amount of money off the top of earnings that were generated by black men. And Strong did sabotage John Connors, the most influential black owner in the East, by denying him many potentially profitable contests. But Strong's defenders claim that this had more to do with the Royal Giants' proximity to Strong's homebase than it did with Connors' race.

Just as Nat Strong had seemingly cemented his grip on the talent-weak world of eastern blackball with the acquisition of the Brooklyn Royal Giants, the Lincoln Giants appeared on the scene. Started by white boxing promoter Jess McMahon, who had once had a financial interest in the Philadelphia Giants, the Lincoln Giants were built to win, and to survive in, Nat Strong's New York. McMahon's Giants skirted Strong's monopoly by buying property for their home field in Harlem, which was dubbed Olympic Field. Capitalizing on the connections he had made playing with the Philadelphia Giants, McMahon hired Sol White away from Brooklyn to build his team. Like Rube Foster in 1910, White put together a dynamo in his first season. White brought over two young stars he had recruited for the Philadelphia Giants—blindingly fast center fielder Spottswood Poles and the greatest slugger of the upcoming generation, catcher Louis Santop—as well as the stellar third baseman from the Giants, Billy Francis. White landed another top-flight young talent, left fielder Jimmie Lyons, who had speed comparable to Poles' (the two were probably the fastest outfield tandem in blackball history). Most impressively, White lured not only Lloyd but the great "Home Run" Johnson and rock-solid Pete Booker from Foster's ranks. White carried the still-dependable southpaw Dan McClellan along with him from Brooklyn to anchor a pitching staff that included the two best pitching prospects to emerge in black baseball since Foster, "Smokey" Joe Williams and "Cannonball" Dick Redding.

The Lincolns did have to deal with adversity in their inaugural season, as Sol White left the team midseason, heading back home to Bellaire, Ohio (for all intents and purposes retiring), and team captain John Henry "Pop" Lloyd took the reins—not a popular selection with all the players. Nevertheless, the Lincoln Giants won more than 85 percent of their games in their inaugural season. They had four players who batted .400 or better: Poles (.400),

in the same game meant that perhaps the two greatest shortstops in the history of baseball were on the field at the same time. The older Wagner had just only one hit, a triple, but that was more than Lloyd could manage against the great Johnson, going 0–4. The Lincolns did score three runs off Johnson, but the major leaguers tallied five against McClellan.

From 1911 to 1913, there were, in effect, two "major league" black professional franchises. Since

he would more than likely soon be on the roster of one of the black game's two reigning dynasties.

Out west, Foster's club, rechristened the Chicago American Giants before the 1911 season, maintained their dominance in spite of the loss of Lloyd, Johnson, and Booker to the Lincolns. With his stadium's renovation completed, Foster scheduled more home games, which attracted vast crowds. The only thing lacking was formidable competition. The American Giants claimed the City League title in both 1911 and 1912, and in the absence of any other top-flight black team in the region, Foster's club breezed through the rest of their schedule. One memorable highlight was a pitching duel between Foster and Jose Mendez, the Cuban Stars ace, that ended in a 0–0 tie after twelve innings.

Back east, the nucleus of the Lincoln Giants remained together in 1912 and achieved even more spectacular results. Twice they faced major league opponents—the New York Highlanders of the AL and the NL champion New York Giants—and the results were identical. The Lincoln Giants won 6–0 behind the shutout pitching of "Smokey" Joe Williams, who made a habit of overwhelming major leaguers throughout his spectacular career. The only thing missing from the Lincolns' resumé was also notably absent from that of Foster's Giants'—the title of World Champion of Colored Base Ball. That would be bequeathed the following season.

The next year, 1913, saw more of the same for the two juggernauts of black professional baseball: the American Giants trounced their midwestern foes, while the Lincolns were even more impressive in the East on account of their 4–1 mark against major league foes (including a Joe Williams victory over Grover Cleveland Alexander and the Philadelphia Phillies). The much-anticipated late-season showdown between the two blackball dynamos proved anticlimactic, as the Lincoln Giants, led by the superior pitching of Williams and Dick Redding, dominated Foster's club. Overall, the 1913 Lincoln

Lyons (.450), Santop (.470), and, at the top, Lloyd (.475). They toured most of the season, playing few home games, their illustrious lineup earning them games against top-rung minor league teams. The highlight of the season was a showdown with a team of major league all-stars, including Honus Wagner and the American League's top pitcher in 1911, Walter Johnson. The presence of Wagner and Lloyd

1906, there had been a steadily increasing pool of black professional and semipro teams throughout the land, but these clubs functioned as "farm teams" for the high-profile black professional teams. During this three-year span, none of these minor league black teams could reasonably expect to challenge Foster's Giants or the Lincoln Giants; and if one of these clubs developed a transcendent young talent,

Giants won more than 94 percent of their recorded games and clearly deserve a place on any short list of the greatest teams in black baseball history.

Rube Foster didn't panic—he got revenge, reclaiming Lloyd and Francis and pilfering "Smokey" Joe Williams from the Lincoln Giants during the off-season. The exodus from Harlem stemmed from player dissatisfaction with Jess McMahon, which was less about money than personality conflicts. Adding insult to injury, Nat Strong's Brooklyn Royal Giants, led by another Lincoln Giant defector, Louis Santop, jumped up and claimed the Eastern Colored title in 1914. But the season belonged to Rube Foster's troops; the American Giants swept the Royal Giants to claim the National Negro Championship.

By 1915, Lloyd and Williams had returned to Harlem (though Francis stayed with Foster) to play for the Lincoln Giants. In a typically odd blackball plot twist, McMahon had sold the Lincoln Giants to a pair of investors but retained control of the players. The Lincoln Giants reasserted their dominance over the Royal Giants and proceeded to a ten-game championship series against the American Giants. Perhaps appropriately, given the seemingly absurd shuttling of players between New York and Chicago every off-season, the series ended in a five-all draw. The Lincolns' other ace, Dick "Cannonball" Redding, distinguished himself in the series, winning three games, including one shutout.

The most significant development in the upper echelon of black baseball in 1915 was the evolution of two midwestern franchises into professional teams capable of challenging Foster's American Giants: J.L. Wilkinson's All-Nations barnstorming troupe and a previously "minor league" black franchise, the Indianapolis ABCs.

The All-Nations team emerged from the midwestern blackball circuit, which had been trailblazed by the Page Fence Giants in the mid-1890s. After the quick rise and fall of the Algona Brownies in 1903–1904, the next black team from the plains

to develop into a regional drawing card was the Topeka Giants. The Giants' approach to barnstorming was much like that of the Page Fence Giants: the team would arrive in town a few hours before their game to drum up interest among the townsfolk, trying to create a festival environment (organizing a pregame parade, if possible). And, à la Page Fence, they often clowned around on the field, though, like the Page Fence nine, they almost always won against small-town opponents. Unlike Page Fence, though, the Topeka Giants were never one of the elite teams in black baseball; they never seriously challenged Rube Foster's Chicago teams. In the 1890s, the Page Fence Giants had represented one of the few opportunities for black ballplayers to earn a living from baseball; by the

1910s, there were numerous professional black teams and their ranks were expanding. In fact, the Kansas City Giants, owned by black entrepreneur Tobe Smith, were well established by 1910. Based in a city with a sizable and expanding black community, Smith's Giants did not rely so much on barnstorming. In fact, they had their own stadium. The K.C. Giants quickly supplanted the Topeka Giants as the top black club on the plains. And in 1910, another Kansas City pro black team, the Royal Giants, also rose to prominence. Meanwhile, in St. Louis, the proprietor of a popular bar in the black community, Charlie Mills, organized that city's first successful black professional team, named, of course, the St. Louis Giants. But by the mid-1910s, the emerging black power on the

✳ ✳ ✳ ✳

OPPOSITE: *The 1915 Indianapolis ABCs featured (back row, from left) Russell Powell, Ben Taylor, Dick Redding, Bingo DeMoss, Morten Clark, Dan Kennard; (middle row, from left) Oscar Charleston, Dicta Johnson, C.I. Taylor, Jimmie Lyons, Tom Allen; (front row, from left) George Shively and James Jeffries.* **ABOVE:** *Oscar Charleston in a later incarnation, as a Homestead Gray.*

western touring circuit was a barnstorming squad that smacked of gimmickry, the All-Nations team.

As the name implies, the All-Nations was not just an all-black team, it was multiracial. Seemingly making light of segregation, the All-Nations team had players from a number of different ethnic groups: white, black, Latin, Native American, Chinese, and so on (usually a pair from each "race"). Also aboard was a woman named Carrie Nation, who usually played first base. Of course, faked ethnicity was a part of the baseball barnstorming scene (e.g., Cuban Giants), as was exaggerated ethnicity (e.g., the long-bearded Jewish House of David team); gender-bending was prevalent as well (there were numerous "all-woman" teams that were really men in drag). But owner J.L. Wilkinson wanted authenticity. Thus, the Latins were really Cuban, Carrie Nation was indeed a woman, and no one wore blackface. And while he was at it, Wilkinson recruited some fine ballplayers.

An Iowa native, Wilkinson became one of the most important figures in Negro league history. J.L. was the son of the president of Highland College in Des Moines. But young Wilkinson's passion was baseball: he pitched for Highland College and also played semipro ball on the side, using the pseudonym Joe Green lest he incur his father's wrath. Eventually acknowledging his identity, Wilkinson pitched on small-town Iowa teams, some pro, mostly semipro. In the twilight of his career, he became a player-manager for a Des Moines semipro team. Wilkinson grew frustrated with the job. Whenever he developed a good young player, a minor league team would simply take the player away. Familiar with black touring teams from playing against them, and aware of the novelty value of fielding a black team, Wilkinson organized the All-Nations in 1912. The barnstorming team and its accompanying burlesque show (wrestlers and musicians were a part of the caravan) were an instant hit on the midwestern circuit.

Wilkinson proved to be a magnanimous owner, paying his employees well; as a result, he was able to attract quality players. At the end of the team's first season, Wilkinson struck gold, signing a legendary Latin hurler, the "Cuban Mathewson," Jose Mendez. This attracted Cuba's other top star, outfielder Cristobal Torriente, who played for the All-Nations in 1913 (and again in 1916 and 1917). Wilkinson proved to be an astute judge of talent, signing young black southpaw John Donaldson in 1913; Donaldson quickly became the top lefthanded pitcher in blackball. When Mendez started to experience arm trouble after 1914, Wilkinson moved the multitalented Cuban to shortstop and brought in another young top-flight black pitcher, Bill "Plunk" Drake. One of the All-Nations' white pitchers, Virgil Barnes, went on to the major leagues. With this aggregation of talent, the All-Nations became one of the best baseball teams in the Midwest, regardless of race, and one of top teams and biggest draws on the black baseball touring circuit. Indeed, the All-Nations won two of three from Rube Foster's American Giants in 1915, and the following season topped Foster's club again, as well as the other emerging black team in the Midwest, the Indianapolis ABCs.

The ABCs' rise to prominence was considerably more mundane than the All-Nations', but it was spectacular nonetheless. The franchise was a prime example of a second-rung black professional team. Not much of an attraction on the road, though it provided adequate competition to regional minor league and semipro teams, the team drew large crowds at home on special occasions, like when Rube Foster brought his team to town. Small crowds meant less money, and this meant the ABCs were doomed to lose their best players to the top-rung black teams, which could pay higher salaries.

This all changed in 1914, when Tom Bowser, a white man, bought the club and turned it around almost overnight by hiring manager Charles I. Taylor. The new manager brought the nucleus of his old team, the West Baden (Indiana) Sprudels, with him to Indianapolis, just as four years earlier he had brought his team to West Baden from Birmingham, Alabama. This core of players included Taylor's younger brother, Ben, an excellent first baseman and quality pitcher; a great young second baseman, Bingo DeMoss; and a righthanded ace, sinker-ball pitcher "Dizzy" Dismukes. An acute judge of talent and a master at teaching players the nuances of the game, by the following season Taylor had built the ABCs into the first team to seriously challenge Foster's western dynasty since upstart St. Paul in 1909. He strengthened his team by signing the St. Louis Giants' star infielder, Frank Warfield, for the season, but the key addition was a rookie center fielder, Oscar Charleston, who was so awesome that he single-handedly transformed the ABCs into contenders. Indeed, the young ABCs challenged the American Giants for the 1915 regional title, but Foster's veteran club prevailed in the closely fought series.

Unfortunately, a midseason brawl overshadowed the ABCs' on-field accomplishments. Second baseman Bingo DeMoss was so incensed at a close call during a game against a team of white all-stars that he ran at the umpire, even throwing a punch. Then Oscar Charleston, who had rushed in from center field, leveled the umpire with one blow. A veritable riot erupted, with fans pouring onto the field. DeMoss and Charleston spent the night in jail. The riot led to the banning of interracial games in Indianapolis. Rube Foster, ever the sermonizer, castigated Taylor's team for inappropriate behavior. The two managers then maintained an antagonistic dialogue in the black press for more than a year, leading up to their 1916 rematch.

The 1916 Indianapolis ABCs were even stronger than they had been the previous year, adding another first-class rookie, third baseman Dave Malarcher, and (late in the season) a ringer, pitching ace Dick "Cannonball" Redding.

Meanwhile, Foster's American Giants had a familiar face back in their lineup in 1916, John Henry Lloyd, who rejoined a core lineup that had been together for a half decade: catcher Bruce Petway, center fielder Pete Hill (probably the greatest blackball outfielder before the arrival of Oscar Charleston), Frank Duncan in left, and fastball pitcher Frank Wickware.

A ridiculous conflict tainted the much-anticipated best-of-nine showdown between the ABCs and Foster's Giants. The teams split the first two games, but Foster pulled his team off the field during game three when the umpires would not allow him to wear a fielder's glove while standing in the first base coach's box. Of course, Foster was accustomed to ruling the roost wherever he went in blackball, and he probably viewed the umpires as nothing more than functionaries in his empire. Thus, the conflict was more about the umpires' authority, or, from Foster's point of view, their impertinence toward the de facto commissioner of western blackball, than about a fielder's mitt. At any rate, neither side buckled and the game was ruled a forfeit. However, when the series resumed, Foster once again wore a glove in the coach's box. Taylor objected again, but this time the umpires let play continue. Foster felt that this represented a reversal of the umpires' previous ruling, which effectively annulled the previously forfeited game. Not surprisingly, Taylor disagreed. Thus, when the ABCs won the ninth game of the series (on a dramatic late-inning triple by Charleston), giving them five victories for the title, Foster argued that the series was actually tied 4–4. Regardless, the ABCs were the champs in their own minds and were recognized as such by all except American Giants' partisans. Along with Charleston, the star of the series was Redding, who tossed three victories for the ABCs.

Meanwhile, in blackball's other hemisphere, the Lincoln Giants and the Brooklyn Royal Giants both claimed the regional crown in 1916. Nevertheless,

the Lincolns took the initiative by facing Foster's American Giants (who had, at best, a dubious claim on the western title) in a Colored Championship Series. The Stars moved ahead three games to two, but Foster's staff pitched a shutout in game six and, after spotting the Stars 3 runs, exploded to win game seven 17–7 to capture the series.

Following the 1916 season, Lincoln Giants owner Jess McMahon pulled out of black baseball permanently, and the Lincolns' core of players reformed as the Pennsylvania Red Caps, which would be a decent professional squad for the remainder of the decade. Jim Keenan, the man who bought the Lincoln Giants from McMahon, would rebuild that team into a solid franchise in a few years. (Keenan went on to play a central role in the history of black basketball, as the owner of the first great all-black team, the Harlem Renaissance, in the 1930s.) In contrast to McMahon, Keenan had no intention of challenging Nat Strong's virtual monopoly over the booking of independent baseball games on the eastern seaboard. Heading into the 1917 season, it seemed that black professional baseball in the Northeast was merely a subset of Strong's empire. But just like in 1911, when McMahon's Lincolns came out of nowhere to spoil Strong's apparent consolidation of power, a couple of new teams, one in Atlantic City and the other in Philadelphia, burst onto the eastern blackball scene in 1917—and both were owned by African-Americans.

In American history, the period from 1917 to 1919 is, of course, synonymous with World War I. The war had a major transformative effect on black American society and, consequently, on black baseball. More than 350,000 black Americans served in the military during the war, though they were organized in segregated units. Many prominent black leaders encouraged young black men to enlist, arguing that they would be fighting for an America that would fulfill its promise of "liberty, justice, and equality for all" and, in doing so, providing whites with an unequivocal symbol of black commitment to the nation, which could only engender good will. Meanwhile, the war proved to be a boon to black America's economy, as a plethora of jobs in heavy industry opened up on the home front. With most of these new jobs located in the industrial North, the migration of blacks from the South to the North, already pronounced, increased tremendously. The armament industries hired tens of thousands of new unskilled laborers, and when the United States entered the war, even more factory jobs became available as workers vacated their posts to enlist.

The war years were also a time of increasing racial tension. Race riots even broke out on military camps. And white workers who feared that blacks were stealing their jobs occasionally expressed their fears through violence. Still, such incidents were not commonplace, and in general, the war years were a time of renewed hope for black America.

The war, and the massive demographic transformation that it brought about, had a direct impact on black baseball, as even more black teams could be supported in the northern population centers. The most conspicuous example of the northern migration's impact on black baseball was the case of a team called the Duval Giants from Jacksonville, Florida, which moved en masse to Atlantic City in 1916. Two black politicians, Tom Jackson and Henry Tucker, brought the team north and rechristened it after Atlantic City's white mayor, Harry Bacharach. Thus were born the Bacharach Giants,

* * * *

Marcus Moziah Garvey was a proponent of black separatism, and his social theories energized many African-Americans in the first part of the twentieth century. In contrast, Rube Foster believed that the Negro National League had to be a separate, black-owned and –run enterprise, but envisioned a day when black and white baseball would intermingle.

who soon established themselves as one of the East's top black professional teams.

In 1917, another all-black team, the Hilldale club from Darby, left the ranks of the amateurs. The team's owner, Ed Bolden, a black clerk in the Philadelphia main post office, had used the black media to build interest in his amateur team. Raiding the rosters of local sandlot clubs, Hilldale became a Philadelphia power, even landing a few exhibitions against Connie Mack's Athletics. Thus, the Hilldale Daisies, as they were sometimes called (in reference to the flowers in a field alongside the Hilldale trolley line), began to fill the void created by the disappearance of the Philadelphia Giants and the other professional teams that had made Philadelphia the blackball mecca of the century's first decade. Hilldale's first professional squad included some veterans Bolden had enticed away from other teams, including center fielder Spot Poles, finesse (spitball) pitcher Doc Sykes, leadoff hitter and right fielder Otto Briggs, and catcher Bill Pettus. And at the end of the season, Bolden brought in "Smokey" Joe Williams, brilliant young shortstop Dick Lundy (the Bacharachs' top star), and slugger Louis Santop to bolster his lineup for exhibition games against a barnstorming team of major league "all-stars" (i.e., midlevel players plus a few stars). Bolden's real coup was signing Santop for the entire 1918 season.

With the Bacharachs and Hilldale as new stops on the eastern blackball circuit, 1917 was a promising year, and the increase in the black population led to sizable crowds; however, no official eastern champion was determined. Meanwhile, out west, "Pop" Lloyd stayed with the American Giants, and second baseman Bingo DeMoss joined him to form perhaps the greatest middle infield in black baseball history. Foster also added lefthanded Cuban hurler Luis Padrone and one of black baseball's best pitchers, Dick Redding. The American Giants were once again a sublime team. C.I. Taylor's young ABCs, who lost their ace Dismukes and third baseman Malarcher to

the draft, and DeMoss to their hated rivals, offered no resistance as Foster's club reclaimed the western title. The American Giants also manhandled the eastern teams they faced, once again establishing themselves as blackball's top team.

One year later, however, the American Giants were also derailed by the war. Dick Redding left for military service. John Henry Lloyd ended his two-year tenure on Foster's Giants when he refused to leave his defense job to report to spring training; he signed with the Brooklyn Royal Giants instead. The draft nabbed starting left fielder Jude Gans and fireballer Frank Wickware, the cornerstone of Foster's staff over the previous decade. Foster also fired a starting pitcher, Tom Williams, for breaking the team's strict rules forbidding drinking. Foster compensated for these losses by adding two great Cuban stars—Cristobal Torriente, a lefthanded power-hitting outfielder with a rifle for an arm, and Jose Mendez, a long-armed hurler whose easy windup masked his phenomenal fastball—and the American Giants proceeded to win the Chicago City League and dominate the blackball scene once again.

Racial tension continued to increase throughout the United States during the war years and it spilled over into games between white and black teams, including contests involving major leaguers. Many white players behaved as if it were an unfathomable disgrace to lose to blacks. And since the top black teams were defeating both major league clubs and off-season "all-star" teams with greater frequency,

* * * *

LEFT: *Catcher and sometime outfielder Louis Santop spent the majority of his long and illustrious career with Hilldale.*
OPPOSITE: *Judge Kennesaw Mountain Landis, first commissioner of major league baseball, whose lasting contribution to the history of baseball may be that he helped keep the game segregated for decades.*

major league owners began to call for an end to these lucrative but demoralizing sideshows. Since the major leaguers (especially the more racist players) probably expected to easily rout the black teams, they often had a hard time coping with defeat. Rather than trying to preserve a one-run lead with the bases loaded in the ninth inning against Hilldale, Boston Red Sox pitcher Joe Bush destroyed the ball and then walked off the field and forfeited the game, such was his fear of losing to blacks. More vulgar displays of racist sportsmanship did occur but were infrequent, probably because of the large numbers of black fans who attended these games. Nevertheless, the potential for violence at games with biracial audiences began to intimidate some organizers.

Still, as bad as racial tensions were during the war, black America was unprepared for what transpired immediately after the war. From the late spring through the summer of 1919, the worst race riots of the twentieth century exploded in cities throughout the United States. Mobs of angry whites went on rampages in black neighborhoods, destroying property and lynching blacks; in most instances, the law looked the other way. White claims of black

provocation were usually pure fiction. In St. Louis, the riots started when a young black boy who was playing in the water on a makeshift float drifted into the whites-only section of the beach and was lynched. Blacks fought to defend themselves but were usually routed. In the end, hundreds of blacks were killed throughout the nation.

The white rage of 1919 has routinely been attributed to a fear of losing jobs to blacks, whom whites believed would work for lower wages. Yet the riots occurred against a backdrop of massive layoffs of black workers, and their replacement by whites. Although fear of unemployment, rank racist hatred, and the horrible carnage of the European war (returning soldiers probably had few qualms about violence and had an abundance of pent-up fear to unleash on scapegoats) were all contributing factors to the white-on-black violence, what was probably most threatening to white men who returned from Europe to find an influx of blacks in their cities was the notion that blacks would feel so much more comfortable in the North than they had in the South that they would cease to behave subserviently to whites, thereby ruining the advantages (both psychological and economic) that white racists enjoyed in their relationship with blacks. Progressives roundly condemned the behavior of the rioters and reiterated their support for the black struggle for equality, but after the summer of 1919, any hopes blacks had of attaining social equality through appeals to white sympathy seemed ill-founded.

Black baseball teams must have brushed up against some scary situations during the summer of 1919, though none of the top teams were involved in any violent incidents. When Rube Foster's American Giants reached Chicago following spring training in 1919, the team's home field, Schorling Stadium, had been transformed into a tent city for the National Guard, which had been called in to quell the riots. It was against this backdrop—of a virulent racist backlash that had spread terror throughout black

America—that Rube Foster decided the time for waiting was over. Black America had to take control of its own institutions; it was time for black baseball to be run by blacks.

However, even after the riots, Foster was not espousing black separatism, which was understandably in vogue. Marcus Garvey's call for black pride, for African consciousness, for a return to the homeland, and especially for responding exclusively to the needs of the black community, was at the peak of its influence following the riots. And Foster's organization of the Negro National League (NNL) must have appealed to many separatists, but that was not Foster's motivation. His model was drawn from the teachings of the great black educator Booker T. Washington. Washington called on blacks to build institutions that would actively benefit the race, thus contributing to the proof, supported by ever-increasing evidence, that blacks merit treatment as equals. Thus, the stated goal of Foster's NNL was the desegregation of the national pastime, which would be a significant step on the path toward racial equality in the United States. In fact, in 1920, just before the start of the NNL's inaugural season, Foster visited Keenesaw Mountain Landis, the newly appointed, first-ever commissioner of baseball, to ask if the majors would accept two all-black teams. Landis, who would remain a staunch opponent of integration during his twenty-four-year tenure, unequivocally rejected the proposal, and Foster went forward with his new league.

The NNL was hardly the first attempt to form a black "major" baseball league. In fact, it wasn't even Foster's first try. In 1910, He had had one of the black backers of the Leland Giants, Beauregard Mosely, approach other clubs in major midwestern and southern cities about joining an all-black league. Mosely enticed seven clubs to sign up, two from Kansas City and one each from St. Louis, Columbus, Louisville, Mobile, and New Orleans—plus the Leland Giants. Mosely's rhetoric was aggressive: the league was forming because blacks were "already forced out of the game from a national standpoint," and the success of the league "would of itself force recognition from minor white leagues to play us and share in the receipts." The project collapsed before any games were played because of a lack of funding. From Mosely's efforts, Foster learned that it would take substantial funding to start a league and that assertive language that might scare away investors should be avoided.

The biggest advantage Foster had a decade after Mosely's abortive effort was that the recent proliferation of successful black professional teams made the ground more fertile for a large-scale black baseball league. Not only were there more black pro teams, but many of these were quality teams that had experience on the road and were based in large cities with growing black populations—perfect conditions for a league modeled on the "majors."

During the 1919 season, Foster was more concerned with the general welfare of black baseball than with the on-field success of his Chicago American Giants. He knew a successful league had to have strong franchises and be located in the major markets. Detroit was a rapidly growing metropolis and industrial boomtown, and black people were swarming there, but it had no history of big-time blackball. However, a wealthy black Detroit man, Terry Blount, decided to try to form a top-flight team. Blount had the money to do it; he was a hugely successful numbers runner in the black community. These gambling pools were illegal but well established, and so many blacks bet on them every day that the person running the operation invariably became very rich. Rube Foster wanted the owners of black baseball teams to be respectable businessmen, not gangsters like Blount. But the sad truth was that few, if any,

people in black America had as much money as the top numbers men. So Foster not only grudgingly accepted Blount, he did everything in his power to see to the success of the Detroit Stars.

Indeed, Foster's generosity was the story of the 1919 blackball season, as he built up Detroit's team at the expense of his own. Foster moved four players

from his own roster to Detroit's, and not just any players, but Jose Mendez and some of the American Giants who had been the nucleus of Foster's team since 1911, catcher Bruce Petway and outfielders Pete Hill and Frank Duncan. Likewise, Foster sat approvingly by as the Stars signed up former American Giants pitcher Frank Wickware and talented young third baseman Dave Malarcher when they returned from the war. With clearance from Foster, Detroit also added John Donaldson, the All-Nations' great southpaw; Frank "the Weasel" Warfield, the ABCs' slick-fielding second baseman; and a top prospect in the outfield, Floyd "Jelly" Gardner. With a quartet of players—Petway, Hill, Duncan, and Wickware—who had been at the

heart of the American Giants' decade-long western dynasty and were not yet past their prime, it was no wonder that the Stars knew how to win. As Detroit rolled over the semipro, minor league, and "lesser" black teams in the Midwest, a series with Foster's club loomed on the horizon.

The American Giants had a few new faces in 1919. Foremost among these was center fielder Oscar Charleston, who was the heir apparent to "Pop" Lloyd's mantle as black baseball's best all-around player. As great as Charleston was, however, the 1919 American Giants were weakened by the departure of many of their top players to Detroit. Indeed, the Stars rolled over the American Giants. The showdown was not an officially declared championship matchup, but the result meant that for the first time in the American Giants' nine-year history, another team could claim the undisputed western title. Still, Rube Foster had been behind the Stars' success, and he achieved what he desired. The Detroit franchise was a huge hit, garnering a $30,000 profit in its first season.

Foster was planning to start his black major league in 1920, but circumstances and logistics dictated that it would be a midwestern league; the eastern powers would not be included. The reasons for this were twofold: one, because the long-distance train rides were costly and could bankrupt some teams; and two, Foster was at odds with the most powerful man in eastern blackball, booking agent Nat Strong. Foster's feud with Strong was long-standing and seemingly irreconcilable. Strong still controlled most of the booking arrangements on the eastern blackball circuit, and he used this power against any team that tried to challenge him. Safely outside Strong's jurisdiction, Foster's American Giants tried to avoid playing on Strong's fields whenever they toured the East Coast. Foster resented not simply that a white man had a stranglehold on eastern blackball, but that Strong was a cunning, power-hungry white man who not only stood in the way of Foster's ambitions but also promised to be a formidable foe. In the black press, Foster repeatedly called for black entrepreneurs to take control of black baseball from white men who "own, manage, and do as they feel like doing in the semipro ranks with underhand methods."

There were four top-level black franchises in the East at the dawn of the 1920s: the Brooklyn Royal Giants, owned by Strong; the Lincoln Giants, who were not as powerful under James Keenan's custody as they had been when owned by Jess McMahon; the Bacharach Giants, who had relocated to New York City in 1919; and the Hilldale club of Darby, Pennsylvania, near Philadelphia. (A fifth pro team, the Cuban Stars, was the weak stepchild among the touring blackball teams. Underfunded and without a home field—or town—the Stars inevitably lost their top talent to the highest bidder.) All four teams featured name stars. Player-manager "Pop" Lloyd led Brooklyn; the great "Smokey" Joe Williams still pitched for the Lincoln Giants; up-and-coming superstar Dick Lundy played short for the Bacharachs; and Hilldale featured the awesome power-hitting catcher Louis Santop, whose tape-measure home runs made him a folk hero. But none

❋ ❋ ❋ ❋

OPPOSITE: *Men from the 369th Colored Infantry are served chicken at the 71st Regiment Armory after the parade celebrating their return on February 17, 1919. Unfortunately, the war had exacerbated racial tensions in the United States, which spilled over into violence following the soldiers' return.* **RIGHT:** *The race riots of 1919 were the worst in the history of the United States. Here a group of onlookers witnesses the aftermath of a riot in Chicago that left three men dead.*

of these teams had the depth of talent that Rube Foster's teams had had year in, year out.

Ed Bolden, the ambitious owner of Hilldale, seemed intent on assembling a great team. And Hilldale had become tremendously popular in Philadelphia during the late 1910s, often outdrawing the Phillies and A's. Bolden expanded the stands at his ballpark to seat eight thousand spectators, and more fans flocked to see the Daisies. Hilldale, consequently, attracted many major league teams, which were struggling financially during the war, and the Daisies more than held their own in these exhibitions (though on these occasions they frequently bolstered their lineup with ringers like "Smokey" Joe Williams and Dick Lundy). Bolden was raking in the dough, and in blackball, a cash-rich owner willing to invest in players usually meant a new dynasty was in the making.

Bolden's ascendancy would eventually make Nat Strong very uneasy. Back in 1916, after Jess McMahon had bowed out of blackball, Strong's control over the business side of eastern independent baseball, and his Brooklyn Royal Giants' dominance of eastern blackball, were virtually unchallenged. When Hilldale and the Bacharach Giants appeared on the eastern scene the next season, both clubs were willing to play by Strong's rules on the business side of the ledger, though they didn't mask their ambitions on the field. Still, the Royal Giants remained superior to Hilldale and the Bacharachs in 1917 and were the de facto eastern champs. The following season, Strong countered the loss of Santop to Hilldale by hiring Lloyd to manage and play, bringing back "Cannonball" Redding and signing a sharp rookie third baseman, Oliver Marcelle. Once again, the Royal Giants looked like the strongest team in the

East; but when the Bacharach Giants folded midyear, most of their top players joined Hilldale, making the Daisies more formidable. Brooklyn and Hilldale both racked up victories the remainder of the season, but since no championship showdown was arranged, neither club could lay claim to the eastern title.

Strangely, it was the collapse of the Bacharach Giants that produced turmoil in Nat Strong's kingdom. While Hilldale was on the rise in 1918, the Bacharach Giants crashed and burned. The Bacharachs had a solid season in 1917, both on the field and at the gate, but not only did the team lose numerous players to the war, Atlantic City attracted fewer visitors during wartime and the team owners closed up shop at midseason. In the off-season, who should step up to buy the club but John W. Connors, the original owner of the Brooklyn Royal Giants.

Of the many people who held grudges against Nat Strong, Connors was at the top of the list. Strong had sabotaged Connors' Royal Giants by charging them an exorbitant amount (far higher than he charged any other team) to play at the Brooklyn Oval (their natural home field) and taking a ridiculously large percentage of the gate and concessions at their games, driving the club to bankruptcy so he could buy it for himself. This time around, Connors had powerful backing—from a black man, no less. Connors, along with Baron Wilkins (a legendary black gangster and Harlem club owner), purchased the Bacharach Giants. Ten years earlier, Wilkins had been a major behind-the-scenes player in the rise of black heavyweight boxing champion Jack Johnson. With Wilkins footing the bill, Connors lured fleet-footed outfielder Jess Barber from Rube Foster's lair, more outfield speed in the person of Spottswood Poles, plus hard-hitting Bruce Pettus off the Hilldale roster, and, in a direct slap in the face to Strong, two legendary superstars who had spent the previous season in Brooklyn: "Cannonball" Redding and John Henry "Pop" Lloyd. But that was

only half the story. Connors and Wilkins were moving the Bacharachs up the coast to New York City, where they had every intention of disturbing Strong's empire.

The year 1919 promised to be an interesting, if undramatic, season in eastern blackball. After all, there was no way in hell that Strong's Royal Giants and Connors' Bacharachs were going to meet on the playing field. Hilldale, the Bacharachs, and the Royal Giants all had fine seasons, none of the three teams distinguishing itself above the others. The Bacharachs played their "home games" in Harlem, but they rarely played in a park with a sizable grandstand. There was, however, one series that was exciting in the extreme. Connors, Wilkins, and Ed Bolden joined forces, pulling strings in their hometowns, and the result was a home-and-home series between the Bacharach Giants and Hilldale Daisies played at Ebbets Field and Shibe Park, homes to the major league Brooklyn Dodgers and Philadelphia A's, respectively. This one memorable coup, however, was an exception, and Connors' Bacharachs were forced to retreat to Atlantic City for the 1920 season. Still, Strong's honeymoon was over. He once more had to contend with a bitter enemy in his midst.

An even more serious, though less pressing, challenge to Strong's influence in blackball was brewing in the Midwest: Rube Foster's organization of the Negro National League. By the end of 1919, Foster had settled on the eight teams, all from the Midwest, that were to play in the inaugural season of the NNL. Foster really wanted to include eastern teams as affiliates of the NNL, but could find no takers because he was not in good standing with either Ed Bolden or John W. Connors. The conflict with Bolden was pretty basic: through 1918, Foster had consistently shunned Hilldale when his team toured the East, playing far inferior teams right on Hilldale's doorstep, because Bolden would not grant Foster his usual 50 percent take of the gate and concessions. Finally, in 1919, the two team presidents

reached a compromise, no longer able to bypass such a high-profile showdown (and fat gate). The American Giants throttled Bolden's Daisies in the first two contests, but the easterners pulled out a controversial victory in the series finale. The scene got ugly during the third game, as the Hilldale fans took their frustration out on Foster's club, a scenario that rekindled the bad feelings between Foster and Bolden. Nonetheless, Foster wanted Hilldale to be associated with his new league and sent Bolden numerous friendly, even flattering, communiqués trying to gain his support. Bolden's response was to raid the American Giants' roster, signing three of Foster's players following the 1919 season. Then the Hilldale owner turned down Foster's invitation to the February 1920 meeting in Kansas City, at which the NNL was officially launched. Foster was appropriately outraged, and as the commissioner (and absolute despot, for all intents and purposes) of the NNL, he declared it illegal for any league team to play Hilldale, the Brooklyn Royal Giants, the Lincoln Giants, or the Bacharach Giants.

Foster's banning of Strong's Royal Giants came as no surprise, and Keenan's willingness to accept Strong's domination made his Lincolns off-limits, but Connors' Bacharachs would seem to be a natural ally for Foster. But when Connors also refused to respond to Foster's overtures, the Bacharach Giants were placed on the NNL blacklist. Connors had never forgiven Foster for raiding his Royal Giants to nab Grant "Home Run" Johnson way back in 1910. Ironically, nine years later, just as Foster was asking for Connors' support, Ed Bolden raided Foster's club, prompting Foster to declare Bolden "a pariah whose selfishness is a blight on black baseball." John Connors undoubtedly felt the same way about Rube, though in Foster's defense, he was calling for the implementation of a reserve clause in the NNL that would bind players to their teams in order to end the confusion caused by players jumping, often in midseason, from team to team.

Still, Connors' distrust of Foster was not unreasonable, given the events of 1910. Foster had been in a bind when he was left without players for his team following the bizarre court decision that awarded the "Leland Giants" name to Foster but the team's players to Frank Leland. With only a few weeks to build a strong team from scratch or lose face in Chicago, he had called on ex-teammates like the Royal Giants' Grant Johnson to help him out. Oddly, in the fallout from Foster's evisceration of the dynastic Philadelphia Giants' roster, the remaining core group of ex-Philadelphians moved en masse with player-manager Sol White to Connors' Royal Giants, and the Brooklyn franchise won its first eastern championship that year. Nevertheless, the vulnerable Connors continued to lose money and Nat Strong was able to buy the club by the end of the 1911 season.

In spite of the Royal Giants' on-field success in 1910, Connors could not forgive Foster for pilfering Johnson. Connors believed that Strong's Machiavellian maneuvers against him were motivated by the racist notion that only white people belonged in positions of social and economic power. Thus, Connors had hoped for, even expected, support from Foster, who at age thirty was already the most powerful black man in baseball, and who so often held forth about the need for mutual support in black baseball, especially among black owners. Instead, Connors felt that Foster had stabbed him in the back. In fact, Foster's powerplay during the 1909–1910 off-season undermined the era's two most significant black owners, Frank Leland and John W. Connors. But Foster's actions were typical. He moved against Leland because he felt constrained by him, and he raided Connors out of desperation. Foster had no qualms about his actions because he believed that he was the only black man with the necessary fortitude and vision to lead blackball to the proverbial promised land. Therefore, he saw it as his duty to advance his posi-

★ ★ ★ ★

The 1916 St. Louis Giants featured (back row, from left) Bill Gatewood, William Drake, Harry Kimbro, Tully McAdoo, Sam Bennett, Lee Wade; (front row, from left) Bunny Downs, Frank Warfield, Dan Kennard, Charles Mills, Richard Wallace, Jimmie Lyons, and Charles Blackwell.

tion in baseball regardless of whether his actions contradicted his proclamations.

For his part, Strong did not sit idly by while Foster was organizing the NNL in 1920. Strong perceived that Foster viewed him not only as a rival but also as the enemy. Thus, Foster's league represented a serious threat to Strong's empire. Even if the NNL didn't include eastern teams, it would likely become the centerpiece of black baseball if it succeeded, thereby diminishing the significance of eastern blackball and potentially elevating Foster to a position of such preeminence that he could reorganize eastern blackball as he saw fit. So Strong acted frantically, though his efforts proved just as futile as Foster's had been when he tried to recruit eastern teams for the NNL. Strong's long-term plan was to organize an eastern Negro league, an initiative that generated very little enthusiasm in the 1910s. Then, wanting to neutralize the threat posed by Connors' reemergence with the Bacharach Giants, Strong tried to form an alliance with Ed Bolden, bribing the Hilldale owner with tremendous incen-

tives throughout Strong's eastern empire. When Bolden turned him down, Strong turned vindictive, reviving the old Philadelphia Giants franchise in an effort to steal Hilldale's fan base. Strong's faux Giants didn't make it through their first season. Thus, heading into 1920, Nat Strong was more insecure than he had been in some time: John W. Connors lurked on the Jersey coast plotting vengeance; Ed Bolden had stood up to him and this new star of the region was rising as fast as ever; and in the Midwest, Rube Foster was laying the groundwork for the future of black baseball, a future in which the games played exclusively by black men would be run by black men.

3

NEGRO LEAGUE BASEBALL

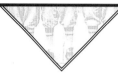

On February 13, 1920, Rube Foster brought together some prominent midwestern black journalists and eight owners of professional black baseball clubs at the Kansas City YMCA in order to officially declare the existence of the Negro National League and determine the rules and regulations of the organization. The eight teams Foster selected for the league (and who anted up the $500 membership levy) were Foster's Chicago American Giants, Terry Blount's Detroit Stars, C.I. Taylor's Indianapolis ABCs, Joe Green's Chicago Giants (descendants of Frank Leland's team), Charles Mills' St. Louis Giants, John Matthews' Dayton Marcos, Abel Linares' Cuban Stars, and J.L. Wilkinson's newly formed Kansas City Monarchs. The inclusion of the first five teams came as a surprise to no one; the final three, however, turned some heads. The Dayton Marcos had been a stable second-tier black franchise for the past decade but had never shown a dramatic improvement like the ABCs had in the mid-1910s. But the league was short on teams, and the Marcos were the oldest stable franchise in burgeoning industrial Ohio, and apparently Foster found owner Matthews trustworthy.

✦ ✦ ✦ ✦

OPPOSITE: *Third baseman Jud Wilson was one of the most feared sluggers of his day. His long career included stints on the Baltimore Black Sox, the Homestead Grays, and the Philadelphia Stars.* **ABOVE:** *The legendary 25th Infantry baseball team was home to several blackball stars. Among those seated here are (front row, from left) unknown, Wilbur "Bullet" Rogan, Lemuel Hawkins, unknown, and Oscar Johnson.*

The decision to include the Cuban Stars club was equally strange. Abel Linares' team, previously known as the Havana Cuban Stars to distinguish them from the New York Cuban Stars, who were owned by Harlem number-running kingpin Alex Pompez and had played thirteen consecutive summers in America. Linares' Stars persevered through numerous logistical problems throughout their history, most notably the fact that the team had no home base; the Stars were on the road all summer long. The club consistently attracted sizable crowds on the road, but the finances of never-ending road trips were troublesome. The Stars were unable to pay their front-line talent—which included superstars Cristobal Torriente and Jose Mendez—competitive wages, and Linares consistently lost his best players to his competitors. Nevertheless, Foster chose the Cubans to play in the NNL. He was probably impressed by the franchise's resiliency, but the determining factor was more likely his friendship with Linares, or even Foster's tremendous popularity in Cuba.

The Cubans did pose a problem: where would they be based? Foster settled upon Cincinnati because two fair-skinned Caucasian Cubans had played for the National League's Cincinnati Reds during the previous decade and both players were very popular with the Cincinnati fans. At the time the players had debuted with the Reds, a wave of hope spread throughout black baseball: the logic went, if these men can play in the majors, then why not a dark-skinned Cuban like Cristobal Torriente, the greatest Cuban player of his generation? And once the likes of Torriente made the majors, then, so the hopeful logic concluded, a black American would soon follow in his path. However, eight years later, some dark-skinned Cubans were arriving in Cincinnati to play in a segregated all-black league. It is unlikely that any black Americans objected to the presence of a Cuban team in an American Negro league, since the dark-skinned Cuban players faced the same racist barrier as black Americans.

Many eyebrows, along with objections, were raised when black fans saw that the owner of the NNL's Kansas City franchise, J.L. Wilkinson, was white. Foster had been consistently outspoken about the need for black baseball to be owned and operated by blacks. Back east, two of the four top black teams were owned by whites, but Foster had been nurturing a black-run environment in the Midwest. And to date, Wilkinson had not operated an all-

★ ★ ★ ★

Rube Foster's drive to win and his commitment to making the National Negro League a success inspired respect in everyone who came into contact with him, although he frequently butted heads with anyone who stood in his way.

black team. His celebrated All-Nations club, which disbanded following the 1918 season, was multiracial. On top of that, the Kansas City team slotted to play in the NNL, the Monarchs, was a first-year team—they had yet to play a game. Wilkinson had already secured the services of black players who would form the nucleus of his new club. He found them en masse, thanks to a tip from his friend Casey Stengel, playing on the "black 25th infantry regiment" team in Fort Huachuca, Arizona. Included in this group was one of the greatest pitchers in blackball history, "Bullet" Joe Rogan, along with outstanding shortstop Dobie Moore, power-hitting outfielder Oscar "Heavy" Johnson, talented southpaw Andy Cooper, and first baseman Lem Hawkins. Wilkinson then added former All-Nations standouts Jose Mendez, Bill "Plunk" Drake, and John Donaldson to the squad.

Why did Foster go against his stated principles and allow a white-owned team into his league? First of all, Foster wanted a team in Kansas City, and that city's two black-owned professional teams from the early 1910s were no longer operating. Second, and most important, J.L. Wilkinson was perceived as a true ally of black baseball in particular, and black America in general. He was a generous owner who genuinely respected his players, regardless of race. Third, Foster understood that the presence of a white man with great connections in midwestern baseball would likely come in handy in terms of booking engagements and receiving better treatment from white baseball organizers. And finally, another team in the league, the St. Louis Giants, was actually owned by a group of white investors who let Charles Mills run the club. Foster's arrangement with Charlie Comiskey, which very few black fans knew about, was not that different from the St. Louis scenario. What was different about the Monarchs was that the white man providing the team's financial backing was also in charge of baseball operations.

At any rate, no one at the Kansas City YMCA meeting objected to the inclusion of Wilkinson's Monarchs, or the Cubans, or the Marcos, or any part of Foster's outline for the league. The league implemented a reserve clause that would bind players to their teams, preventing a player from jumping to another team (at least within the league). As a corollary to the reserve clause, Foster forbade raids on other teams, including black teams not in the league. Foster understood that player movement without compensation to the player's former team had already destroyed numerous black franchises. The constitution also forbade ungentlemanly conduct both on and off the field; those not complying with this statute were subject to fines. And 5 percent of the gate at every league game was to go to the league office. Thus was born the National Association of Colored Professional Base Ball Clubs, which came to be known as the Negro National League. Rube Foster was chairman of both the league's board of directors and its Base Ball Commission, and Foster's booking agency was responsible for scheduling all league games. Foster was, in effect, the ruling body—the benevolent dictator of the league.

Foster set about proving his benevolence, moving players from stronger teams onto weaker teams in order to create greater parity in the league. For instance, Foster decreed that Jose Mendez and pitcher Sam Crawford go from Detroit to Kansas City in exchange for John Donaldson; then he sent one of his American Giants outfielders, Jimmie Lyons, to Detroit. The most conspicuous of these transfers involved the great Oscar Charleston, whom Foster sent from his own American Giants back to the Indianapolis ABCs. This move symbolized Foster's commitment to the success of the league, as he removed one of the greatest players of all time from his own team for the benefit of the league. Personally, Foster might have regretted the Charleston move after the ABCs topped the American Giants 4–2 in the league's inaugural game on May 2, 1920.

All of Foster's careful planning, however, did not produce a smooth debut season for the NNL. Foster wanted all of the league's teams to have eminent domain over their home fields, but this was only true for three of the clubs: the American Giants, Detroit, and St. Louis. The other franchises were reliant upon renting parks from white landlords, and it was often difficult to secure dates for league games. The Cuban Stars failed to find a place to play in Cincinnati, so they spent another entire season on the road. Consequently, the league schedule became quite uneven, a far cry from the one-hundred-game season (each team would play every other team roughly fourteen times) that Foster had envisioned. Still, all eight teams stayed afloat, playing their league games along with a healthy diet of exhibition matches against other competition. Whenever an NNL team got bogged down on the road, Foster would wire money from the league office to get them to the next game. Meanwhile, Foster continued to shift players around the league to increase competitiveness throughout the season. Unfortunately, very little information exists about how the season played out on the field, though at the end of the summer, the Chicago American Giants were declared league champions. More important, Foster's financial records show that all eight NNL teams turned a profit, as did the league itself.

Back east, the top teams played the 1920 season much like any other. Animosity between team owners once again precluded any regional championship playoff. Certainly, one of the highlights of the season came at the end, when a major league all-star team featuring New York Yankees slugger Babe Ruth, whose fifty-four home runs that year shattered the previous major league record (twenty-four) and revolutionized the sport, faced Hilldale at Phillies Park. The Daisies had a slugger of their own, Louis Santop, the most prolific home run hitter in blackball during the 1910s. The major leaguers took the

series, but Santop was impressive, getting three hits to outperform Ruth in the first game. The Bambino, however, bounced back in game two with a towering home run.

The Ruth-Santop showdown was the talk of the town and overshadowed another series taking place simultaneously at Shibe Park, Philadelphia's other major league venue, between the American Giants and the Bacharach Giants. Foster had snubbed Bolden when his club came east, going so far as to visit Darby to play a semipro team. Bolden responded by scheduling Hilldale's encounter with the mighty Ruth on the same days as the Bacharach-American Giants series. The teams split four games, which were played before disappointingly small crowds. The Bacharachs, however, got a measure of revenge when Ruth and company came across town and played them at a soldout Shibe Park. "Cannonball" Redding squared off against Carl Mays (26–11). The Bacharachs knocked Mays all over the park, while Redding contained the major leaguers despite a seventh-inning blast by Ruth; the final was 9–4, Bacharachs.

Foster then countered Bolden's slight by offering an associate membership in the NNL to the Bacharachs. John W. Connors was more than happy to drop an old grudge and accept Foster's offer; after all, Connors had to find a way to survive in an environment dominated by his archenemy, Nat Strong. So Connors and Foster joined forces, united by a common enemy. As an associate member of the NNL on the East Coast, Connors' club would host a set of games with each league team and take an annual midwestern tour to visit the NNL teams. Once allied with Foster, Connors apparently adopted Foster's enemies as his own, as he raided Bolden's Hilldale club for three top players: catcher "Yank" Deas, former American Giant Jess Barber, and superstar shortstop Dick Lundy, who had been one of the original Bacharach Giants only five years earlier.

Ed Bolden actually challenged Connors' raid in court, to no avail. Then, fearing his team's isolation from other blackball powers, he made peace with Nat Strong. However, shortly thereafter, Bolden apparently decided that he was aligned on the wrong side, that it was the NNL and Rube Foster who had history on their side. Bolden wrote an open letter to Foster in the *Philadelphia Tribune*, calling for cooperation between eastern and midwestern blackball. Soon Bolden had paid his tithe to King Rube, and Hilldale was granted an associate membership in the NNL. With the 1921 season on the horizon, the long-divided blackball universe finally seemed to be unifying.

Meanwhile, below the Mason-Dixon line, the Negro Southern League (NSL) was being organized to begin play in 1921. Made up of semipro teams from New Orleans, Montgomery, Birmingham, Atlanta, Jacksonville, Nashville, and Knoxville, the NSL joined Rube Foster's National Association of Colored Base Ball Clubs. In essence, the NSL teams paid dues to Foster as a guarantee against raids by NNL teams. Southern black baseball had been flourishing at the local semipro level for three and a half decades. The top teams would occasionally venture a few hundred miles to meet another vaunted semipro club, but the South had been without a successful professional franchise. This is not surprising since games between white and black teams were not tolerated in the Jim Crow South. Such interracial matchups earned northern black teams more money than games against other black teams, and it's doubtful that any northern black teams could have afforded to travel from region to region without the money earned from playing white teams. Thus, the NSL was not created as a minor league for the NNL, but that's how it functioned throughout the 1920s (and it functioned quite smoothly, at that). Foster had hoped that minor black leagues would emerge to complement the Negro major leagues. Another piece of Rube Foster's blackball puzzle had fallen into place.

The 1921 season was a classic, generating the first great blackball pennant race and a dramatic postseason. The same eight teams that had played in the NNL in 1920 returned for the following season, though the Dayton team relocated to Columbus, Ohio, and the Cuban Stars found a field to call home in Cincinnati. Foster did his best to provide for the league's weak link, enticing "Pop" Lloyd away from the East Coast to be the Columbus Buckeyes' player-manager, and luring wise old Sol White out of retirement to be the team's secretary. The story of the season was the race for the pennant between Wilkinson's Kansas City Monarchs and Foster's American Giants.

On paper, the teams seemed mismatched. The Monarchs had a powerful lineup and a deep and

* * * *

OPPOSITE: *The 1920 Chicago American Giants were the new Negro National League's crown jewel. Featured on the team were (back row, from left) Christobal Torriente, Tom Johnson, unknown, unknown, Rube Foster, Bingo DeMoss, Leroy Grant, Tom Williams, Jack Marshall; (front row, from left) Jim Brown, Otis Starks, George Dixon, Dave Malarcher, Dave Brown, unknown, and John Reese.*
RIGHT: *Gentleman Dave Malarcher, a graduate of New Orleans University, was a reliable utilityman who enjoyed an eighteen-year career in the Negro leagues.*

brilliant pitching staff. Foster's American Giants had a bunch of guys hitting in the low .200s (with the exception of the great Cristobal Torriente) and a decent pitching staff led by young lefthander Dave Brown. But the game is played on the field, not on paper.

Foster had curtailed his tinkering with teams' rosters in the league's second season, and many of the players gravitated back to the teams he had pulled them from. However, Oscar Charleston floated over to the St. Louis Giants for a season, where he topped the league in homers (fifteen), triples (eleven), doubles (fourteen), and stolen bases (thirty-four), and batted .434, second in the league to teammate Charles Blackwell's .448. Charleston, left fielder Blackwell, and pitcher Bill "Plunk" Drake, who posted a 20–10 record, led the Giants to a strong (33–23) third-place finish.

The Monarchs, in contrast, had a plethora of stars. Four Monarch starters batted higher than .350: shortstop Dobie Moore, switch-hitting first baseman George "Tank" Carr, outfielder Oscar "Heavy" Johnson, and pitcher-outfielder Wilbur "Bullet" Rogan. And J.L. Wilkinson had stocked the Monarchs with pitching talent (the brilliance of Monarch pitching would be a recurring theme throughout the franchise's storied history). Rogan, in his prime, was the undisputed ace; other standouts included crafty veteran Sam Crawford, who posted an 8–3 mark for the Monarchs in 1921, and Rube Currie, a young native of Kansas City who had excellent control and a wicked curveball. Then there was the great lefthander John Donaldson, who on his return from exile in Detroit was experiencing arm problems and could pitch only occasionally; he spent the rest of the time playing center field and batting leadoff, where he exploited his exceptional swing. Likewise manager Jose Mendez, a former star pitcher who rarely took the mound, filled in at other positions, and when he played he was still great. The Monarchs had a great season, posting a 50-31 record for a .617 winning percentage.

The Monarchs won with a powerful offense and great pitching; the American Giants won with speed. No team ever played the game of baseball the way Rube Foster's American Giants played it. In retrospect, speed and aggressive base running were emphasized in baseball during the "deadball" era (before 1920); that is, before Babe Ruth revolutionized the game by making home-run hitting central to baseball offense. Foster's American Giants, especially his team in the early 1920s, emphasized speed and base running more than any team in baseball history. They played the game at hyperspeed.

Giant third baseman Dave Malarcher summarized the 1921 American Giants: "We had Jimmy Lyons, Cristobal Torriente, and Jelly Gardner in the outfield. They're all fast. I was on third, I'm fast. Bobby Williams, shortstop, real fast. Bingo DeMoss, second, he's fast. We had George Dixon and Jim Brown catching. Brown was fast, could push and bunt, and hit too. Leroy Grant playing first base was the only slow man on the team. He usually hit way down by the pitcher. See, when James Brown was catching, we had seven men in the lineup could run a hundred yards (100m) in around ten seconds. All speed, and with Rube directing it, it was something. Rube telling us what to do—push it here, hit it by the first baseman, hit over there. He directed your play all the time.

"When you play a diversified game, you don't allow your team to get into slumps, because you are making your breaks. You don't just say, 'We got the breaks today.' You make your breaks."

Clearly, only disciplined players worked for Rube Foster. Pitcher Webster McDonald, who played for Foster's Giants in the mid-1920s, pointed out, "[Foster] was good to you, but you had to listen, you had to learn, or you'd find yourself with one of the weaker clubs in the league."

One skill all Foster players had to master was bat control; bunting and placement hitting were, along with speed, the cornerstones of Foster's offense. He would draw circles in front of the plate, down

* * * *

Cannonball Dick Redding's huge hands gave him excellent ball control, but his trademark was a blazing fastball that even the best hitters found difficult to swat. He was an important part of the 1917 Chicago American Giants. Here, Redding (right) poses with another pitching legend of the Negro leagues, Smokey Joe Williams.

either baseline and have his players practice dropping bunts into the circles. Bingo DeMoss, who batted second behind Jelly Gardner, was perhaps the greatest bunter of all time. Bingo did not square around, but rather held the bat as if to hit until the last possible millisecond, when he would flick the lumber at the ball, often producing a backspin that would cause the ball to change direction and roll backward once it stopped bouncing. Malarcher, batting third, was a renowned clutch hitter and, of course, a great bunter; and the cleanup hitter Torriente, who was renowned for his fearsome line drives, was also an exceptional bunter; because of this combination, first and third basemen could not sneak in to protect against the bunt, fearing for their lives. Lyons once quipped that he no longer remembered what it was like to swing away at the plate since he was called on to bunt constantly.

Actually, the element of surprise was central to Foster's strategy. Malarcher, who would succeed Foster as the manager of the American Giants in 1926, noted, "[Rube] used to say... 'We do what the other fellow does not expect us to do.' This was his philosophy...that in order for a man to put you out going from base-to-base, the other team must make a perfect play. If you can run, if you're fast, he's got to make a perfect play, and if you surprise him, he can't make a perfect play, he can't make it."

The amount of pressure that Foster put on the opposing teams' infielders was intense, and he moved his base runners so aggressively, opening up new holes to exploit in the infield defense, that infielders knew they had virtually no margin for error, and no time to think on any play. Compounding this pressure was the paucity of runs allowed by the American Giants with their strong pitching and sterling defense (it was virtually impossible to hit a ball between the outfielders). Thus, the Giants (literally) raced by the league's competition while posting what must have been an absurdly low slugging percentage. The Giants and the Monarchs moved ahead of the field, and as the Monarchs moved ahead in games played, the Giants began to post the higher winning percentage. In the end, the Giants played nineteen fewer games than the Monarchs, going 41–21 for a .661 winning percentage. The Giants claimed their second straight NNL pennant on the basis of their superior winning percentage. There wasn't much grumbling from the Monarchs about injustice, but Foster's Giants never did play a game at St. Louis all season.

At any rate, following the league season, Foster took his troops, heralded as champions of the West, east for showdowns with the Bacharach Giants and Hilldale. The Bacharachs' two stars, shortstop Dick Lundy and third baseman Oliver Marcelle, were on the left side of their infield. The B's also had a fine rotation, with "Red" Ryan and southpaw "Nip" Winters, but against Foster's Giants the ball was handed to the great veteran "Cannonball" Redding. Foster came to town saying he was going to drop bunts down the third base line to challenge the vaunted Marcelle and run against the heralded arm of catcher "Yank" Deas. However, for the first six innings of the first game, Redding kept the American Giants off the base paths, allowing no hits. Across the way, Foster's ace southpaw Dave Brown simply kept Connors' Giants off the scoreboard. It was a classic duel, but Redding tired first and the American Giants won 3–1. The Bacharachs evened the series the next day, and the two aces squared off again in the decisive game. Brown got the better of Redding again, 6–3, and Foster's club took the hard-fought series.

The Chicagoans headed to Philadelphia for four games against Hilldale at Shibe Park. In spite of losing Lundy, Deas, and left fielder Jess Barber to the Bacharachs, Hilldale had had a strong 1921

season. One of the reasons for Hilldale's continuing success was the presence of another black team in Darby, the Madison Stars, that, in effect, operated as Hilldale's minor league team. Early in the 1921 season, Bolden "brought up" Madison's young third baseman, William "Judy" Johnson, a brilliant fielder and line-drive hitter who would be Hilldale's greatest player over the next decade. However, player-manager Bill Francis was the Hilldale third baseman, so Johnson competed with another youngster, super-quick Jake Stephens, for playing time at short during the 1921 season. Faced with the American Giants' onslaught of bunts and base running, the aging Francis decided he had better go with youth and moved Johnson to third for the series. Likewise, slugger Louis Santop moved to the outfield and the more agile Jim York started at catcher.

The rest of the strong Hilldale starting lineup included speedy leadoff hitter Otto Briggs in right field, second baseman Bunny Downs, first baseman Napoleon "Chance" Cummings, and George Johnson, perhaps the team's best all-around player in 1921, in center field. A crafty young spitball pitcher, Phil Cockrell, who was just coming into his own, was their ace. Foster, of course, planned to run the Daisies out of the park. The strategy worked in game one, as the American Giants stole six bases on their way to a 5–2 victory. However, Hilldale rebounded in game two, winning 4–3 behind the pitching of Cockrell. Game three was a rout, Hilldale 15, Chicago 5, and the hero was young "Judy" Johnson, who ripped a home run and a triple. Johnson was also cementing his reputation as a defensive wizard, brilliantly handling the array of bunts that Foster's players dropped down the third base line. Foster hoped to earn a split in game four, but Phil Cockrell hurled a gem for Ed Bolden and Hilldale won the game 7–1, and the series 3–1.

In spite of his club's loss against Hilldale, 1921 was in many respects the apex of Rube Foster's

career. His was the first black league to not only survive two seasons but prosper, extending Foster's influence across eastern blackball. As a youth, Foster had been a legend in the Southwest, and when he went north his performances in the Colored World Series took on mythic proportions. When he became a manager, his ingenuity and baseball acumen were such that his teams were champions virtually every year. Once he controlled the front office, he built his American Giants into the most profitable franchise in blackball history. And when he organized the NNL, he bucked the odds and oversaw its success.

Up to this point, Foster's career in baseball had been the story of one success after another. But Foster had played hardball to get this far; his ascendance was predicated more on willfulness than cooperation. He had stepped on more than a few toes along the way. Out west, Foster reigned unchallenged as the overlord of black baseball, though some of the region's other owners undoubtedly harbored resentment toward him. Back east, however, Ed Bolden was not yet reliant upon Foster for his survival. Before the 1922 season, Bolden made some grumblings in the black press about Foster's rule forbidding teams affiliated with the NNL from playing against New York's three top black teams—Nat Strong's Royal Giants, Alex Pompez's Cuban Stars, and James Keenan's Lincoln Giants—which were natural rivals for Hilldale. Bolden complained that this rule deprived him of a prime source of revenue and questioned whether it was in his best interest to renew his NNL associate membership. Foster responded with a thinly veiled threat: if Bolden left the fold, his team would be raided into nonexistence. Seeing that the cards were stacked against him, Bolden backed down and signed on again with the NNL, but he spent the better part of 1922 plotting behind Foster's back, laying the groundwork for an eastern Negro league.

The Negro National League began its third season with three new franchises. In St. Louis, Charles

ED. BOLDEN'S PHILA. STARS

Mills' Giants went under and the Stars were born, owned by Dick Kemp, a black numbers man, but run by Dr. Sam Shepard, a former New York Gorhams player. The Stars' lineup resembled the strong Giants team of the previous season—only their best player, Oscar Charleston, was missing. The man who would soon assume Charleston's position in center field, James "Cool Papa" Bell, debuted with the Stars in 1922, but as a pitcher. The rookie earned his nickname when he exhibited tremendous composure while striking out the mighty Charleston to quell a threat in a close game. The Stars struggled to a .500 (23–23) record in their inaugural campaign. Meanwhile, the Columbus Buckeyes disappeared after a not-so-glorious (24–38) one-year existence, "Pop" Lloyd returned east to manage the Bacharach Giants, and the Chicago Giants (descendants of Frank Leland's team) dropped out of the league after posting a feeble 10–32 mark in 1921. Replacing these two franchises were two newly formed clubs from major league cities, the Pittsburgh Keystones and the Cleveland Tate Stars, managed by third baseman "Candy Jim" Taylor.

Black baseball suffered a great loss when C.I. Taylor, the Indianapolis ABCs' mastermind, died on February 23, 1922, at the age of forty-seven. His wife assumed control of the team and hired her brother-in-law, ABCs first baseman Ben Taylor, to manage it. The team responded with a banner year.

It helped that Oscar Charleston rejoined it and had another brilliant season, batting .370 while leading the league in stolen bases and sharing the home run crown with Monarchs outfielder and pitching ace "Bullet" Joe Rogan. Also, Indianapolis southpaw Jim Jeffries was the stingiest pitcher in the NNL in 1922, allowing only 2.84 runs per nine innings. And the ABCs had a sterling young catcher named Biz Mackey, whom C.I. Taylor had tutored the previous two seasons, teaching him the nuances of the game. Possessing a rifle for an arm, Mackey was the consummate defensive catcher: strong, quick as a cat, and knowledgeable about pitching. He could also hit, which he showed in 1922, posting a .361 average and a .630 slugging percentage. Manager

Ben Taylor, probably the top black first baseman at the time, contributed a .358 average. The Taylors' ABCs challenged Foster's Giants for the NNL pennant with a 46–33 record (.582). The Monarchs, meanwhile, had an off year, dropping to fourth, while the Detroit Stars had a solid season and finished third. Rube Foster had kept his American Giants juggernaut intact (and added a young power hitter of note, John Beckwith), and it rolled to a 36–23 record (.610) to remain the only club ever to win an NNL title.

The American Giants also triumphed, in the season's most memorable game, a postseason contest against the Bacharach Giants in Chicago. The teams went to extra innings tied at zero. While Foster used his bullpen, the Bacharachs stayed with starter Harold Treadwell, a control pitcher with a good curve and fastball who threw virtually underhanded. The game wore on, scoreless. Finally, in the bottom of the twentieth inning, Foster directed Dave Malarcher to hit to right field with Cristobal Torriente on second because Foster thought right fielder Ramiro Ramirez had a suspect arm. Malarcher lined a base hit into right, and Torriente was waved home. Ramirez fielded the ball and came

* * * *

OPPOSITE: *Ed Bolden's 1933 Philadelphia Stars included (from left) Jake Stephens, Herb Smith, Casey, Jud Wilson, Pete Washington, Allen, Porter Charleston, Biz Mackey, Ed Bolden, Paul Carter, Rap Dixon, Dick Lundy, Chaney White, Eggie Dallard, Cliff Carter, Webster McDonald, and Tom Finley.*
ABOVE: *Catcher-manager Biz Mackey was one of the legends of the game; he was a member of the great Philadelphia Stars teams of the mid-1930s, but ended his twenty-seven-year career with the Newark Eagles.*

up throwing, but Torriente beat the throw home and Treadwell was the losing pitcher, in a record-breaking loss.

However, all was not well in Rube Foster's universe. NNL attendance was down 25 percent from the previous season, and only Chicago, Indianapolis, Detroit, and Kansas City turned profits. Meanwhile, Foster lost an ally in the East when John W. Connors, no longer able to sustain his financial losses, sold the Bacharach Giants back to the Atlantic City businessmen who had owned them before 1919. Connors had purchased the Bacharachs and moved them to New York City in a gallant effort to combat Nat Strong's control over eastern blackball. Unfortunately, this maneuver ended up reducing the number of teams that the Bacharachs could play against in their own region, eliminating natural rivalries and losing the large crowds that such rivalries attract. Connors left blackball defeated for the second and last time; he had a stroke in 1926 and died at age forty-eight.

Hilldale had a disappointing season, losing seventeen of twenty-eight games against NNL opponents (though one of the Hilldale wins came when Phil Cockrell pitched a no-hitter against the American Giants in Chicago). Also, Ed Bolden still felt it made more sense for Hilldale, a Philadelphia team that was the top black team on the East Coast, to play against the top teams from New York City than to acquiesce to the needs of a midwestern league. So Bolden officially discontinued his affiliation with the NNL after the 1922 season. Foster, as expected, responded with venom, refusing to return the $1,000 deposit Bolden had made as an associate member of the NNL. Bolden knew this meant war, and he went at it full force.

First, Bolden made peace with Nat Strong. Considering Bolden's betrayal of Strong before the 1921 season, Strong had reason to shun him, but the New York booking magnate was more interested in profits than revenge. Furthermore, Bolden's return to Strong's side of the fence was tantamount to a victory for Strong, who could have lost his stake in eastern blackball if the Bolden-Foster alliance had succeeded. In effect, Strong needed Bolden as much as Bolden needed him.

After reaching an agreement with Strong, Bolden outlined his proposal in the press. In the December 1, 1922, *Philadelphia Tribune*, Bolden wrote: "The fans have loyally supported the club and there is little doubt they will continue doing so, but I think they are entitled to better competition among our clubs, and the best way to secure it is through an organized circuit." Thus, Bolden invited the owners of the five other black professional franchises in the East—Strong of the Brooklyn Royal Giants, Alex Pompez of the New York Cuban Stars, James Keenan of the Lincoln Giants, Tom Jackson of the Bacharach Giants, and newcomers Charles Spedden and George Rossiter, the two white owners of the newly professional Baltimore Black Sox—to join him at the Philadelphia YMCA on December

16, 1922, to approve the guidelines for the Mutual Association of Eastern Baseball Clubs (which would be redubbed the Eastern Colored League, or ECL, before the start of its inaugural season). Everything went as planned, and the second Negro major league began preparations for its inaugural season.

Though Rube Foster had envisioned a second Negro league in the East to parallel the structure of the white major leagues, he was less than pleased with Bolden's confederation. To make things worse, some of the eastern clubs began to raid the rosters of the NNL. The ECL had adopted the reserve clause, binding players to their teams, but applied it only to teams within their league. In contrast, the NNL extended the ban to all black ball clubs, in the interests of blackball in general. Thus, no sooner had the ECL been born than the raids began. James Keenan made the first move, enticing the great lefthander Dave Brown to leave Foster's Giants and join his Lincoln Giants (which meant the Lincolns had Brown and "Smokey" Joe Williams on the same staff, arguably the greatest lefthanded pitcher and greatest righthanded pitcher, respectively, in blackball history). Then Ed Bolden went to work, pilfering four front-line NNL players: outfielder Clint Thomas and second baseman Frank Warfield from Detroit; first baseman George Carr from Kansas City; and from Indianapolis, catcher Biz Mackey, perhaps the top young star in the NNL. By the start of the 1924 season, the NNL had lost eighteen players to ECL raids.

The team Ed Bolden put together for the 1923 season ranks among the greatest in blackball history. Gone was player-manager Bill Francis, which allowed "Judy" Johnson to start every day at third. Replacing Francis as player-manager was none other than thirty-nine-year-old John Henry "Pop" Lloyd, perhaps not the franchise player he had been for so long but still a great baseball player (and a patient tutor of young talent). Second baseman Frank Warfield was prototype Rube Foster talent: though

he had never played for Foster, he was fast, a skilled batsman, an exceptional defender, and an avid student of the game. Tank Carr was a Bo Jackson–type athlete, huge with blazing speed. At six feet, two inches (188cm) and 230 pounds (104.5kg), Carr could run one hundred yards (91.4m) in ten seconds; he could also belt the cover off the ball. The diminutive Otto Briggs remained in right field and at the top of the Hilldale batting order, where he consistently hit better than .300 and terrorized opposing catchers with his base stealing. Center field still belonged to George Johnson, another gem who combined speed, defense, a strong throwing arm, and hitting ability. Left fielder Clint Thomas, the new kid in the outfield, possessed all the same attributes, and was six years younger.

Hilldale did have a serious problem at catcher: the team had two of the greatest catchers black baseball had yet produced, the incumbent Louis Santop and the regent Biz Mackey. Actually, Santop was no match for Mackey as a defensive catcher, and the effects of a career behind the plate were beginning to show on Santop's body. However, Santop's reputation was based on his power-hitting, which remained awesome. Manager Lloyd had to find a way to work both superstars into the lineup, so he split their time behind the plate and also played them in right or left field or at first base on occasion, allowing them both to have full seasons. The Hilldale pitching staff was not as phenomenal as the everyday lineup, but it was very solid. Phil Cockrell, the feisty spitballer with a live fastball and good control, remained a top-flight hurler and a cornerstone of the staff, but by 1923 southpaw Nip Winters had become the team's ace. Winters was six-foot-five (196cm) and threw with considerable velocity, but his forte was an exceptional curveball. A new member of the Hilldale staff, a submarining righthander named Holsey "Scrip" Lee, had a brilliant 1923, establishing himself as the club's third starter. Also of note was another small hurler, five-foot-eight-inch

(173cm) Red Ryan, who threw hard and also featured a knuckleball and forkball.

This overwhelming roster blew away their competition all year long. The team ran away with the ECL crown with a 32–17 record (.673). The Cuban Stars were a distant second with a .575 winning percentage, and Brooklyn placed third, going 18–18. The Bacharachs and Lincolns had disappointing ECL campaigns, ending up fourth and fifth, respectively, and the newcomers from Baltimore brought up the rear. But the relative strength of the ECL teams is apparent considering that Hilldale went 105–26–6 over the rest of their schedule, a .766 winning percentage (.802 if the ties are not factored in). And the competition Hilldale faced outside the league was not all semipro teams and weaker black clubs. In fact, Connie Mack somehow sidestepped the ban imposed by Commissioner Landis against major league teams playing against black teams, as Mack's Philadelphia A's played a six-game series against Hilldale after the regular season. Hilldale had once again captured the imagination of Philadelphia's black community, as well as those of many of the city's white baseball fans, so the showdown with the A's was widely anticipated. It was no contest: Hilldale won five of the six games, a result that brought exultation to black Philadelphia but probably hardened Judge Landis' resolve to outlaw Negro-league-versus-major-league showdowns.

The individual statistics for the 1923 Hilldale Daisies speak for themselves. Nip Winters went 32–6 with a 2.44 ERA in ECL games; Cockrell and Lee

* * * *

OPPOSITE: *The World Champion Kansas City Monarchs of 1924 included (from left) George Sweatt, Bill Drake, Carroll Mothel, Bill McCall, Frank Duncan, Lemuel Hawkins, Cliff Bell, Dobie Moore, William Bell, Jose Mendez, Bullet Joe Rogan, Newt Allen, Harold Morris, Heavy Johnson, and Newt Joseph.*

both posted impressive 24–8 marks; and Ryan went 20–11. "Judy" Johnson batted .391; the thirty-nine-year-old Lloyd posted a .418 average in league play; Warfield hit at a .339 clip and stole sixty-seven bases; Carr did it all, with twenty-one HRs, thirty-nine SBs, and a .354 average; Briggs hit .342 and nabbed fifty-four bags; George Johnson was at .376 and fifty SBs; and Thomas added twenty-three homers to go with his .373 and fifty-six steals. The catchers made do with their reduced playing time,

though Mackey seemed to have the better year. Biz led the ECL with a .433 batting average, and over the course of the season the young catcher blasted twenty home runs, hit an amazing .423 and registered a seismic .698 slugging percentage. The only offensive statistic available for Santop is that he hit a not-too-shabby .364. It's amazing that Hilldale ever lost; in fact, the only logical explanation for their forty-three losses is that such a team must have consistently faced other team's aces.

Back in the venerable NNL, the rest of the league had to wonder if someone besides Foster's Giants would ever win the league. Besides losing ace Dave Brown, Foster returned his 1922 champions intact; the ABCs, the previous year's challengers, were in disarray. Oscar Charleston remained in Indianapolis, but Mackey made a widely publicized exit, as did slugging player-manager Ben Taylor, who left to try to build the Potomacs, a new club in Washington, D.C., into a power. Detroit seemed to be

in a holding pattern as it lost two dynamic players, Warfield and Thomas, to Hilldale, but it gained a transcendent young talent, Norman "Turkey" Stearns, who had previously roamed the outfield and hit massive home runs for Montgomery in the Negro Southern League. Both the Cuban and St. Louis Stars remained middling clubs, while both of the previous year's new franchises, the Pittsburgh Keystones and Cleveland Tate Stars, had failed and were replaced by the Toledo Tigers and Milwaukee Bears, neither of which would complete the season.

This left the Kansas City Monarchs, who were coming off a disappointing 1922 NNL campaign, to try to unseat Foster's dynastic Giants.

Actually, the American Giants fell as much as they were toppled. The absence of Dave Brown exposed a vulnerable pitching staff; crafty right-hander Tom Williams was Chicago's only top-quality hurler and he was hardly an ace. Also, Foster seemed so preoccupied with the troubles befalling the league (declining attendance, falling revenue, and failing franchises) that he wasn't really available

to work his magic for his team. The starting eight were as kinetic as ever, but the team's 41–29 (.586) league record was good enough only for third place.

The ABCs recruited some decent young talent to play alongside the great Charleston. Of special note was catcher Larry "Iron Man" Brown, who inherited Biz Mackey's starting role and turned out to be a great defensive catcher himself. Indianapolis went 45–34 (.570) to finish just behind Chicago.

Since their inception in 1919, the Detroit Stars had featured a core group of veterans led by catcher-manager Bruce Petway, one of the cornerstones of Foster's Giants in the 1910s. Slowly a new generation of Stars began to replace the vets, the most distinguished of whom were switch-hitting shortstop Orville Riggins, right fielder Clarence Smith, southpaw ace Andy Cooper (who led the NNL with fifteen victories in 1923), and the great Turkey Stearns (who blasted onto the scene, hitting .353 with sixteen homers in fifty-seven league games for an astounding .737 slugging percentage). With their mix of veterans and newcomers, the Stars posted a 40-27 (.597) record to claim second in the league.

J.L. Wilkinson's Kansas City Monarchs fully matured in 1923. Despite losing a great player, Tank Carr, to Hilldale, the Monarchs finally realized Wilkinson's vision of a power offense complemented by great pitching and solid defense. Actually, the Monarchs of the mid-1920s had exceptional infield defense and only adequate outfield defense, which suggests that Wilkinson may have had Rube Foster's club on his mind when he designed his own. But then, the Monarchs were nothing if not a quirky team—a *great* quirky team. Spearheading their improvement over the previous year was the growth of many young players. In the infield, the two Newts—second baseman Newt Allen and third baseman Newt Joseph—completed their first full season on either side of the Monarchs' brilliant all-around shortstop, Dobie Moore. The Newts were defensive

* * * *

OPPOSITE: *The 1922 Indianapolis ABCs, with manager and owner C.I. Taylor (center) and Oscar Charleston (front row, second from left), look serene in what is probably a preseason photograph, but soon the team would be devastated by the death of Taylor. By 1924 this charter NNL team would disappear altogether, done in by the loss of its leader and the player raids conducted by the clubs of the newly formed Eastern Colored League.*

stalwarts who developed into solid hitters, usually batting around .280, but capable of posting a .330 season. Moore, on the other hand, featured all the skill and talent you could want in a baseball player. He had a howitzer for an arm and terrific range at shortstop; he could gun-out runners at first from deep in the hole. Moore consistently led the team with an average above .350 while also hitting for power. Moore ranks among the top shortstops in Negro league history, even though his career was tragically cut short in 1926, when he was shot in the leg under mysterious circumstances by a woman he may have been involved with. The combination of the bullet wound and the damage Moore did to his leg when he jumped off a balcony trying to escape his assailant left him unable to play baseball anymore. But three years before that tragic night, in 1923, Moore was a wonder to behold on a baseball diamond.

Another developing young Monarch was catcher Frank Duncan. Like Allen and Joseph, Duncan was in the lineup more for his defense than as a run producer. Duncan was not only a sharp receiver, he was a great handler of pitchers, which made him invaluable in Wilkinson's scheme.

Following the loss of Tank Carr, first base remained a problem for the Monarchs; rather than sacrifice his infield defense by putting one of his outfield sluggers at first, however, Wilkinson stuck with light-hitting gloveman Lem Hawkins or utility man George Sweatt, who could fill in anywhere but catcher or pitcher (as could manager Jose Mendez, the legendary Cuban pitcher who found some life in his weary arm in 1923, collecting eight wins against two losses). And former pitching ace John Donaldson rarely took the mound due to a tired arm, but did crack the starting lineup occasionally since he still hit for a high average and covered a lot of ground in the outfield. This wasn't the case with most of the Monarch outfielders, particularly six-foot (183cm), 250-pound (113.5kg) Oscar "Heavy"

Johnson. However, "Heavy" came of age in 1923, pounding NNL pitching for a league-leading eighteen homers in only forty-six games while batting .380. The Monarchs' other outfield slugger was none other than their pitching ace, Wilbur "Bullet" Rogan, whose sixteen home runs in 1922 tied him for the league lead with Oscar Charleston, and who followed that up with a .416 average in 1923. (When Rogan was on the mound, one of the Monarchs' two valuable utility men, George Sweatt or Carroll "Dink" Mothell, would start in the outfield.) The third starting outfielder, Hurley McNair, was a five-foot-six (167.6cm) switch-hitting powder keg who sprayed laser-beam line drives all around the ballpark, batting .354 with eleven homers during the 1923 NNL season. While Rogan and McNair were not as much of a defensive liability as "Heavy" Johnson, they would never be mistaken for Oscar Charleston when chasing fly balls. Thus, the Monarchs' offense featured four good, but not great, hitters—Joseph, Allen, Duncan, and the first baseman—who set the table for the Monarchs' four big bats: Johnson, Rogan, McNair, and Moore.

The other half of the Monarchs' master plan was great pitching, which Wilkinson had always featured on the great All-Nations teams during the 1910s. Rogan, of course, was the ace of the staff in the mid-1920s, though he posted an unimpressive 12–8 record in 1923. Two young hurlers stepped up in 1923: Bill "Plunk" Drake, who had pitched for the All-Nations in 1915, posted a 9–7 record in his first full season with Kansas City; and Rube Currie, a six-foot-four-inch (193cm) righthanded control pitcher who featured a wicked curve and went 14–7 during the NNL campaign. And manager Jose Mendez, the "Black Diamond," was always available to step to the fore and rescue his troops at the most dramatic moment. But that wouldn't be necessary until October 1924.

Rube Foster categorically dismissed all overtures from the East about staging a postseason

Colored World Series, pitting the respective champions of the NNL and the ECL against each other. Foster had no desire to cooperate with a black baseball league with a majority of the teams owned by white men, and he had no intention of doing so as long as ECL teams continued to raid NNL rosters. Unfortunately, Foster's brainchild was fading fast. The ECL had flourished in its inaugural season and was expanding from six to eight teams in 1924; the logical place for a new major league team to look for its players was an already existing major league. Reflecting this, the new ECL teams both had player-managers who had come from the NNL.

Oscar Charleston assumed his first managerial post with the Harrisburg Giants, as the club prepared to enter the ECL. Simultaneously, Charleston's former manager Ben Taylor was poised to oversee his second-year Washington Potomacs' entry into the young league. Both of these young managers had previously been with the Indianapolis ABCs, so it is no surprise that the ABCs lost more players (ten) to the ECL than any other NNL team. Both Charleston and Taylor called on former teammates to help their new teams. Pitcher James Jeffries, for instance, followed Charleston to Harrisburg. Not all of the raids, however, involved ABCs. Indeed, Ed Bolden stole from a more formidable adversary, J.L. Wilkinson, improving his pitching staff by signing the Monarchs' up-and-coming hurler Rube Currie.

The balance of power in black baseball was shifting east, and as the curtain was about to rise on the 1924 season, the NNL was in disarray. True to what had become an NNL tradition, the seventh and eighth teams in the league had failed each year. In the 1923–1924 off-season, however, only one new team had formed, the Cleveland Browns, organized by none other than Sol White. Foster wanted very badly to have an eighth team (the white major leagues had eight teams each), especially since the ECL was expanding to that size in 1924. So Foster reached into the Negro Southern League

and drafted the Birmingham Black Barons to join the NNL. This incursion into the deep South was a last-resort maneuver by Foster since it not only increased travel expenses but also meant that NNL clubs had to cope with the draconian Jim Crow race laws. But the Barons had been a stable franchise and their fan base was bound to increase with their entry into the big time. The Barons' presence in the league also helped Foster cope when the Indianapolis ABCs, their roster depleted by the ECL raids, folded shortly after the beginning of the 1924 season. With NNL teams already contending with the long haul down to Birmingham, Foster called on another NSL team, the Memphis Red Sox, to fill in. The stopgap measure worked, and eight teams completed the NNL season, but Foster realized he had to do something more to save his league. After all, how long would the Detroit Stars and the K.C. Monarchs, the only two NNL franchises making money besides Foster's Giants, be willing to sacrifice their profits in order to support weak franchises in an unstable league?

Taking stock of the situation, Rube Foster decided to bury the hatchet and try to make peace with the ECL. So Foster and J.L. Wilkinson met with Ed Bolden during the 1924 season. Foster wanted reparations for the player raids and was looking for Bolden to extend the ECL's reserve clause policy to the NNL, thus ending the raids. Foster also wanted to coordinate interleague exhibitions so the NNL teams would have access to the large eastern markets. He even wanted Bolden to allow those games to be coordinated by Foster's booking agency. Bolden granted none of these wishes. Happy with the ascendance of the ECL and his booking arrangement with Nat Strong, Bolden didn't consider hosting NNL teams to be very alluring, and he certainly saw no reason for ECL teams to travel to the Midwest. Bargaining from a position of power, Bolden even rejected Foster's plea to outlaw raids on NNL rosters. The two sides did agree to hold a black World Series

every autumn between each league's champion. However, rumors persisted that Foster, incensed at Bolden's unwillingness to grant any of the NNL direcor's wishes, only agreed to cosponsor the World Series when Wilkinson informed him that if his Monarchs won the NNL again (and they were in first place), they would play the ECL champion in a postseason series anyway. So Foster acquiesced in order to secure some of the series revenue for the league.

The Monarchs did repeat as NNL champs, posting a record-breaking 55–22 (.714) league mark. However, the Monarchs needed to play at such a clip to stay ahead of Foster's Giants, who had returned to form. In fact, the American Giants recorded their highest winning percentage yet, .671 (49–24). The rest of the NNL trailed far behind the front-runners, though the Detroit Stars had another solid season (37–27, .578) to finish third, and St. Louis' young Stars (40–36, fourth place) showed promise. The league's southern contingent acquitted itself respectably, with Birmingham (32–37) doing slightly better than Memphis (29–32). Linares' Cuban Stars had a lousy NNL campaign, though not quite as awful as Sol White's Cleveland Browns, whose main accomplishment was completing the season.

The race at the top of the league was exhilarating. Chicago stayed on K.C.'s heels throughout the season, but Wilkinson's club just kept winning. The American Giants, who still had the same starting eight as in 1921, received much-needed pitching help from veteran Cuban southpaw Luis Padrone, who led the western circuit with a 2.83-runs-per-game average. Foster's club still had a shot at the pennant when the Monarchs rolled into Chicago for a late-season four-game series, but the home team needed a sweep. Foster's veterans responded to the challenge, playing brilliantly and winning the first three games. The American Giants had all the momentum heading into the Sunday afternoon finale at soldout Schorling Park, but the Monarchs had Joe Rogan on the mound. The Kansas City ace shut down the American Giants in the early going, as the Monarchs built a big lead. Then Rogan "pitched to the scoreboard," willing to sacrifice a run for an out in order to contain Chicago's racetrack offense, and Kansas City coasted to a 9–5 victory that essentially wrapped up the pennant.

The Monarchs' personnel was similar to the previous season's. Pitchers Will Bell Sr. and Cliff Bell assumed more prominent roles on the staff in the absence of Rube Currie, and proved up to the task, going 10–2 and 4–1, respectively. The club's two top players were absolutely stellar. Rogan, the hero in Chicago, was brilliant both on the mound and at the plate, topping the league with a 16–5 record and 2.37 ERA while finishing second in batting with .412. Teammate Dobie Moore had one of the greatest offensive seasons in Negro league history, leading the league in doubles, slugging percentage (.694), batting average (.463, best in NNL history), and tying slugger Turkey Stearns for the home run crown with ten. As the Monarchs headed east for the start of the first interleague black World Series, they trusted that Rogan and Moore would play brilliantly, but they knew they'd need someone else to step up as well if they hoped to beat their vaunted foes, the Hilldale Daisies.

Whereas the great pennant race in the NNL had forced the Monarchs to win as many games as possible, Hilldale had posted a comparable record, 47–22 (.681), while running away with the ECL title. Like the Monarchs, Hilldale didn't do much tinkering with the lineup that had led their league the previous season. Player-manager "Pop" Lloyd was gone, however, replaced at shortstop by the slick-fielding, light-hitting Jake Stephens; second baseman Frank Warfield assumed the managerial duties. Apparently, Lloyd, who was generally well liked throughout his career, had not been popular with the Hilldale players. No such conflict existed on the 1924 Hilldale

team. The only hitch in the Hilldale juggernaut was the trouble experienced by pitcher Rube Currie, whom Bolden lifted from the Monarchs to add depth to his staff: Currie struggled to a disappointing 1–5 record in his first season in the East. In contrast, Hilldale's all-star lineup had no such hitches as Santop, Mackey, J. Johnson, Warfield, Carr, Briggs, G. Johnson, and Thomas were all as consistently brilliant as ever.

✳ ✳ ✳ ✳

Shortstop John Henry "Pop" Lloyd had one of the longest and most successful Negro league careers, batting .353 over a nearly thirty-year career. Seen here in a Hilldale uniform in 1923, Lloyd left for the Bacharach Giants in 1924 and therefore missed by one year the opportunity to play in the inaugural Colored World Series. Unfortunately, Hilldale, which lost to the Monarchs, could have used the prolific bat of Lloyd (who lead the ECL in hitting in 1924).

While Bolden's dynamo raced off with the ECL pennant, the second-place finishers, the Baltimore Black Sox (30–19, .612), established themselves as a quality club. The nucleus of the team was a trio of talented youngsters: hard-nosed first baseman Jud Wilson, a fierce lefthanded power-hitter whose specialty was vicious line drives; shortstop John Beckwith, who was a dead-pull hitter with power and consistency (he batted .403); and a fleet-footed outfielder taken from the Indianapolis ABCs, Christopher "Crush" Holloway, who hit .331 in the leadoff spot. At third base, the Black Sox had another top-flight young talent, Henry Blackman. An exceptional fielder whose acrobatic plays made him a crowd favorite, Blackman was batting .333 in late July when he fell ill with a throat infection; tragically, he did not recover and within two weeks he was dead from apparent liver failure.

The ECL's top hitter was none other than forty-year-old Pop Lloyd, who compiled an amazing .444 average with the Bacharach Giants. Lloyd did, however, make one concession to age, as he moved to second base and let Dick Lundy play shortstop. Alas, the Bacharachs had lost Oliver Marcelle to New York's Lincoln Giants before the 1923 season, and pitcher Dave Brown and third baseman Marcelle led Lincoln to a third-place finish in 1924, ahead of the Bacharachs. Both expansion teams made it through the season, though Oscar Charleston's Harrisburg Giants (26–28) did better than Bill Taylor's Washington Potomacs (21–37). Nat Strong had brought both of the greatest black pitchers from the 1910s, Smokey Joe Williams and Dick Redding, to Brooklyn (16–25), but the two veterans couldn't keep the Royal Giants from a disappointing sixth-place finish in the ECL. The top pitcher in the East in 1924 was on the top team: Hilldale's Nip Winters led the circuit in wins (19–5) and ERA (2.84).

The 1924 Colored World Series was a seminal event in the history of the Negro leagues. The best-of-nine series drew headlines in black newspapers throughout the land. Anticipation ran high for the showdown between the two back-to-back league champions, and the series more than lived up to its billing. In fact, the Hilldale-Monarch series in the autumn of 1924 ranks among the most dramatic postseason matchups in all of baseball history.

The first two games were played in Philadelphia. Rube Foster made the trip east to preside over the series as co-commissioner alongside Ed Bolden. Foster understood that it was in his own best interest, as well as the NNL's and black baseball's in general, to (temporarily) bury the hatchet and present to the world an image of two black major leagues coexisting harmoniously. Thus, Foster (begrudgingly) shook hands with Bolden at home plate before game one. More than fifty-three hundred fans came to Shibe Park on October 3, 1924, to root for their hometown Daisies in the first-ever NNL versus ECL world series contest. The partisan crowd went home disappointed, as the day belonged to Monarchs ace "Bullet Joe" Rogan, who contained the powerful Hilldale offensive and also collected

two hits off Hilldale starter Phil Cockrell in the 6–2 Kansas City victory. Attendance increased to more than eighty-six hundred for game two on Sunday afternoon. The fans left happy, as Nip Winters pitched a complete game shutout and the Daisies pounded out eleven runs to even up the series.

The teams traveled to Baltimore for games three and four. Foster and Bolden had decided to play games three and four, and, if necessary, eight and nine in the cities whose teams finished in second place. Besides the obvious appeal this plan had for Foster, the rationale for adopting it was twofold: it would bring Negro baseball's greatest spectacle to more than two cities; and it would hopefully increase overall attendance since few black fans anywhere had enough disposable income to attend more than one game per week. However, the initial experiment with neutral sites was a disaster, as game three attracted a meager crowd of 584 in Baltimore. The few fans who were present witnessed a classic battle. After nine innings, the score was tied 5–5. In the top of the eleventh, Newt Allen doubled for the Monarchs and Joe Rogan, who had pitched the

whole game for Kansas City, singled to drive in Allen. But in the bottom of the inning, Rogan could not close out the game, as Hilldale rallied to tie the score. The teams completed two more innings as dusk fell. Neither team scored and the game was called a tie; Rogan had pitched thirteen innings in vain.

A larger crowd showed up for the Sunday game in Baltimore, though it was still much smaller than the crowd that had packed the stands in Philadelphia the previous week. It was another nail-biter. With the game knotted at three in the bottom of the ninth, Hilldale loaded the bases with two outs and scored the winning run when Newt Allen made a wild throw after fielding a grounder. The winning pitcher for Hilldale was ex-Monarch Rube Currie. The teams headed west with Hilldale ahead two games to one.

Five days later, the teams' two aces, Nip Winters and Joe Rogan, took the mound at Kansas City's Muehlenbach Stadium. Rogan took a 2–1 lead into the eighth when Hilldale loaded the bases, courtesy of one hit and two Monarch errors, with no outs.

But Rogan induced two ground ball force-outs at home and then struck out Winters to preserve the lead. The score was still 2–1 in the bottom of the ninth. Rogan got off to a poor start, hitting leadoff man Otto Briggs, but he bounced back, getting Hilldale manager Frank Warfield to pop up. Then Biz Mackey lined a single to center field, where Carroll "Dink" Mothell, who usually started when Rogan was on the mound, misplayed the ball, allowing Mackey and Briggs to advance to second and third. With Judy Johnson on deck and the light-hitting John Lewis at bat, the Monarchs chose not to intentionally walk the batter to set up a force play at every base. Lewis hit a ground ball to shortstop Dobie Moore, who wanted to throw home. But hurrying in order to peg the speedy Briggs, Moore bobbled the ball and then threw wide to first, pulling Hawkins off the bag. The score was tied 2–2 with runners on first and third and only one out. Judy Johnson stepped up to the plate and promptly hit a Rogan pitch over Mothell's head in center. Johnson rounded the bases for an inside-the-park home run and a 5–2 Hilldale lead. Winters closed out the ninth

allowing one run, and the Daisies of Darby had a 3–1 lead in the series.

The Monarchs had their backs to the wall going into game six, and Hilldale seemed determined to keep up the pressure: Judy Johnson tripled to bring in two runs in the top of the first inning. But K.C. came out swinging, and Joe Rogan got the big hit in a three-run rally by the home team. Once again, the game was close throughout. With the teams deadlocked at five in the bottom of the eighth, Dobie Moore collected his third hit of the game with a single to right. Then first baseman George Sweatt shot a ball past the outfielders and Moore raced all the way from first to score the go-ahead run. When Hilldale failed to rally in the ninth, the Monarchs were back in the series. Game seven was on Sunday afternoon at a packed Muehlenbach Stadium. Ed Bolden called on ace Nip Winters to start on one day's rest; Bill Drake got the assignment for Kansas City. The Daisies led 2–0 in the fourth when Dobie Moore singled to right, sending Newt Joseph around to third. Then the Monarchs executed a perfect double steal, as Joseph raced home when Moore

drew a throw at second. Pitcher Drake then singled home Moore to tie the score. Hilldale moved back ahead by a run, but K.C. rallied to tie the score in the bottom of the eighth. Hilldale got a couple of runners on with one out in the ninth, and it was evident that Drake had nothing left. Having used

* * * *

Opening day for the first-ever Colored World Series took place on October 11, 1924, and featured Kansas City of the NNL and Hilldale of the ECL. The Monarchs are (from left) Boyd, McNair, Joseph, Morris, O. Johnson, Rogan, Allen, Mendez, Moore, W. Bell, Hawkins, Duncan, C. Bell, Mothel, McCall, Drake, and Sweatt; the men in suits are (from left) Wilkinson, Dr. Smith, Spedden, Pompez, Foster, and Bolden; the Hilldale Club are (from left) Santop, Winters, Currie, Lee, Carr, C. Johnson, J. Johnson, Ryan, Mackey, Allen, Campbell, Lewis, Thomas, Cockrell, Briggs, Warfield, Stevens, and Lambert.

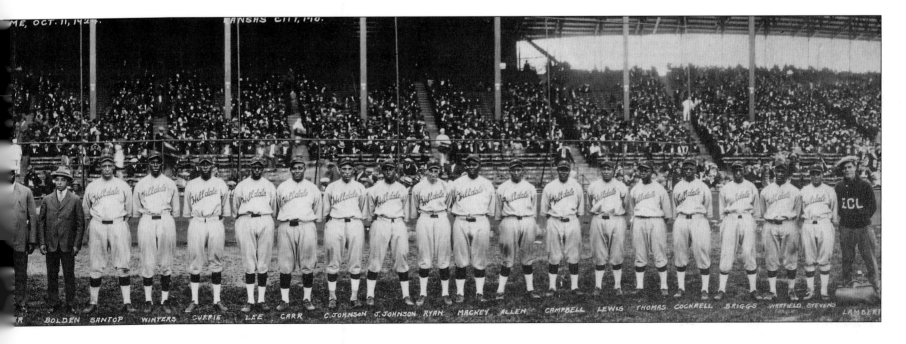

Rogan in relief of Bell the day before, Monarchs manager Mendez was short on options, so he called his own number. One of the game's greatest pitchers only a few years earlier, he had performed well in recent years as a spot starter, but he had not pitched, under a doctor's orders, since he had undergone surgery a couple of months earlier. The first batter he faced was former Monarch Tank Carr; Mendez struck him out in three pitches. The aging Cuban then got Winters to fly out. The game went to extra innings, and Mendez, who had had a blazing fastball in his youth, used a wide array of off-speed pitches to baffle the Daisies for three more innings. In the bottom of the twelfth, George Sweatt got his second clutch triple in as many days and came home on Joe Rogan's single to give the Monarchs a 4–3 victory. The series headed to Chicago even at three games apiece.

An African prince attended the first game at Schorling Stadium, which matched Monarch ace Rogan against ex-Monarch Rube Currie, the winning pitcher in game four. Rogan was sharp, but so was Currie. The game was scoreless until the sixth, when Warfield singled for Hilldale, Mackey sacrificed him to second, and then Santop came through with an RBI single. Hilldale added an insurance run and Currie took a 2–0 lead into the bottom of the ninth. In the lore of black baseball, the events that followed have a tragic resonance similar to Fred Snodgrass' boner in 1908 that cost the Giants the National League pennant, or more recently, Bill Buckner's flub in the sixth game of the 1986 World Series. Currie retired the first batter in the ninth, then Rogan singled, but Currie rebounded to retire the next batter on a ground out. Then Moore legged out an infield single, moving Rogan to third. McNair followed with a clean base hit, scoring Rogan, and when Currie hit Heavy Johnson to load the bases, the walls seemed to be caving in on the ex-Monarch. Catcher Frank Duncan stepped up to the plate. Miraculously, Currie induced Duncan to hit a high pop-up behind home

plate. Catcher Louis Santop had room to make the catch, but it bounced off the side of his mitt, giving Duncan and the Monarchs new life.

Duncan proceeded to rip Currie's next offering right at third base; unfortunately for Hilldale, Biz Mackey, not the sure-handed Judy Johnson, was at the "hot corner" and the ball scooted through his legs. Moore and McNair scored and K.C. won 3–2 to take a 4–3 lead in the series.

After the game, Hilldale manager Frank Warfield gave Santop a tongue-lashing for muffing the pop foul. Even in his early days, "Top" was not considered a very good fielding catcher, but his bat always atoned for his defensive lapses. Meanwhile, Mackey, a great backstop, ended up at third because shortstop Jake Stephens had been unable to handle the sharp curveballs thrown by the K.C. pitchers. So Warfield moved Judy Johnson to short, where he had some experience, and tried Mackey at third. John Lewis had started a few games behind the plate, but Warfield wanted Santop and all three of his regular outfielders in the lineup. Of course, Warfield should have been yelling at himself; if he had used Stephens as a defensive replacement in the ninth, he could have moved Johnson to third, Mackey behind the plate, and Santop to the dugout, vastly improving the defense and probably not losing the game on a dropped foul ball.

Nip Winters took the ball to try to end Hilldale's three-game skid in front of more than six thousand fans on a Sunday afternoon. The game was nip and tuck all the way, but Winters got stronger as the game wore on, while the Monarchs were forced to use an assortment of pitchers to try to contain Hilldale. The score was knotted at three heading into the ninth when Hilldale broke through for two runs. Winters set the Monarchs down in the ninth for his third win of the series, and the series was tied once again. Going into the ninth game, Hilldale had more than just momentum on their side, because the talented but thin Kansas City pitching staff was

exhausted. Scrip Lee, Hilldale's crafty righthander with a submarine delivery, was set to start the decisive game, whereas the Monarchs were in a quandary as Rogan, Bell, and Drake were all fatigued.

It was a gray, blustery October day in Chicago for game nine. The temperature had dropped into the thirties when the Monarchs took the field led by their manager, Jose Mendez, who walked to the mound. In front of a small crowd of about fifteen hundred fans (the small number was a result of the weather and the fact that it was a weekday), Mendez and Lee were both brilliant, matching each other frame for frame. After seven innings it was 0–0. Mendez was absolutely masterful, fooling the Hilldale batters with a wide array of breaking balls and an occasional perfectly placed fastball. Lee, meanwhile, baffled the Monarchs' bats with his deceptive motion, sharp curves, and sneaky fastball.

Mendez worked a flawless eighth. Lee took the mound and Dobie Moore worked the count full before smacking a single to center field. Moore advanced to second on a sacrifice. The next batter doubled into the corner, scoring Moore. Lee then walked the next batter and gave up a scratch single to Mendez to load the bases. Newt Allen, who had struck out in his three previous at-bats, shot a bullet down the third base line into the corner of the outfield, clearing the bases with a triple. McNair singled in Allen for the fifth run of the inning. In the top of the ninth, McNair made a great catch on a long fly ball into the right field corner by pinch-hitter Nip Winters for out number one. Otto Briggs followed with a ground out. Mendez then gave up his first walk of the game to Frank Warfield, only the third Hilldale player to reach base. Biz Mackey followed with a Texas Leaguer—a little looping pop fly—in shallow left field, which Dobie Moore raced out and caught for the final out. The Kansas City Monarchs were the Colored World Champions.

The Monarchs were the toast of black America. The celebration went long into the night in Chicago.

Rube Foster boasted that Mendez had consulted with him before the final game about who should pitch and that Foster told Mendez to take the mound himself. Foster even claimed that he told Mendez, "You go in there, and if you don't know what to throw, look over at me and I'll tell you." He also claimed that he followed up this proposal by sitting in the Monarchs' dugout and essentially calling the game for Mendez. Whether apocryphal or not, this tale betrays that Foster had come to view the Monarchs' hard-fought, dramatic triumph as his own. It was also significant that the NNL, which had seemed to be weakening, had triumphed over the ECL. Moreover, the series had been a financial success. The ten-game odyssey had generated a $30,000 profit, which was split among the leagues, the two teams (the greater share going to the winners, of course), and the second- and third-place teams in each league. At the end of the 1924 season, such issues as the ECL's player raids on NNL teams and the instability of the marginal franchises still loomed over blackball, but in the afterglow of the brilliant World Series, the future looked bright.

As it turned out, the 1924 World Series was probably the pinnacle of blackball in the 1920s. At the time, two black major leagues were up and running, having gotten over the hurdle of surviving more than one season, and there was little doubt about their continuing the following year. The leagues had troubles, but none that couldn't be overcome. Or so it seemed. At the end of 1925, by contrast, Ed Bolden declared that the season had been "one of the most disastrous years for black teams in the last ten."

As noted, prospects were good for the 1925 season, and it was a successful year on the field of play, if not for teams' finances. Out west, the Negro National League once again fielded an eight-team league, the two southern teams, Birmingham and Memphis, returning for their second seasons. The only team from 1924 to disappear was the Cleveland

Browns, who had failed to make ends meet in their first season. Rube Foster took charge of this situation, and under his guidance, Mrs. C.I. Taylor reformed the Indianapolis ABCs. Hoping to reestablish a quality franchise in a city with a blackball tradition, Foster once again proved his commitment to furthering blackball by sending some of his American Giants to play for Mrs. Taylor. While he

* * * *

Third baseman Judy Johnson's .364 average in the 1924 Colored World Series was just slightly better than the .343 he posted over the regular season, though the Daisies lost the series to Kansas City. In 1925, Johnson was even better in the regular season (.390) and Hilldale went on to win the World Series rematch with the Monarchs.

was in Indianapolis overseeing these maneuvers, Foster almost died taking a nap in a hotel room with a leaky gas furnace. He was found unconscious after someone smelled the fumes. Following this incident, Foster, whose young daughter had recently died, began to act erratically, to the increasing concern of those around him.

Before the season began, Foster and the rest of the league owners decided to implement a split-season structure in the NNL. The teams would compete for first place through midseason, and then the teams would start afresh and a second pennant race would commence. Then the first-half winner and the second-half winner (or runner-up if the same team won both halves) would face off in a best-of-seven series to determine the league champion. This structure insured against diminishing crowds at second division teams' home games late in the season, and it also created a potentially profitable postseason series.

The NNL's first-half title went to the prohibitive favorites, the defending world blackball champion Kansas City Monarchs. However, the Monarchs had lost one of their key players, slugger Oscar "Heavy" Johnson, to the ECL's Baltimore Black Sox. Nonetheless, the Monarchs outclassed the rest of the league with an amazing 31–9 (.775) mark. Their traditional rivals, Foster's Giants, provided no competition, falling to fourth place at 26–22. In order to help build a solid foundation for the ABCs franchise, Foster had broken up the starting eight—who had been together for half a decade—and sent Bingo DeMoss, one of his two greatest everyday players (the other being Cristobal Torriente), to Indianapolis along with one of his two top catchers, George "Tubby" Dixon. This act of generosity proved costly. The Detroit Stars finished ahead of the American Giants in third (26–20) but were still not able to make the leap to serious pennant contender. The only team that did challenge the Monarchs was the St. Louis franchise.

The Stars were the story of the 1925 NNL season, finishing a strong second (31–14, for a .689 winning percentage) in the first half, and winning the second half of the regular season to earn a place in the first-ever NNL championship playoff. The Stars were owned by Richard Kent, a black man who had made his money running numbers. Under Kent's stewardship, St. Louis became a perennial power in the West, and at the heart of their success were two brilliant young talents: center fielder James "Cool Papa" Bell and shortstop Willie Wells. The legend of "Cool Papa" Bell is such that he has earned the appellation the "fastest man ever to play baseball." He certainly possessed blinding speed and used it to tremendous advantage on the field. Extremely aggressive on the base paths, he would take Rube Foster's style of play one step further, going from first all the way home on a bunt. (This isn't merely the stuff of myth because if Bell knew he could beat the throw to third [on Foster's first-to-third play], and that the catcher had chased after the bunt and was not at the plate but in the infield, Bell could just keep running and in all likelihood reach home before the catcher was back there with the ball to tag him out.)

Bell also used his speed to advantage in the massive center field in the Stars' home park. Not only could he run down fly balls, but he also became the master of the inside-the-park home run when he shot a line drive over or past the center fielder.

Teammate Willie Wells, who turned twenty during the 1925 season, was an exceptional fielder who was rapidly developing into an exceptional hitter. When a bullet wound ended Dobie Moore's career prematurely in 1926, Wells was able to establish himself as the third of the three transcendent Negro league shortstops, following in the footsteps of Pop Lloyd and Dick Lundy. The careers of Wells and Bell, who was only twenty-two himself, would span the remaining twenty-one years of baseball's segregated era. In 1925, however, they were merely the

brightest young stars on the NNL's up-and-coming team, which posted a 38–12 record to top the Monarchs' 31–11 and win the second-half title.

* * * *

When Willie Wells broke in with the Detroit Stars in 1924 he was just twenty and a raw talent. But his skills were honed by the great manager Candy Jim Taylor, brother of C.I. Taylor, and by the late 1930s, when this photo was likely taken, he was a respected manager himself as well as one of the greatest shortstops in the history of the game. His career batting average over twenty years was .328.

The American Giants improved on their first-half performance with a 28–18 mark, but Foster recognized it was time to bolster his depleted club with youth. By the following spring, Jimmy Lyons, Cristobal Torriente, first baseman Leroy Grant, and shortstop Bobby Williams were gone from Chicago, leaving Dave Malarcher at third, "Jelly" Gardner in the outfield, and James Brown behind the plate as the only holdovers in a new era. Detroit had the league's two top batting stars in 1925: first baseman Edgar Wesley, who led the NNL with a .416 average, and his slugging teammate "Turkey" Stearns, whom he tied for the most home runs in league play with eighteen. As a team, unfortunately, their second half was no better than their first (27–20). Of the NNL's other four teams, Indianapolis, Memphis, and Birmingham were firmly rooted in the NNL second division during both halves; the Cuban Stars had a respectable year (22–25), especially considering they were once again virtually homeless.

The big news in the league was that attendance continued to decline. Even though all eight teams stayed afloat throughout the season, many owners were becoming impatient with Foster's dictatorial rule over a league in apparent decline. In fact, Detroit owner Terry Blount confronted Foster with his complaints and declared that he would no longer stand silently by while Foster, in effect, ran the Detroit team (into the ground, in Blount's opinion). In retaliation for Blount's insubordination, Foster canceled many of the games that the Stars had scheduled through his booking office, and when Blount suffered great losses because of this, he certainly wasn't going to get bailed out by the NNL. During the 1925 season, Blount could no longer sustain the losses and sold the team to a group of black Detroit businessmen whom Foster had already rounded up in anticipation of Blount's defeat. Still, Foster was not to blame for the troubles plaguing the NNL; in fact, his obsessive attention to every detail of the league's operation remained its greatest asset, the ethics of Foster's Machiavellian parlor politics notwithstanding. Even as the league struggled financially, Foster's willfulness and unrivaled stature among blackball fans was such that they seemed to ensure the continued operation of the NNL.

The decline in attendance afflicting blackball had little to do with mismanagement; rather, it had its roots in one of the defining characteristics of black America, poverty. At the beginning of the 1920s, the expanding northern black communities experienced a modicum of prosperity stemming from the income earned by black men both in the military and at the many unskilled industrial jobs either created by the war economy or left by white workers who joined the armed forces. But in the years following the war, black workers were laid off in droves as military production slowed and white veterans returned to the job market (exercising their inalienable right to take away any job held by a black man). While the 1920s were an era of unprecedented prosperity in white America, the northern black communities fell back into their usual state of chronic economic depression.

As World War I faded into the past, there was a decrease in disposable income in the black community, which meant there was less money to spend at the ballpark. And confusing matters for league organizers was the relative success of both leagues' first two seasons. Given the logistical problems experienced with inaugurating any such undertaking, it's understandable that they would believe that things could only improve once the kinks had been worked out. Foster and Bolden both believed that if black baseball was made more accessible to black fans, its popularity would surely increase. However, in retrospect, both the NNL and ECL prospered initially by offering fans long-awaited matchups between the top black teams in the Midwest and on the East Coast. Once these matchups lost their novelty, they weren't in demand as much as they had been. However, the rivalries between the top teams

continued to generate large gates, thus expectations were high for the 1925 postseason.

The matchup in the inaugural NNL championship series was a natural rivalry if there ever was one. At the time, St. Louis was a major league city par excellence, with teams in both the NL and AL (the powerful Cardinals and the anemic Browns, respectively), while Kansas City was just a stop on the minor league outback to the world of white baseball. The opposite had been true in black baseball: Kansas City had a more vibrant blackball scene than St. Louis before World War I (K.C. had four pro teams in the mid-1910s). Since the war, Wilkinson's Monarchs had posted baroque win-loss records every season, finishing at or near the top of the standings in all six years of the NNL's existence. They were seeking their third consecutive league title, and, of course, they were the defending "colored" world champions. The Stars' resume, on the other hand, showed one winning season in the NNL before 1925 (40–36 the previous year). The Monarchs were looking not only to defend their status as the top team in the region against the youthful upstarts backed by big-city money, but to secure a place in the mythology of their hometown, which craved acknowledgment as a significant urban center and thus relished any victory over St. Louis. The Stars wanted to complete a storybook "breakout" season by toppling the legendary Monarchs and staking a claim to blackball greatness.

The Stars certainly had the brain trust to educate their young talent: their manager/third baseman was Candy Jim Taylor, brother of the deceased C.I. Taylor of ABCs fame, who was living proof that baseball smarts ran in the family. The team's former manager, Bill Gatewood, another C.I. Taylor understudy, pitched for the team; and veteran Sam Bennett, who mainly played catcher for the 1925 Stars, had in his prime been a brilliant and innovative outfielder. According to blackball legend, Bennett was not only the first outfielder to master

the technique of taking his eye off a fly ball in order to run as fast as possible to the spot where he determined the ball would land, where he'd turn and make the catch, but he also tutored Tris Speaker, considered the greatest white defensive outfielder of the era, in the tricks of the trade. This crew of veterans molded the likes of Bell and Wells into complete ballplayers and students of the game. Gatewood, who coined Bell's nickname, suggested he abandon pitching when he experienced arm trouble, and learn to hit from the left side of the plate to take better advantage of his speed. Wells went from a weak hitter to one of the best in the game in two short seasons under Taylor's guidance. And when Wells became a manager late in his career, he passed what he had learned from Taylor onto the next generation of black batters—most important, that the only way to improve as a hitter is to practice hour upon hour upon hour.

Taylor, like his older brother, preached hard work and fundamentals, and considering the Stars' on-field success, the message must have gotten through to the team's stable of talented youngbloods. The average age of the Stars' starting lineup in 1925 was around twenty-five. Alongside Bell in the outfield were Wilson "Frog" Redus (twenty) in left, a disciplined batsman who posted a .385 average in his first full season in St. Louis, and Branch Russell (an old man, at thirty) in right, a consistent .300 hitter. At the infield corners were third baseman Dewey Creacy (age unknown, probably around twenty-five), who batted .326 and had a knack for knocking balls over the short left field fence in St. Louis; and first baseman Willie Bobo (early twenties), a talented gloveman and a power hitter. Catcher Mitchell Murray (late twenties) was a defensive stalwart (though his arm was merely adequate) and an excellent clutch hitter.

Second base was something of a question for the Stars, one they would answer the following season with the arrival of John Henry Russell, an exceptional fielder and a disciplined batsman who, like

Murray, often came through in the clutch. In 1925, the Stars made do with journeyman infielder Eddie Watts or forty-one-year-old manager "Candy" Jim Taylor, who primarily had been a third baseman throughout his career. The Stars were never renowned for their pitching staff the way the Monarchs or the American Giants (of 1926–1927) had been, but they had some quality arms. Young but crafty, Roosevelt Davis was best known for his spitballs and use of an emery board to doctor the baseball. Davis posted an 11–3 NNL record in 1925 to establish himself as the Stars' ace. Another youngster, Eggie Hensley, had a wicked curveball and was

maturing rapidly. Three veterans also contributed on the mound: Percy Miller, Deacon Meyers (who occasionally played second base), and former manager Bill Gatewood.

Though on paper the Stars' lineup wasn't comparable to Hilldale's or the Monarchs', especially considering that Wells was not close to being the hitter he would be in a few years, manager Taylor guided this group to the second highest winning percentage (.726) in NNL history to date. Unfortunately, the best (.756) was posted by the very team they had to face in the playoffs, the defending Negro World Champion Kansas City Monarchs. Wilkinson's

team, however, had relied more than ever on pitching in the absence of slugger Heavy Johnson, who had signed with the Baltimore Black Sox before the season. Ironically, the position abandoned by Johnson was filled by the speedy Wade Johnston, who had returned to the Monarchs after leaving to play with Baltimore in 1924. A natural leadoff hitter, Johnston had a fine season in 1925, batting .313, but he provided none of Johnson's clout. The pitching staff more than compensated during the regular season: Rogan was nothing short of spectacular, leading the league in both wins (15–2) and ERA (2.17); Bill "Plunk" Drake, Will Bell, Sr., and

Cliff Bell had solid seasons; rookie Nelson Dean went 12–4; old man Mendez contributed a 3–1 mark; and an eighteen-year-old phenom from Leavenworth, Kansas, named Chet Brewer showed great promise, though he was used sparingly.

The seasoned Monarchs were prohibitive favorites against the young Stars but, as it turned out, the series was fought tooth and nail through seven games. The difference was one man, Wilbur "Bullet Joe" Rogan. The Monarchs' ace won game one, 8–6. Rogan made a brilliant catch in center field in game two, but the Stars evened the series with a 2–1 victory. Rogan moved Kansas City back ahead, going the distance in the Monarchs' 5–4 game-three triumph. Then the Stars captured games four and five at home and the series moved on to Chicago with St. Louis only one victory away from pulling the upset. Heading into the bottom of the ninth inning of game six, the Stars were up 4–3, only three outs away from advancing to the World Series. But the Monarchs refused to go quietly. With runners at second and third and only one out, manager Jim Taylor decided to walk Dobie Moore to create a force out at every base. K.C.'s hottest hitter, Joe Rogan, who already had three hits that day, was up. Rogan

✴ ✴ ✴ ✴

OPPOSITE: *The 1929 Baltimore Black Sox featured (back row, from left) Eggie Clark, Pud Flournoy, Scrip Lee, Oliver Marcelle, Jesse Hubbard, Merven Ryan, Pete Washington, Bill Force; (front row, from left) Rap Dixon, Cook, Gomez, Frank Warfield, Jud Wilson, Dick Lundy, and Lamon Yokeley.* **ABOVE:** *Pitcher Wilbur "Bullet Joe" Rogan was one of the fearsome 25th Infantry Wreckers, the club that dominated warball during World War I. J.L. Wilkinson wisely snatched up many of the best players from that squad when he was assembling his Kansas City team.*

promptly rapped his fourth hit, scoring two runs, and the series was down to a final game.

In a scene reminiscent of the previous season's World Series, game seven was played in frigid conditions in Chicago. But it was Rogan's heat that froze the Stars' bats—he hurled a shutout as the Monarchs triumphed 4–0 to capture their third straight NNL title. The moment belonged to Rogan, who had pitched three complete game victories and led the Monarchs' offense, batting .500 over seven games.

So Kansas City headed east for a rematch with Hilldale in the World Series. Ed Bolden's Daisies had blown away the rest of the ECL for their third straight pennant, proving more dominant than ever with a .775 winning percentage (45–13). The ECL had only seven teams in 1925; the Washington Potomacs had dropped out of the league and moved to Wilmington, Delaware, though not before manager Ben Taylor had absconded with a few of his players. Taylor and company joined forces with the

other ECL expansion team from the previous season, Oscar Charleston's Harrisburg Giants, producing a first-rate club that finished second in the ECL with a 37–18 record (.673). Taylor and Charleston had been teammates on the ABCs, and much like St. Louis in the NNL, Harrisburg had the feel of a C.I. Taylor ball club. In this case, that meant solid fundamental baseball and twenty-eight-year-old center fielder Oscar Charleston.

Charleston had perhaps his greatest season ever in 1925, leading the ECL in hits, doubles, homers (twenty), slugging percentage, and batting average (.445). Other than Charleston and the thirty-seven-year-old Taylor, who played first base and hit .327, the only notable players on Harrisburg were right fielder Cliff Jenkins (.317), who hit in the leadoff spot; second baseman Rap Dixon (.357), who batted second; and, most notably, power-hitting shortstop Walter "Rev" Cannady (.386, with eleven homers), who hit in the cleanup spot following Charleston. Mack Eggleston (.301) was a solid catcher, but third base and left field were filled by an array of journeymen and utility men throughout the season. It is a testimony to Charleston's and Taylor's skill as motivators and teachers that the players who filled in generally posted better numbers in Harrisburg than elsewhere during their careers. Likewise, Harrisburg got the most out of a ragtag pitching staff that included Ping Gardner (9–3), who threw underhanded; two ex-ABCs, Charles Corbett (8–1) and Daltie Cooper (6–3); youngster Clifford Carter, who would become the staff's ace in a few years; and Lefty Gisentaner (5–4), who had a mangled pitching hand that he took advantage of to develop some unorthodox breaking balls.

Finishing just behind Harrisburg in the standings were the Baltimore Black Sox at 31–19 (.620). The Black Sox expected to challenge Hilldale after their second-place finish the year before and their off-season acquisition of Heavy Johnson. They only improved by half a game over their 1924 total. The middle of the Black Sox lineup was a veritable mur- derers' row, with Jud Wilson (.395), John Beckwith (.402), and Heavy Johnson (.345) batting third, fourth, and fifth, respectively.

In Wilson and Beckwith, the Black Sox had two of blackball's more confrontational personalities, and they both missed games in 1925 because of this quality. Wilson, who was built like Hercules, had a wicked temper. He played with unbridled pas- sion and hated to lose, and if he felt he was being cheated, he was capable of spectacular violence. Some of the brawls he was in are the stuff of legend. Once it took three cops using billy clubs to get him under control; another time he stopped his assault on an umpire only when a teammate threatened him with a bat. Off the field, Wilson was a pleasant, soft- spoken man, but his reputation was such that his reticence was widely perceived as brooding. Even his teammates considered him intimidating. Thus, the slugger was the perfect man to frame for a vio- lent crime; this is exactly what happened in the middle of the 1925 season, causing him to miss some games before the real perpetrator was caught.

Beckwith, meanwhile, was more incorrigible than passionate. Possessing talents comparable to Wilson, the six-foot-three (191cm), 220-pound (100kg) pull-hitting infielder was a drinker who brawled both on and off the field, and though he often managed the teams he played on, he had no work ethic to speak of and his apparent lack of con- viction frustrated teammates. Beckwith was having a tremendous year in 1925; in late July he was lead- ing the ECL in home runs. But then he beat up an umpire so severely following a disagreement that he had to leave Baltimore or face arrest. Beckwith rejoined the team a few days later, but shortly there- after he quit for the remainder of the season over a contract dispute with Black Sox management, and Pete Hill returned as skipper.

The Black Sox' most versatile player, Chippy Britt, who doubled as a pitcher (5–4) and as the

front-line catcher (batting .345), was also one of the great brawlers in Negro league history. In fact, Britt and Wilson (though not Beckwith) made up half of a group deemed the Big Four of the Bad Men, alongside Oscar Charleston and Vic Harris (a spray- hitting left fielder who left Foster's Giants at the age of twenty in 1925 to begin a twenty-three-year affiliation with an independent club called the Homestead Grays). In 1931, this fearsome foursome was united on the Homestead Grays, dropping the 1925 Black Sox to second place on the list of meanest teams in blackball history, even though Baltimore's speedy leadoff hitter Crush Holloway (.289 in 1925) was also a renowned pugilist whose aggressive slides initiated more than a few brawls. Even without the loss of Beckwith, the Black Sox didn't have enough offense (though they had a lot) to compensate for their lack of top-flight pitchers. Their two best hurlers in 1925 were Bob McClure (12–4) and Joe Strong (11–6), two good, but not great, righties. Thus, Baltimore posed no threat to Hilldale.

As for the Bacharach Giants, they remained a .500 club in ECL competition, but they made a significant step in the right direction when they reacquired third baseman Oliver Marcelle from the Lincoln Giants in midseason (forming a dream infield of Marcelle, Dick Lundy, and the venerable Pop Lloyd). Nat Strong's Brooklyn Royal Giants had little to boast of, as they struggled to a 13–20 (.394) league mark. Alex Pompez's New York Cuban Stars finished in sixth at 15–26 (.366), but they did have a budding superstar in twenty-year-old second base- man Martin Dihigo.

As for the Lincolns, they suffered a terrible drop-off from a decent third-place campaign in 1924 to a disastrous last-place finish (7–39, .152) in 1925. In the off-season, James Keenan and the Lincolns' front office had decided to rebuild the team with youth and released the great Smokey Joe Williams, who was turning forty that April. Thus,

Williams, who remained a great pitcher, finally moved on from his Harlem lair, where he had spent the previous twelve seasons, to become the ace of the Homestead Grays. The Lincolns, after all, had another superstar hurler in lefty Dave Brown, who, like Marcelle, was just entering his prime and would provide a solid foundation for the new Lincolns. Alas, that plan was laid to waste after Dave Brown became a fugitive from justice.

Brown was not considered a disciplinary prob- lem as a player, and he was well liked by his team- mates, who found him congenial and good-humored. Persistent rumors circulated that he had been fleeing the law when he signed on with Foster's Giants in 1918, and it was whispered that Foster had paid $20,000 under the table to law enforcement officials to cancel a warrant for Brown's arrest on charges of highway robbery. Brown apparently went about his life without incident when, early in the 1925 baseball season, he went to a Harlem nightclub, where he met teammates Oliver Marcelle and Frank Wickware. An argument ensued between Brown and another man, apparently concerning cocaine; a fight broke out and Brown killed the man. The next day, police investiga- tors dropped in on the Lincoln Giants before game

* * * *

OPPOSITE: *The Kansas City Monarchs pose with members of the House of David baseball club in front of the Kansas City bus (known to the players as Dr. Yak) during a barnstorming tour of Canada in 1934. Included here are (back row, from left) Bullet Joe Rogan, Newt Joseph, Newt Allen; (middle row, from left) Chet Brewer, J.L. Wilkinson, George Giles, Frank Duncan, Carroll Mothel, Sam Crawford, House of David player, Charles Beverly, Andy Cooper; (front row, from left) Hurley McNair, House of David player, Eddie Dwight, and another House of David player.*

time. Brown was nowhere to be found. Marcelle and Wickware, who had not witnessed the fight, were brought in for questioning and later released. Brown was never heard from again. Wanted by the FBI, the great lefthander laid low for a while, but as the summer wore on, Negro leaguers got wind of rumors that a sharp southpaw going by the name of Lefty Wilson, who had been pitching for semipro teams in the Midwest, was actually Dave Brown. The following season, Wilson showed up on Bob Gilkerson's Union Giants, a midwestern barnstorming team. In 1927, he was with a white semipro club in Bertha, Minnesota. Some historians seem quite confident that Wilson was in fact Dave Brown. If so, he played

in Sioux City, Iowa, in 1929 and for Little Falls, Minnesota, in 1930, after which no further record of him exists. According to most accounts of the Dave Brown mystery, he met a violent death somewhere in the western United States, perhaps in Denver, but no documentation exists to support this claim. The only thing that's certain is that the Negro league career of Dave Brown, perhaps the greatest left-handed pitcher in blackball history, came to an abrupt end in early 1925. Without Brown as a cornerstone of their rebuilding process, the Lincolns soon realized there was no point holding Marcelle captive and traded him to the Bacharachs. The Lincolns completed the season in substandard form.

At the other end of the ECL spectrum, the Hilldale juggernaut kept rolling along. Not much had changed from 1924 except that manager/second baseman Fred Warfield and slugger Louis Santop never made amends after the tongue-lashing Warfield gave Santop after the ninth game of the World Series; consequently, Santop's role on the team had diminished considerably. Thus, Biz Mackey, perhaps the greatest defensive catcher in Negro league history, became the starting backstop. Other than that, it was business as usual for Hilldale, as Bolden's troops swept through their ECL schedule in record-breaking style, going 45–13 for a .775 average. Ace Nip Winters, who lead the circuit with a 3.40 ERA, collected twenty-one of those victories. Of course, it was a rare day that Hilldale didn't light up the scoreboard. The only respite for opposing hurlers was shortstop Jake Stephens, who shored up Hilldale's infield with his superb glovework but batted only .229, and the pitchers (except for Winters, who batted .345). Speedy leadoff man Otto Briggs had another good year (though his batting average is unrecorded), Frank Warfield hit a solid .314, Judy Johnson led the club with a .392 average, Biz Mackey hit .350 with power, Clint Thomas chimed in at .351, center fielder George Johnson batted .327, and Tank Carr stole twenty-four bases in league play to complement a .367 batting average.

Hilldale wanted nothing more than to avenge their World Series loss from the year before, so the Darby Daisies had to be elated when Kansas City snuck by St. Louis, setting up a rematch. And the likelihood that the Hilldale team would fulfill their mission became much greater when the Monarchs lost their most important player, Joe Rogan, to an injury suffered while playing with his infant son. The child, not understanding the consequences, had stuck a pin into his father's knee. The injury required emergency surgery, and while Rogan traveled with the team throughout the series, in hope of a miraculous recovery, he could do no more than cheer on his teammates from the dugout. The loss of Rogan promised to be devastating; not only was he one of the Monarchs' top two sluggers, along with Dobie Moore, he was also the team's pitching ace. Even with Rogan in the lineup, the Monarchs figured to be less potent than the previous year with the loss of Heavy Johnson's bat. The departed slugger had contributed a solid .296

* * * *

In a rare action shot from the period, the mighty slugger Judson Ernest "Boojum" Wilson unleashes his swing. Jud Wilson was a feared slugger and a fierce competitor whose brooding demeanor was intimidating even to his teammates. He had a tremendous 1925 season with the Baltimore Black Sox (although the team fell to the mighty Hilldale juggernaut), batting .395 with six home runs, three triples, and fourteen doubles.

average in the 1924 black fall classic, in which the Monarchs had needed every last bit of production to eke out a victory.

The Hilldale-Monarchs rematch in 1925 started out as thrilling as the previous year's series. The Monarchs gave the ball to Cliff Bell for game one, while Hilldale countered with Rube Currie. Both were brilliant and the score was knotted at two after nine innings. Bell buckled first, as Hilldale tallied three runs in the twelfth to take the opener. Then, in a manner reminiscent of the classic encounter between these foes twelve months earlier, K.C. bounced back behind the pitching of rookie Nelson Dean, defeating Phil Cockrell and the Daisies by the score of 5–3. Hoping to keep up the momentum, and perhaps spook Hilldale with memories of their failure in the last year's climax, the Monarch manager Mendez played his trump card in game three, calling his own number. So the venerable hero of the previous October climbed the hill and was as sharp as a razor. But Hilldale's ace, Nip Winters, was up to the challenge. After nine innings, both clubs had managed only one run. Then Judy Johnson led off the tenth with a sharp single off of Mendez. Moments later Clint Thomas sent a ball to the gap and Johnson raced home with what held up as the winning run. Hilldale had faced, and conquered, the ghost of its greatest defeat.

The Monarchs desperately needed to win game four, their final "home" game, lest they head east in a deep hole. But it was not to be, and the Daisies took a 3–1 lead in the series for the second straight year. In game five, the Monarchs turned to Cliff Bell for a reprieve, while manager Fred Warfield handed the ball to Rube Currie. Once again, a tight pitcher's duel ensued. Through eight innings the game was even at 1–1. If K.C. could only have broken through for a run, they could have climbed back into the series; but Currie dismissed the NNL champs in the top of the ninth. In the bottom of that inning, Biz Mackey sent a towering blast to deep right field that bounced high off of Shibe Park's tall right field fence and pulled up with a double. The Daisies sacrificed Mackey to third, K.C. intentionally loaded the bases, and then the pinch hitter lofted a fly ball to the outfield. Hilldale was a win away from the blackball title.

The Monarchs were gamers and put up a good fight the next day, but Phil Cockrell, who had lost the first Monarch-Hilldale World Series game a year earlier and suffered the Daisies' only series setback that season, outpitched William Bell to claim his first World Series victory. After a long year in which they mulled over what might have been, Hilldale had won their Colored World Championship, closing out their nemesis with four straight victories. As for the Monarchs, they could only wonder what might have been had the great Rogan been able to play. In spite of the lopsided 5–1 tally, the series was so closely contested that there was little to distinguish between the teams' stats. Hilldale, with its impressive slate of .300 hitters, had only Mackey (.375), Carr (.310), and Briggs (who had the same number of hits, twelve, as the year before, but in four fewer games) above that marker. Dobie Moore led the Monarchs' offense, batting .364. The standout performer, if there was any, was Hilldale hurler and ex-Monarch Rube Currie, who won his two decisions, both complete games, one of which went twelve innings, to post a 1.29 runs-per-game average.

After the series, the Hilldale players and their faithful followers in Darby celebrated boisterously, and the eastern black media railed mercilessly against the Monarchs and the NNLers (i.e., Rube Foster and his ilk), who, they felt, had boasted so arrogantly after K.C. had won by only the slightest of margins the previous autumn. One mock eulogy read, "In loving memory of the Kansas City Monarchs

(infant prodigy of the National League and only child of J.L. Wilkinson), who held the title of world champions of the diamond until its sudden death and violent death at the hands of the clan of Darby, better known as Hilldale...Kansas City departed this life at the tender age of one year."

While the partisans of the ECL in the black press apparently savored the blood-feud-type passion that informed the two-decade-old East-versus-West struggle for the soul of blackball, it didn't prove to be such a big hit with the average blackball fan on its return engagement. Relative to the first interleague World Series the previous year, attendance plummeted at the 1925 postseason black baseball championships. Actually, the Stars-Monarchs Negro National League Championship Series (NNLCS) proved to be a bigger draw than the Colored World Series, the event which both Rube Foster and Ed Bolden had been hoping would reverse the downward trend in blackball revenue. The series managed a profit of only $6,000, down from $52,000 the year before. Both the Monarch and Hilldale players were off salary for the series, playing instead for their World Series share, which they anticipated would be comparable to their checks in 1924 ($308 to the winners, K.C., $193 to the losers, Hilldale). A year later, Bolden's players collected a mere $69 each, while Wilkinson's men were rewarded a paltry $57.64. Likewise, the series offered little for the two leagues' coffers, which it was important to have stocked when weather cancellations or a string of disappointing gates occasionally left a league team stranded without the means to return home or to continue a road trip.

Furthermore, word came down from Judge Landis' office that he would no longer remain lax in prosecuting major league clubs that defied the ban on playing against Negro league teams. (The ban extended to all "non-organized" clubs, but Landis' rhetoric and timing made it obvious that he meant no more games against colored teams.) The problem

stemmed not merely from the fact that major league teams had resumed playing all-black teams with greater frequency, but from the fact that black teams were winning with greater frequency. Most notably, Hilldale played a three-game set against Connie Mack's Philadelphia A's just after the close of the 1925 AL regular season.

The young A's had finished the 1925 season in second place, ahead of Ruth's Yankees, and behind the Washington Senators, led by Walter Johnson, who won the pennant by eight and a half games. It was during this season that the A's trio of future hall-of-famers came of age. Sluggers Jimmy Foxx and Al Simmons and ace Lefty Grove would become the backbone of the Athletics' three straight AL pennants and two World Series victories from 1929 to 1931. Having clinched the ECL, Hilldale was biding time and waiting for the NNL playoffs to conclude. Needless to say, the series at Shibe Park, an intracity showdown, provided Ed Bolden with his biggest paydays of the year (and a handsome reward for Connie Mack as well). The results were eye-popping. Hilldale didn't just top the A's, they thrashed them, including an 18–3 rout. In 1925, Foxx, Simmons, and Grove were no match for Mackey, J. Johnson, and Winters. Such victories by the upper-echelon black teams (unsupplemented by ringers from other clubs) over intact white major league teams were not yet the rule, but they were no longer the exception. Clearly, Hilldale and the Monarchs were among the world's elite professional baseball teams.

Landis and much of the white baseball power structure had seen enough; the increasingly common losses to all-black teams were becoming more conspicuous and more of an embarrassment. Landis put his foot down and kept it down this time. After 1925, there were no more games between teams from the majors and the Negro leagues. From that point on, the only teams composed exclusively of major leaguers who played against Negro league teams were off-season major league "all-star" teams, some of which were deep with talent, but most of which had a few front-line stars and a bunch of backups in need of extra income. Thus, Landis not only deprived clubs like Bolden's and Foster's of the big paydays generated by games against the local major league teams, he also deprived blackball of its most meaningful tool for comparing itself with major league ball, which set the standard—for better or worse—for baseball around the world.

The very fact that the top black clubs seemed reliant upon the revenue generated by the rare game against a major league team spoke tomes about the financial prospects of the Negro leagues. After six full seasons of the NNL and three ECL campaigns, the Negro leagues were an unqualified success on the playing field. But in spite of the considerable organizational ingenuity of the leagues' organizers, most notably Rube Foster but also Ed Bolden and others, they were a financial morass. The two northern Negro leagues were successful not merely because they brought competitive black baseball to fans in the urban North, but also because the Negro leagues contributed greatly to an increase in the number of top-flight black ballplayers in America. By calling for the maintenance of fourteen to sixteen top-flight blackball teams, all populated with experienced baseball coaches and managers who were especially well versed in developing unrefined talent (important because black prospects did not have an extensive minor league system in which to refine their talents), the Negro leagues groomed the broadest, best-skilled, and most knowledgeable generation of black baseball players to date. And this generation of players, as long as the size of the leagues remained roughly the same, set a new standard of quality at each position that every young black player knew he must attain in order to make the big time. In other words, this broad base of teams did not result in a significant thinning of talent among the top clubs, but rather in the development of more high-quality black players.

In the economics of blackball, the supply of quality product was not the problem in 1925—it was the lack of demand. This probably has more to do with the declining state of the black American economy in the mid-1920s than with a drop in baseball's popularity among blacks. At any rate, in 1925, virtually no Negro league team turned a profit, with the possible exception of Foster's Giants and perhaps Nat Strong's Brooklyn Royal Giants, since these teams had their games arranged by their owners' booking agencies. Then again, Ed Bolden's Hilldale Daisies had a special under-the-table arrangement with Strong, virtually eliminating their booking levies, yet the Hilldale company needed to borrow money just to open its doors for the 1926 season—and this team was a regional dynasty that had just won its first national title and had shared in a huge gate from a three-game exhibition series against the local white major league team. Simply put, the system was failing.

Ed Bolden said as much following the 1925 season; however, the titular head of the "colored" senior circuit, Rube Foster, was not likely to admit such a thing. On the one hand, turning a profit was never Foster's primary motivation (and unlike Bolden, Foster seemed to anticipate, and thus accept, that his vast undertaking would run in the red). Nor was he driven to run a baseball franchise because the national pastime was his true love and he wanted to spend his entire life in the game, even if that meant tightening his belt. No, the Negro National League had to survive, according to Foster, because it was a vehicle to advance black America, a vehicle to develop the skills of African-Americans on the most symbolically American space of all, the baseball field. In this way, all Americans regardless of race or creed would plainly see—as a white shortstop flips to a black second baseman, who forces the Dominican base runner as he pivots and throws on to the white southerner playing first—that racism was ignorance. Furthermore, in Foster's own experience, he was the

only person he knew with the fortitude to complete such a project, so there could be no second-guessing.

On the other hand, Foster was losing his mind and was increasingly unable to assess the performance of the league he had founded. He began to have isolated fits of irrational behavior during the second half of 1925, which recurred with increasing frequency throughout the first half of 1926, until his wife called the police in August when he was destroying all the furniture on the ground floor of their house. The police came to the Foster residence, subdued the father of the Negro leagues, and took him to a state mental institution, where he would reside for the remaining four years of his life.

It's virtually impossible to establish exactly what caused Foster to lose control of his mind in this manner, but it seems reasonable to assume, from the fervency he exhibited as he organized all branches of his black baseball empire, that this minister's son was cracking under the inordinate amount of pressure he was putting on himself to fulfill his destiny as a latter-day Moses who would lead his people to the promised land. And this pressure probably increased as NNL attendance declined, revenue fell, teams' debts grew, and as his associates became more skeptical about the direction of the league (as perhaps he had as well).

Before Foster became stranded inside his unconscious, he had passed the reins of his baseball club over to his longtime third baseman and understudy, "Gentleman" Dave Malarcher, who had functioned as the interim skipper in 1925 while Foster recuperated from his asphyxiation in Indianapolis. Foster still oversaw the club's player movements, and in the off-season he orchestrated the youth movement that saw the dismantling of the American Giants' longtime nucleus. Cristobal Torriente was gift-wrapped and sent to J.L. Wilkinson for utility man George Sweatt, a lifelong Foster devotee. Jimmy Lyons and Leroy Grant were simply released and they both retired. And then Foster made one last stab at resuscitating the Indianapolis ABCs, who had outdone the Lincoln Giants' season of futility with a 4–33 record in the second half of the 1925 NNL campaign. With the ABCs left for dead, second baseman Bingo DeMoss and catcher George "Tubby" Dixon returned to Foster's lair in the off-season, but he sent them right back to Mrs. C.I. Taylor for the 1926 season, this time accompanied by shortstop Bobby Williams. Thus, only manager-third baseman Dave Malarcher, catcher James Brown, and left fielder Jelly Gardner remained from the American Giant lineup that had garnered the first three NNL pennants and had remained unchanged for five consecutive seasons, from 1920 to 1924.

Foster's fire-sale/charity handouts were not done haphazardly; he knew he wasn't likely to win any more pennants with an aging lineup that had won with speed. Foster had a different vision for the new team he was building. He hadn't won a pennant since Dave Brown headed east after the 1922 season, so he began to focus on acquiring some top-flight young arms during the 1925 season. He picked up a sinker ball pitcher named Webster McDonald when the latter's hometown Wilmington Potomacs bit the dust at midseason; and he landed a crafty, diminutive righty from Eutaw, Alabama, by the name of Willie Powell. Foster was impressed with both pitchers' composure and wide repertoire of pitches as they helped the American Giants to an improved second-half showing. (Note that neither of these two prospects showed up on Mrs. Taylor's doorstep, though Foster did send a young quality arm to the ABCs in the form of Buck Miller.) Following the 1925 campaign, Foster had to be delighted when he signed none other than Rube Currie, Ed Bolden's star pitcher during Hilldale's recent World Series triumph. With McDonald, Powell, Currie, and incumbent spitballer George Harney, who was just coming into his own in 1926, Foster had the makings of a nifty little staff, though it was still missing two crucial elements: a formidable southpaw and a superstar.

Foster had to look no further than his own family to find someone who combined all the above-mentioned qualities in one neat twenty-two-year-old package. Bill "Willie" Foster had masterful control over a large repertoire of pitches, with an especially wicked change-up. Willie and Rube were technically half-brothers, but the twenty-five-year age difference between them gave their relationship more an uncle/nephew feel. When Willie first tried out for the American Giants in 1923, brother Rube sent him away, telling the nineteen-year-old, "That's no life for you, don't play baseball." Rube Foster was adamant about his own children receiving a college education, and felt the same way about his half-brother. But Willie was not about to stop playing

★ ★ ★ ★

Oliver Marcelle was the most popular as well as one of the most valuable players on the mighty Bacharach Giants of the mid-1920s. He is considered one of the very best third basemen in blackball history.

ball. Resentful of Rube's treatment of him, he signed on with the Memphis Red Sox, one of the NNL's two southern teams, though he also continued attending college in the off-season. A rift existed between the two distant brothers, but it was not that significant. In fact, the young southpaw spent some time with Rube's American Giants during both the 1924 and 1925 seasons, where his "uncle" tutored him in the nuances of pitching. Willie spent the balance of the 1925 season with the Birmingham Black Barons, the NNL's other southern team. Willie missed the first half of the 1926 season in order to remain in Tennessee and complete his college education. He finally joined the American Giants full-time in the second half. Of course, Rube was no longer the manager. Willie had completed his apprenticeship in the South, and by 1926 he was fully mature and ready to take center stage.

Heading into the 1926 NNL season, the Monarchs and the St. Louis Stars were the co-favorites, expected to capture the two postseason berths and settle the score in a rematch of the last season's playoff. Both teams figured to be stronger than they had been during the previous season. The Stars added Mule Suttles, a classic righthanded, pull-hitting, cleanup slugger who was tailor-made for St. Louis' home park, with its 250-foot (76.2m) left field fence. John Henry Russell, a brilliant fielder and solid hitter, filled the void at second base, giving the Stars a well-rounded, maturing starting eight of Bell, Redus, Wells, Suttles, Bobo, Creacy, Murray, and Russell. Kansas City, meanwhile, more than filled the hole created by "Heavy" Johnson's departure by acquiring Cristobal Torriente to play center field. Thus, Joe Rogan could move to first base when he wasn't on the mound. The Monarchs' lineup looked as formidable as ever, with Johnston, Allen, Moore, Torriente, Rogan, McNair, Joseph, and Duncan.

J.L. Wilkinson's club did, however, suffer a significant, and ultimately tragic, loss in the off-season, as manager-pitcher (and ace-in-the-hole) Jose Mendez fell victim to the tuberculosis epidemic that struck Havana in the wake of the great hurricane that devastated the Cuban capital during the winter. Mendez, of course, had been a fixture of the nonsegregated winter league in his native Cuba, where he was a national hero.

Nonetheless, the Monarchs rolled to the first-half pennant in the NNL, posting an impressive 35–12 (.745) mark. St. Louis remained respectable with a 29–18 (.617) record, but this was only good enough for fourth place, and was only one half-game better than the revitalized ABCs (28–18, .609). The revamped American Giants placed third, 28–16 (.636), behind slugger Turkey Stearns and the Detroit Stars, who made their best showing to date, 33–17 (.660). The top five teams' inflated records were at the expense of the Cuban Stars, the Dayton Marcos, and the Cleveland Elites, who were a combined 18–101.

Not surprisingly, the Dayton and Cleveland teams folded before the second season began, which in turn brought Indianapolis and Detroit back to earth, finishing fourth and fifth, respectively, with 15–25 (.375) and 13–23 (.361) records. The Cubans brought up the rear at 10–20 (.333). St. Louis improved to a .645 (20–11) clip, but Bell, Wells, and company had to be disappointed with their third place given their success in 1925. The Monarchs had little to prove in the second half, and figured to fall off when Cristobal Torriente was suspended for a handful of games for nightlife excesses; even more serious, brilliant shortstop Dobie Moore's career came to a sudden end when he was shot in the leg following a lover's quarrel. Still, the Monarchs had a new star on the mound in nineteen-year-old Chet Brewer, who posted a 12–1 record, and the KC juggernaut continued to roll along, posting 21 wins and only 7 losses. Nonetheless, the second-half flag was claimed by the reconfigured American Giants, led by a stellar Bill Foster, who hadn't joined the team until partway

* * * *

Superstar shortstop Dick Lundy poses in his civvies with a friend. He was the best player on the great Bacharach Giants teams of the mid-1920s.

through the first half, but proved unbeatable by late summer as he posted an astounding 26 straight wins (including some non-NNL contests). In spite of Foster—and it's a truism of postseason baseball that one hot pitcher can make all the difference in a series—the dynastic Monarchs were prohibitive favorites in the best of nine NNL playoffs.

Through five games, Kansas City held a commanding 4–1 advantage. The star of the early part of the series was Joe Rogan, who had assumed the team's managerial duties in Jose Mendez's absence. He earned the win in each of the first two games as a relief pitcher, and accounted for the game-winning RBI in game two. Brewer pitched a shutout in game three, before former Monarch Rube Currie earned

the American Giants their first victory of the series in game four. Rogan captured his third decision of the series, in an 11–5 romp over Chicago ace Bill Foster in game five. However, Chicago fought back as Currie outdueled Brewer in game six. Then the Monarchs self-destructed in the bottom of the ninth inning of game seven, as Chicago pushed across two runs—via a couple of walks, an infield single, a costly error by the usually sure-handed first baseman Lem Hawkins, and a passed ball—to claim a 4–3 victory.

With the Monarchs' series lead down to 4–3, the season came down to one day. If KC prevailed in game eight of the series, the Monarchs captured the pennant, but if Chicago won, the second game of the day would follow immediately after. The teams sent their respective aces, Bullet Joe Rogan and Bill Foster, to the mound for game eight. The pair pitched superlatively, as the game remained scoreless through eight innings. Foster closed out the Monarchs in the ninth; then his teammates scratched out a run in the bottom of the inning to take the game, 1–0, and pull even in the series.

Between games, manager Malarcher held a team meeting and asked his players who they wanted to take the mound, and the Giants anointed the red-hot Foster. Foster told Willie Powell, the scheduled starter, "I'll go in and go as hard as I can as long as I can." Powell retorted, "Go ahead, I know you can take them. You take them and I'll stay ready."

When Monarch manager Rogan saw Foster warming up before the game he walked up to Foster and asked, "You going to pitch?" The young southpaw answered, "Yeah, I'm going to pitch." Rogan fired back, "Well, I'm coming back." And according to some accounts, he literally walked up to Chet Brewer, who had been warming up, and took the ball from his hands. Even if this detail is apocryphal, it was clear that Rogan's innate competitiveness got the better of him as he promptly went out and was rocked for a flurry of runs in the first frame. He then settled down and shut out Chicago the rest of the way, but irreparable damage had been done, as nobody was scoring off Bill Foster on that day. The American Giants won the nightcap 5–0, to take the series and the NNL pennant in dramatic fashion, 5 games to 4. Bill Foster had done his half-brother Rube Foster proud, echoing the legend's mythic performances in Philadelphia a full two decades earlier by hurling an improbable 18 consecutive shutout innings for a pennant-winning double-header sweep that swung the balance of power in western blackball away from the Monarchs and back to the Foster family and the Chicago American Giants.

The Monarchs were stunned; having needed only one more victory to take their third straight pennant, they dropped four in a row. Apparently the American Giants were ill-prepared for their shocking victory, as they had made no preparations to travel east for the Colored World Series. Dave Malarcher's crew had to run home, pack their bags, and rendezvous at the train station before they could really celebrate their NNL pennant.

Chicago's foe from the Eastern Colored League was the Atlantic City (Bacharach) Giants, who like the American Giants had leapfrogged over the favored teams of their league—in this case, Hilldale, Harrisburg, and Baltimore. In fact, 1926 was the first time in the ECL's four-year history that Hilldale failed to win the league title. The Daisies dropped off to a respectable but uncharacteristic 34–24 record, and third place. Even more disappointing than the Daisies were the Baltimore Black Sox, who plummeted to an 18–29 mark and a sixth-place finish. For the second straight season, runners-up honors in the ECL went to the Harrisburg Giants (25–17), led by the ever-sensational Oscar Charleston. Posting impressive turnaround seasons were the Eastern Cuban Giants, who finished fourth with a 28–21 mark, and the fifth-place Lincoln (New York) Giants (19–22), led by the ageless John Henry Lloyd, who had come over from the Bacharachs

as a player-manager and hit .349. The Brooklyn Dodgers stumbled to 7–20, while the Newark Stars lost 10 of 11 league games before disbanding in midseason. Thus, the Atlantic City Giants, known by most blackball fans simply as the Bacharachs, won the pennant with a relatively modest 34–20 mark.

Two things about the Bacharachs would have made Rube Foster proud. First, the team's ascendancy brought a whole new cast of players into the blackball limelight, breaking the Monarch-Hilldale Giant-American Giant monopoly on blackball prominence, proving that the game's talent base had expanded to support more than two or three elite teams. Second, the Bacharachs played an exceptionally heady, intelligent brand of baseball, epitomized by the team's superstar, shortstop/manager Dick Lundy. A brilliant all-around player, Lundy hit .329, an impressive clip for an ECL campaign in which offensive production was generally down, and one that, in the words of historian John Holway, would "surely have won MVP if there had been a vote that year."

The less conventional part of the Bacharachs' brain trust was first baseman Napoleon "Chance" Cummings, who carefully studied opposing batters and frequently strolled to the mound to advise the Bacharach pitchers. Cummings was, in essence, a second catcher, as well as a second manager. Lundy and Cummings occasionally clashed, but Cummings more often than not dispensed excellent advice and was superb in the field and posted a respectable .289, batting second in the order.

The Bacharachs were practically as heady at the other six day-to-day positions, and rock-solid when the ball was in play. The team's two other top stars were third baseman Oliver Marcelle, who batted .289 in the third position, and fleet-footed center fielder Chaney White, who hit .295 in the clean-up position, batting in front of Lundy. One of blackball's best (and best-loved) players in the mid-twenties, Marcelle was stellar in the field, had great

range and a quick and accurate arm, and was a prime offensive asset at bat and on the bases. In a clear demonstration of how popular and respected Marcelle was, a 1952 *Pittsburgh Courier* poll found Marcelle, not future Hall of Famers Judy Johnson or Ray Dandridge, the best third baseman in Negro League history.

Chaney White was just coming into his own in 1926. In three previous seasons in the ECL, spent mostly with the Bs, he had hit leadoff and posted impressive (.385, .352, and .358, respectively) averages. He had also taken full advantage of his blazing speed on the base paths (with the exception of the 1924 season, when he was hindered by leg injuries). White's average dipped when he moved to the clean-up spot, but his increased power numbers and RBIs more than compensated.

Replacing White in the leadoff spot was the speedy, versatile left fielder Ambrose Reid, who had filled in at third base in 1924 when Marcelle was on "sabbatical" with the Lincolns. Filling out the Bacharachs air-tight infield was Cuban Romando Garcia, who inherited second base when Pop Lloyd moved on to the Lincoln Giants. Garcia was excellent in the field, which compensated for his modest batting average. Hitting seventh, ahead of Garcia, was veteran backstop William "Fox" Jones, so-called because of his diminutive size, who was a decent hitter, had a strong arm (if not a rifle), and handled pitchers well. Right fielder Luther Farrell rounded out the Bs' starting lineup. An important part of the team's make-up, Farrell was a power hitter who could clear the bases, which were often full. Farrell was in his prime in 1926 and posted an impressive .320 mark. A burly man who did not have great range in the outfield, Farrell more than made up for this deficiency with his shotgun arm (which was also put to terrific use on the mound, as he was used as a spot starter and, occasionally, in relief). Before 1926, Farrell's duties had been split between right field and the mound, but by their pennant-winning season the

Bs had enough pitching talent that Farrell's skills as a hurler could be held in reserve, though manager Lundy found it hard to resist using the fire- and spitball-throwing Farrell in the postseason.

The Bacharachs' ace was a young, sidewinding right hander by the name of Arthur Chauncey "Rats" Henderson, who had a blazing fastball and, even more impressive, one of the great curve balls of all time. His distinctive sidearmed release made it virtually impossible for opposing batters to distinguish between his fastball and his curve, which broke "off the table" at seemingly the last moment. Henderson had been with the Bs as early as 1923, but had split to Chappie Johnson's non-league-affiliated touring team in 1924. This prompted the Bacharachs to offer Henderson $375 per month to pitch for them in 1925; Rats took the money and returned to Atlantic City as one of the highest-paid players in eastern blackball. He was well worth it: Rats was brilliant in 1926, posting a 15–5 record.

The team's second starter in 1926 was southpaw Red Grier, a finesse pitcher who kept batters off balance and was brilliant throughout the campaign, going 12–2. Also of note on the staff was Hubert Lockhart, a well-educated young man who would go on to teach at the collegiate level, though in 1926 he was just an up-and-coming hurler who split his six decisions during the regular season.

With the blackball universe accustomed to the dominance of the Monarchs and Hilldale, few knew what to expect from an American Giants-Bacharachs Colored World Series, especially since the Monarchs had seemed a lock to take the NNL pennant only a couple of days earlier. But the two upstart teams proved worthy adversaries, producing an exciting, closely contested series. Just how evenly matched the two league champions were was made clear in the first contest: a 3-all draw, in which the teams' two aces, Chicago's Bill Foster and Atlantic City's Rats Henderson, squared off. Foster seemed to get the better of the pitching duel, as Henderson was

chased with the Bs trailing 3–2, but Luther Farrell came in from right field, providing brilliant relief, and Chaney White pulled the Bs even with a clutch RBI just before nightfall. The next day Chicago exploded for seven runs in the first two innings, chasing Bacharach starter Red Grier. But Willie Powell was shaky as well, and Atlantic City came roaring back. Manager Malarcher summoned Rube Currie from the bullpen. The crafty veteran stifled the rally, and contained the Bs the rest of the way for a dramatic 7–6 win.

The third game, played in Baltimore, proved the most memorable of the series. Manager Lundy decided to bring back Grier for a second consecutive start, since he had barely worked up a sweat in game two—a quirky selection. Things did not start auspiciously for Grier, who walked the first man he faced, speedy "Jelly" Gardner, who then proceeded to steal second. But Grier bore down and struck out left fielder Sandy Thomson. He induced the next batter to ground out, but Gardner advanced to third. Chicago's clean-up hitter that day, catcher Jimmy Hines, then reached out and poked a Texas Leaguer towards left center that seemed destined to drop, but Dick Lundy made a miraculous over-the-shoulder catch. Inspired, Lundy's troops rallied for 4 runs in their half of the first. Grier cruised through the next two innings, assisted by a brilliant stab by first baseman Chance Cummings. Chicago starter Webster McDonald settled down as well. In the fourth Grier gave two more free passes, but escaped unscathed, thanks to a brilliant throw-out by catcher Fox Jones. In the fifth, Grier walked Malarcher, then induced two ground-outs and looked to be out of the inning, but Cummings booted a routine grounder by the pitcher. Grier then walked Gardner to load the bases, but masterfully closed out the frame by getting Thomson to hit a weak grounder. In the top of the sixth, at 4–0, Grier's no-hitter was preserved by a second defensive gem, by second-bagger Garcia on a sharp grounder. The Bacharachs effectively

put the game away with 6 runs in the sixth, but the fans stayed to witness the wizardry of Grier and the infielders.

First baseman Cummings was uncharacteristically making an adventure out of some routine balls, and committed his second error of the day with two out in the seventh. Grier, however, retired the next batter on a lazy fly to right. Grier walked Gardner again, Jelly's third base-on-balls in the game, to start the eighth, but then shut down the rest of the side easily. George Sweatt began the ninth with a roller to Lundy, who tossed across the diamond for out number one. Next up, Malarcher stung the ball down the third base line, where Oliver Marcelle made a sensational play to save Grier's gem, rifling the ball to Chance for the second out. Only weak-hitting Sanford Jackson stood between Grier and blackball immortality, but the Chicago shortstop was no more up to the task than his teammates. Jackson feebly dribbled a grounder to Garcia, who flipped it to Cummings. The first-ever World Series no-hitter was complete. As the following day's *Atlantic City Press* noted, "Marcelle, Lundy, and Garcia pulled off some of the most phenomenal fielding we have seen through these long years," some of which "bordered on the impossible." Of course, the Bacharachs' magical 10–0, no-hit performance only counted for one win, knotting the series at one-all.

✷ ✷ ✷ ✷

OPPOSITE: *The St. Louis Stars of 1928 featured (back row, from left) Jim Taylor, Clarence "Spoony" Palm, Theodore Trent, Mule Suttles, James Williams, Eggie Hensley, Willie Wells, Henry Williams, Dewey Creacy; (front row, from left) bat boy, James Russell, Cool Papa Bell, Branch Russell, Richard Cannon, Roosevelt Davis, Wilson Redus, and Luther "Old Soul" McDonald.*

Game four failed to loosen that knot, as a show-down between the club's respective aces once again merely produced a draw (4-4), the key moment coming when Lundy ripped a bases-loaded triple off of Bill Foster. Game five of the now "first to five wins" series (as opposed to a "best of nine" set, which might fail to produce an adequate number of decisions) did actually generate a winner, as Dick Lundy continued his hot hitting, sparking a 6-run rally with a double, and his team took advantage of a gutsy performance by its no-hit wonder, Red Grier, to post a 7–5 triumph. Chicago pulled even with a dramatic 5–4 victory in game six, in which Bill Foster went the distance for his first World Series victory.

This could have sparked an irreversible swing in momentum, but the Bacharachs bounced right back a few days later in game seven. Lundy put Rats Henderson on the mound, and the embattled ace rewarded his faithful skipper by hurling a complete-game shutout to earn his first postseason win. The Bs then turned to Grier, looking for some more magic to lift them to a commanding 4–2 series lead, but Chicago once again pulled even with a 6–3 victory behind a strong relief effort by Webster McDonald.

The ninth game (which, of course, would have been the ultimate finale if not for the two ties) was played the next day. In this contest, the superior depth of the American Giant staff proved decisive. Having used his ace, Henderson, and his hottest pitcher, Grier, the previous two days, and feeling Hubert Lockhart wouldn't be ready until the next day, Lundy was short on options. Malarcher, meanwhile, called up a fresh arm, in the person of George Harney, and the young spitballer came through to give Chicago its first lead in the series since the second game.

In the wake of this triumph, Malarcher had to like his hand, as he had his ace, Bill Foster, rested and ready to go in game ten. And, indeed, Foster was in control throughout, shutting out the ECL champions. But Atlantic City's Lockhart had matched American Giant's ace goose egg for goose egg through eight frames. Foster thwarted the Bacharachs in the top of the ninth despite Oliver Marcelle's third hit of the game. Lockhart took the mound with no margin for error, but the American Giants were the masters at "manufacturing" runs, true to Rube Foster's tutelage. To the dismay of the gallant Lockhart, they pushed a run across without the benefit of a solid hit and captured the championship. The Bacharachs limped home, having lost three games to let the title slip through their fingers. Still, they had acquitted themselves honorably in their first postseason appearance, and, if the team could keep its nucleus whole, figured to challenge for the ECL title in 1927.

Next October, the Colored World Series was a rematch for the second time in its four-year history,

as the American Giants and the Bacharachs repeated as NNL and ECL champions, respectively. Though blackball revenue continued to decline, both of the top Negro Leagues managed to field a full complement of teams at the top of the season. Out west, Chicago squeaked by Kansas City (32–14, .696, to 36–18, .667) to claim the first-half title. St. Louis had once again played superbly (32–19) but fell short, while Detroit posted another strong first half (28–18). The Western Cubans (15–23) and Cleveland (10–37) brought up the rear. The two clubs that had been "called up" from the Negro Southern League—the Birmingham Black Barons (23–29) and the Memphis Red Sox (19–25)—proved surprisingly competitive in their role as replacements for the defunct Indianapolis and Dayton teams.

In fact, the Black Barons proved just how fertile the South was as a wellspring of black baseball talent when they captured the second-half pennant. Unfortunately, due to the general decline in the league's infrastructure (the product of both the revenue crisis and Rube Foster's inability to oversee league operations) no official standings from the second half survive. Yet, the Black Barons' success was clearly due to first-rate talent; indeed, the team had almost limitless potential. Their general manager, Rube Foster understudy Big Bill Gatewood, took full advantage of his club's promotion to big-time blackball to recruit some of the South's top young stars—most notably, a six-foot, four-inch (193cm) beanpole of a pitcher with a blazing fastball by the name of Leroy "Satchel" Paige. At the top of the season, Paige was with the Chattanooga Black Lookouts, the NSL team he had joined the previous season, but Gatewood was aware of the legend that was building around the flamethrower and wanted him on the Barons. So Gatewood enticed the Baron's owner to travel to Chattanooga with him to sign the young prodigy, and Satchel was starting for the Barons by late June.

This is not to say the young buck carried the upstart NSL exiles to the pennant. In fact,

Birmingham already had two veteran ace pitchers, junkball master Sam Streeter and sidearm flame-thrower Harry Salmon. Furthermore, the Barons had two star batsmen, Red Parnell and Nish Williams, both of whom hit .400 in the NNL that year. So Paige was merely supplementary, or worse, as he was knocked around his first month or so. But then the kid acclimated himself to blackball in the big time, and, exhibiting the uncanny pinpoint control that would become one of his trademarks, finished the regular season with a flurry of brilliant showings that were instrumental in catapulting the Barons to the second-half pennant. In the final five-game set of the season, against the Cuban Giants, with the Barons virtually needing a sweep, Paige threw a complete-game shutout to win the second game. Then, in the season-ending double-header, Satch relieved Salmon in the first game, trailing 5–4. Paige shut down the Cubans the rest of the way and Birmingham rallied to win 6–5. Then Gatewood told Paige to go back out there for the nightcap, and he proceeded to hold the Cubans to 2 runs on six hits, while his mates circled the bases for 7 runs. Satchel finished with an 8–3 mark, a better than four-to-one strikeout-to-walk ratio, and yielded just over 3 runs per nine innings. Most significantly, when the chips were down, the future legend came through to lift his team to the pennant.

Gatewood chose to bypass his hottest pitcher in the playoffs and go with his two veteran hurlers, so both Salmon and Streeter started two games. And that was the extent of the series as, in the pressure of the postseason, the American Giants thoroughly outclassed their southern foes, sweeping the Barons in four straight. Gatewood's decision not to pitch Paige was not as irrational as it may look, as the wiry youth had a long, awkward delivery that, though it effectively fooled batters, left him in terrible fielding position and very susceptible to bunts and steals, which, of course, were specialties of the American Giants. Indeed, when Paige entered the

second game with the Barons clinging to a 5–4 lead, the American Giants reached him for 6 quick runs. Satchel proved more effective in game four, but he had inherited a deficit that the Barons were unable to erase. Paige and the Barons had to be thrilled with their success in 1927, but the day still belonged to Dave Malarcher and his well-schooled defending world champions.

Meanwhile, the ECL was showing signs of decline, as only six clubs started the season. The most notable absence was the Lincoln Giants, as John Henry Lloyd's team chose to play independently in 1927. The ECL tried to stimulate fan interest and cope with anemic late-season crowds in the same manner as the NNL—that is, by adopting a split-season format. However, the Bacharachs made the notion of a playoff for the pennant laughable, by winning both halves of the season with 29–17 and 25–18 marks, respectively. Baltimore finished second in the first half, but then fell to fifth. Harrisburg garnered runners-up honors in the second half, after placing fourth. The eastern Cubans ran a respectable third, but then stumbled to fifth; while the once-mighty Hilldale Daisies were the Cubans' mirror-image, rising from fifth to third. The Brooklyn Royal Giants, meanwhile, could hardly take solace in the fact that they matched the Bacharachs in consistency by bringing up the rear in both seasons.

Unfortunately for the ECL champs, the World Series proved to be a carbon copy of the previous year, at least insofar as the American Giants won 5–3 in spite of a Bacharach pitcher hurling a no-hitter. The two repeat pennant winners' rosters included most of the same significant players as they had the year before, though the American Giants starting lineup did have a somewhat new look to it. The one conspicuous absence was offensive sparkplug Jelly Gardner, who had jumped to the Lincoln Giants at midseason following a dispute with Malarcher. Gardner's departure took some of the finesse out of the Giants' attack, though this was more than compensated for by the maturing of two young stars: outfielder Walter Davis, who hit .399 during the 1927 campaign, and shortstop Pythias Russ, a natural all-around talent who seemed destined for blackball superstardom (but would succumb to tuberculosis, dying tragically in 1929), and became a fixture in the clean-up spot, hitting behind Davis.

Meanwhile, the most significant shake-up in the Bacharachs' ranks was in the pitching staff, as Lundy had to replace Red Grier, who fell ill during the season and, mysteriously, never returned to pitching. Also, Hubert Lockhart was largely ineffective in 1927. Fortunately, in the off-season the Bs had bolstered their staff by signing Jesse "Mountain" Hubbard, a veteran finesse and junkball pitcher who had persevered through serious arm trouble during a ten-year career spent largely with the Brooklyn Royal Giants. (In his younger days, Hubbard almost landed a tryout with the Detroit Tigers since he was half-Indian and could probably have been "passed-off" as non-black. In the end the Tigers had been unwilling to take the risk.) Hubbard had a solid year, going 8–3. Still, Hubbard and the ever-solid Rats Henderson were not enough, so manager Lundy called on right fielder Luther Farrell to double as a starting pitcher, and Farrell responded with a sterling 17-win season. The Bs' postseason prospects once again seemed dim when Henderson suffered a season-ending injury just before the World Series. As the Bacharachs' lack of pitching depth had been their downfall a year earlier, they were praying for a miracle in the rematch.

In sharp contrast to the 1926 Colored World Series, the 1927 blackball fall classic started out as anything but tight. The series opened in the Midwest and the defending champion American Giants swept the first four games (making it seven straight postseason wins over the Bs). But no sooner had the clubs reached Atlantic City than the pendulum swung in dramatic fashion: Luther Farrell pitched a no-hitter to earn the Bacharachs their first victory of the series. While Farrell's dominance of the Chicago batters recalled Grier's gem from the previous autumn, much about the circumstances surrounding Farrell's performance was different: Farrell's no-hitter occurred in a one-run game, not a blow-out; the Bacharachs managed to score two runs while being no-hit in the 1927 series, due to errors; and, finally, Farrell's historic performance came in a seven-inning contest due to a late afternoon rain storm.

Still, Farrell's inspirational outing apparently rejuvenated the Bs, who, following a day off due to more rain, clawed back from a few runs down to earn a draw in the next contest. Then Farrell returned to garner a second straight victory in an 8–1 rout. Atlantic City showed they were back from oblivion with a third straight win. Unfortunately for Lundy's troops, Bill Foster stood in the way. The American Giants' southpaw ace had been absolutely spectacular all year long, posting an eye-popping 32–3 mark (21–3 in NNL contests), and no amount of Bacharach momentum could faze him—for the second straight year Foster clinched the Colored World Series with a complete-game, one-run, shutout victory.

As bleak as the financial ledgers of blackball looked, only an ardent pessimist would have guessed that Bill Foster's 1927 championship-clinching shutout would be the last Negro League World Series contest for fifteen years, but that is what happened. The clearest sign of the ill health of blackball was the paltry World Series winners' bonus earned by each American Giant in 1926 and 1927. Both years a full share hovered around $25—a pathetic sum, especially compared to the $308 reaped by each triumphant Monarch, or the $189 consolation for each Daisy, only three years earlier. And, unfortunately, the declining gate for the Colored World Series was hardly an isolated problem, as it was symptomatic of a crisis that had advanced beyond merely threatening a few weak franchises. By 1928, the structure of organized blackball itself—which Rube Foster, Ed Bolden, and so many others had struggled to create and sustain—was crumbling.

The game's leaders were also failing. Former Philadelphia postal clerk Ed Bolden, who had valiantly fought for—and won—control over blackball's eastern franchise, suffered a nervous breakdown in 1927, much as his greatest rival/mentor had the previous year. Such were the pressures of operating a Negro league (which, it shouldn't be forgotten, were among the largest black-operated enterprises in what remained a fundamentally racist society).

Why did the 1920s Negro leagues decline so soon after they were established? There is, of course, no simple answer, though the brutal economic realities of black American life in the mid- to late 1920s certainly played a major role. Black America had undergone a major transformation in the first quarter of the twentieth century, highlighted by a massive migration of southern blacks into northern cities. And the increased availability of industrial jobs during World War I both heightened the motivation of blacks to move north and effectively contributed to a short-term (relative) prosperity in the burgeoning northern black communities. This situation created the fertile ground in which men like Rube Foster and Ed Bolden sowed the seeds and nurtured the growth of the Negro leagues. It was assumed, with good reason, that these black communities would only continue to grow in size in the near future—and no one doubted at the time that baseball would remain hugely popular among all varieties of American males. But, alas, it turned out that the once-fertile ground would soon be unable to sustain what Foster and Bolden had planted, for the simple reason that the general prosperity of northern blacks would decline precipitously in the mid-1920s.

Given the overall boom occurring in 1920s white America, this seems hard to reconcile. But socioeconomic forces being what they are, the overall prosperity of white America did not necessarily generate a parallel effect within black America, and indeed often caused the inverse. With the onset of such a recession, the pool of blackball's potential paying customers—which was not large to begin with—shrank considerably, and blackball's chances of generating enough revenue to keep sixteen "major league" teams afloat were increasingly slim. Try as they might, not even crafty Ed Bolden or visionary Rube Foster could effectively counter these macroeconomic trends.

Bolden, for what it's worth, saw the writing on the wall as early as the end of the 1925 season, which he declared "one of the most disastrous years for black teams in the last ten" at a time when many of the men associated with the Negro leagues were patting themselves on the back for completing another full season with a minimum of defections. By next spring, Bolden had to scramble to arrange emergency financing just to keep his championship Hilldale club on the field. And following their 1925 triumph, the Daisies unexpectedly degenerated, even though Holden had kept the team's core intact. The only notable departures were veteran pitcher Rube Currie, who was past his prime, and legendary slugger Louis Santop, who had been reduced to pinch-hitting duties by 1925; in fact, the only significant absence was center fielder George Johnson. Manager Frank Warfield's squad still included the likes of Biz Mackey, Judy Johnson, Otto Briggs, Clint Thomas, Tank Carr, Jake Stephens, Skip Lee, and ace Nip Winters—all of whom were still in their prime.

So why did Hilldale free fall in the standings in 1926 and 1927? No doubt part of the problem was a lack of pitching depth. In addition, the team had a history of infighting and disruption on and off the field that probably compounded with incipient financial insolubility sufficiently to distract the players. At any rate, Hilldale's failures on the diamond also meant empty bleachers, and thus barren coffers versus escalating debt. It was becoming increasingly evident that the ECL, Bolden's life work, was doomed to collapse. In September 1927, suffering

from nervous exhaustion, Bolden committed himself to a local hospital.

Unlike Foster, Bolden soon recovered his sense of psychic balance and was back trying to reclaim his preeminence in eastern blackball. Having been stripped of his position as president of the ECL while he was in the hospital, he managed, through strength of will alone, to wrestle this title away from Isaac Nutter (the new African-American owner of the Bacharach Giants, which Tom Jackson had put up for sale) in time for the start of the 1928 campaign. No sooner had Bolden resumed control of his duties than he announced he was pulling his Hilldale club out of the league. The remaining ECL owners scrambled, trying to make do by bringing the one-year-old Philadelphia Tigers into the fold. The 1928 ECL season sputtered along for a few weeks before it was officially terminated. The member clubs fended for themselves that summer.

The situation out west was not quite as chaotic. The NNL's structure had proven resilient through eight seasons, surviving even in the absence of its chief architect, Rube Foster (whose name remained on the stationery, though he was a figurehead, in the manner of Lear, or less poetically mad King George). Still, major fissures were becoming apparent as the league began the season with only five teams for the first time in its history. The most conspicuous absentee was a charter club, the Kansas City Monarchs, one of the top two franchises in the region. Owner J.L. Wilkinson had simply grown too frustrated with losing money when he felt certain he could turn a profit if the Monarchs were free to barnstorm. Gone as well from the ranks of the NNL were the Memphis Red Sox and the lowly Cleveland Hornets, leaving only the dynastic American Giants, the St. Louis Stars, the Detroit Stars, the West Cuban Giants, and the previous season's Cinderella team, the Birmingham Black Barons. In spite of the thinned ranks, both halves of the season were completed, though no official standings are extant. The St.

Louis Stars, led by all-time greats Willie Wells and James "Cool Papa" Bell, captured the first-half flag, and the defending back-to-back blackball champion American Giants took the second.

Manager Candy Jim Taylor's St. Louis Stars had perhaps the most stable cast of characters in the history of the Negro leagues, over the span of seven years from their emergence as serious contenders in 1925 until the franchise's demise in 1931. As of 1928, the Stars' everyday starting lineup had remained unchanged since opening day 1926, with the exception of catcher Mitchell Murray, who moved on after the 1927 campaign. This group, which was just reaching its stride in 1928, consisted of first baseman/slugger Mule Suttles, John Henry Russell at second, superstar shortstop Willie Wells, Dewey Creacy at third, solid all-around players Branch Russell and Frog Redus in right and left, respectively, and the sublime speedster Cool Papa Bell in center. Furthermore, St. Louis' two top starting pitchers, Roosevelt Davis and Eggie Hensley, had come of age with the gang and were aboard for the long haul. These Stars would stake their claim to the title of best in the West as one decade closed and the next one dawned.

Of course, until the Stars dethroned the reigning world champions they were little more than pretenders to the throne. In the playoffs, the Stars jumped out to an auspicious start by taking game one; Mule Suttles, who had had a disappointingly mediocre (by his standards) regular season (12 homers, .256), came through with a double and a triple against Bill Foster. The American Giants fought back, and the series remained tight throughout: after six games, the teams were tied. And

* * * *

OPPOSITE: *The mighty bat of Mule Suttles was the lynchpin in the St. Louis Stars' NNL-pennant winning drive in 1928. Over twenty-two years, Suttles batted an amazing .329.*

though the Stars had proven they could win against Foster, Dave Malarcher and the Giants had to feel pretty good that their ace, who had provided dramatic series-winning victories in the previous two years' pennant and series drives, was on the mound in game seven. But Suttles once again led the way with two clutch hits against the brilliant southpaw, and the St. Louis Stars triumphed to win the 1928 NNL title. The victory marked the first time in the nine-year history of the league that a team other than the American Giants or the Monarchs won the NNL pennant.

By the following spring the league had once again replenished its numbers. The Memphis Red Sox and Kansas City Monarchs were back, and all seven teams completed the entire season. The return of the Monarchs proved more than a little significant as Kansas City thoroughly dominated the NNL field, becoming the first team since the institution of the split-season format to win both halves. The Monarchs took the first half with a 28–11 clip, just better than the defending champion Stars' 28–14. In the second half, the Monarchs made history, becoming the first club to win an NNL race with a winning percentage (.850, 34–6) more than a hundred points higher than the second-place team—and this in spite of the fact that the Chicago American Giants posted the second highest winning percentage (.743, 26–9) in its storied league history. The Stars fell to third (28–16) in the second half. No postseason series was played and no one argued when the Monarchs were declared league champions without one, their first NNL crown in four years.

The Monarchs had clearly reasserted their preeminence in midwestern blackball. KC's overall winning percentage (.784, 62–17) qualified as the highest to date in Negro league history. J.L. Wilkinson's team played the same type of ball they had won with in the mid-1920s, which shouldn't be surprising since many of the faces remained the same. Five of the starters were holdovers from the mid-1920s dynasty: catcher Frank Duncan; the two Newts, Allen and Joseph, at second and third, respectively; former utilityman Dink Mothell, who had settled in at first; and the ever-brilliant slugger/outfielder/pitching ace/manager Joe Rogan. The most significant loss was shortstop Dobie Moore, one of blackball's top all-around stars and a true "impact" player (he was hitting .381 at the time), whose career was ended by a debilitating gunshot wound suffered in late May 1926. If not for Moore's absence, the balance of power in the NNL may never have swung back to Chicago in 1926 and 1927.

The Monarchs' new superstar in 1929 was their "other" mound ace,

Chet Brewer (having more than one genuine pitching phenom was a recurring motif throughout the Monarchs' long and storied history). The right-hander not only racked up a 17–3 record, but also hurled 31 consecutive scoreless innings in league play. Brewer featured a vast array of pitches and deliveries, plus considerable velocity and exceptional location; and he was always thinking on the mound, aware of a batter's strengths and weaknesses, and of just how to set him up given the sequence of pitches and the outcome of previous at-bats. And he was only twenty-two years old. Unfortunately for this

great Monarch team, their sweep of the NNL season—and the fact that there was no Colored World Series in 1929—meant they didn't get to play in the postseason, no doubt depriving them of a golden opportunity to add to their legend.

The lack of a Colored World Series in 1929 was not due to the absence of a major blackball league, as was the case in 1928. Shortly after the rapid demise of the Hilldale-less ECL in 1928, negotiations began between Ed Bolden and the other owners of ex-ECL franchises. The eventual result was a "new" league called the American Negro League

* * * *

When the teams of the ECL started drastically altering their player rosters in the late 1920s, Ed Bolden made sure to retain the services of mighty catcher Biz Mackey, seen here.

(thus bestowing on blackball its own "American" league to complement its "National" league and complete its parallel to the major league universe). The new league consisted of five former ECL franchises—Hilldale, the Bacharachs, the Cubans (East), the Baltimore Black Sox, and the Lincoln Giants (who had left the ECL following 1926 and prospered as an independent team)—and the Homestead Grays, a club based in western Pennsylvania that had prospered as an independent team since 1912 and was widely recognized as being on par with the top-tier Negro league teams (if not, perhaps, the pennant winners).

Two of the staple franchises from the ECL were notably missing from the ANL: the Harrisburg Giants, who had disbanded after the 1927 season; and, more significantly, Nat Strong's Brooklyn Royal Giants. Strong had never made his franchise's performance in the ECL much of a priority, often canceling league games with little notice in favor of other more lucrative engagements, in the process rekindling the hatred of the other ECL owners (save Bolden). Still, Strong was secure in the lucrative position of the ECL's de facto booking agent, thanks to his alliance with Bolden. After Strong effectively sacked the ECL by deviously pulling his marquee franchise out of the league before opening day 1928, the other owners informed Bolden in no uncertain terms that they would not join a league that included the Royal Giants. And though Strong wouldn't be entirely out of the picture, since he still handled the scheduling for Alex Pompez's Cuban Stars, his diminished role helped lure the previously independent Lincolns and Grays into the ANL fold.

The reshuffling of the league was accompanied by considerable player movement among teams. In the process, Bolden finally broke up the nucleus of his once-championship club (though he wisely held onto Biz Mackey) and maneuvered to bring two future Hall of Famers, Oscar Charleston and Martin Dihigo, to Philadelphia. The group didn't click until the second half (finishing a sorry 15–20 in the first), and even then their 24–15 mark only earned them second place. Faring much worse was the Atlantic City franchise, which barely resembled the club that had swept to consecutive ECL titles in 1926 and 1927. Most notably absent were the stars

who had shared the left side of the infield and had been the foundation of those championship teams, Dick Lundy and Oliver Marcelle. What made Lundy and Marcelle's departure even more conspicuous was that while their old team plummeted to the lower rungs of the second division (next-to-last at 11–20, then last at 8–25) their new team, the Baltimore Black Sox, won both half seasons with 24–11 and 25–10 marks.

The Black Sox didn't just have Lundy and Marcelle, though. Indeed, the other half of what was dubbed the "million-dollar-infield"—former Hilldale manager Frank Warfield at second base and torrid slugger and longtime Black Sox player Jud Wilson at first—certainly contributed more than their fair share. Also of note were right fielder Rap Dixon, the proverbial complete ballplayer and a certified star, and Pete Washington, who put his blazing speed to spectacular use in center. But the Black Sox' lethal everyday lineup was only half the story, because Baltimore had also collected a stable of first-rate arms that included a fine supporting cast of Red Ryan, Scrip Lee, Jesse Hubbard, and number-two man Pud Flournoy, a stocky southpaw. And late in the season, the team's general manager enticed a certain Leroy Paige to hop over from Birmingham for a stint. But the man on the mound in Baltimore was, unequivocally, crowd favorite Laymon Yokely, a flamethrowing right-hander who came of age in 1929, much as Chet Brewer had in KC, and (matching Brewer) rang up 17 wins.

The 1929 Black Sox undoubtedly belong on the short list of all-time Negro league teams. Thus it is especially unfortunate that they didn't get to face the NNL-champion Monarchs in a postseason showdown. Then again, the lack of a Colored World Series would prove to be the least of the Black Sox', or the rest of eastern blackball's, worries. The stock market crash of October 1929 decimated the nation's (and especially that region's) financial institutions, which meant that organizations like Ed Bolden's,

which would have closed shop long before if it hadn't been able to borrow money at the top of each season, were doomed. Knowing he wouldn't be able to raise the money to rent the stadium he had built, Bolden sold the Daisies before the 1930 season. Hilldale did field a team in 1930, as did most of the region's top franchises, but owners couldn't always make payroll, and players began to roam, hoping to find a steady income. Perhaps due to their experience as independents, Homestead and Lincoln stayed afloat throughout 1930. Indeed, as a consequence of the two teams' relative stability and the excess of "free agents," both clubs became veritable all-star teams (though some appearances were mere cameos). These two dynamos did meet in the early autumn to determine the (unofficial) championship of eastern blackball.

Of the competing squads, Homestead had a greater resemblance to the team it had been the previous season, while Lincoln acquired the lion's share of recently footloose ringers. Thus, it was a fine victory for longtime Grays like feisty outfielder Vic Harris and the ancient but still wondrously effective flamethrower Smokey Joe Williams. It must have been particularly gratifying for their top prospect, a young power-hitting catcher named Josh Gibson. Homestead's victory, in retrospect, reads symbolically, the triumph signifying a shift in the balance of power in eastern blackball to forces outside of those that had once dominated the ECL. Indeed, the Grays, thanks in large part to their rookie catcher, were destined to rule eastern blackball for much of the next decade and a half. The Lincolns, in contrast, wouldn't even field a team in 1931.

Meanwhile, back in the Midwest, the NNL moved into its second decade of operation. In spite of a dearth of funds, the NNL was able to stay afloat, in contrast to its eastern counterpart, in large part because of the strict guidelines that Rube Foster had laid down regarding ownership and booking arrangements—guidelines that effectively insured that member clubs, and the overall league operation, would not become beholden to outside financiers. And remarkably, the NNL actually added a franchise in 1930, the Nashville Elite Giants.

Heading into 1930, prospects looked good for the defending champion Monarchs. The previous season Kansas City had found the proverbial missing piece of the puzzle in the person of pitching prodigy Chet Brewer. Nonetheless, in 1930 the Monarchs learned the hard way that Joe Rogan was still "the man," as their all-purpose superstar missed the majority of the season due to illness. The club had a solid first half, finishing with a 31–14 (.689) record that would have thrilled most teams, but was unacceptable by Monarch standards since St. Louis, at 41–15 (.732), topped it. The Monarchs then stumbled to a fourth-place finish in the second half, while Detroit's Stars nipped their St. Louis namesakes by one game (24–7 to 22–7) to force a playoff for the league title. Detroit had managed only a .500 record in the first half of the season; its dramatic improvement in the late summer was, no doubt, related to the return of Turkey Stearns, the franchise's signature superstar. A Star since 1923, Stearns had interrupted his tenure in Detroit for a New York tour, joining the Lincoln Giants in spring 1930. Fortunately for Detroit, its prodigal slugger got homesick and returned, lifting the club to its first-ever division crown.

The battle of the Stars, St. Louis vs. Detroit, was billed as a showdown between the NNL's two top sluggers—both with barnyard monikers—Mule Suttles and Turkey Stearns. St. Louis, trying to win its second NNL flag in three years, was heavily favored, and rightly so, given the likes of Willie Wells and Cool Papa Bell. Also, St. Louis, not known for great pitching, entered the series with two hot pitchers: Ted Trent, a curveball artist who had anchored the staff since he came of age in 1928 with a 21–2 season; and recently acquired

Ted "Double Duty" Radcliffe, who had originally come over from Detroit in the off-season to be St. Louis' regular catcher. When injuries thinned the Stars' staff late in the year, Radcliffe decided he could do a better job than some of the men he was catching, and proceeded to prove it by 10–2. Radcliffe happened to be the nephew-in-law of former teammate Turkey Stearns.

The series defied expectations, as Detroit not only provided St. Louis with a good tussle, but seemed in control after defeating Trent in game five to take a 3–2 lead, with games six and, if necessary, seven to be played in Detroit. Stearns and Suttles, meanwhile, didn't disappoint, as both sluggers were crushing the ball. Stearns hit a mammoth home run in his first at-bat in game six, and then knocked in 2 runs late in the game to knot the score at 3. But St. Louis added a run and held on to win 4–3. Through six games Turkey Stearns was absolutely awesome, driving in 11 runs while hitting .591 (13–22), with two homers, four doubles, and a triple for an unbelievable 1.136 slugging percentage. Alas, when the dust settled after game seven, it couldn't have mattered to Stearns that his final stats were slightly better than Suttles'. When it mattered most, in the one game for all the marbles, Stearns had "worn the collar," going 0 for 5, and the St. Louis Stars had escaped Detroit with their second NNL championship in three years.

A third St. Louis title came the following year, as the Stars finished atop the standings in both halves of the season. While the Stars were worthy champions, it's difficult to assess the season because it was clearly played out against a backdrop of impending doom. The league had contracted to only six clubs, which included only three real teams— St. Louis, Detroit, and Chicago—and three makeshift fill-ins—the Cleveland Cubs, the Louisville White Sox, and a reformulated Indianapolis ABCs. The Monarchs were not only not in the NNL, but J.L. Wilkinson had disbanded the team at the end

of its 1930 campaign. KC remained moribund until a restless, fully recovered Joe Rogan persuaded Wilkinson to reassemble the club in August. But wily old Wilkinson, who had his roots in barnstorming, recognized that touring the heartland—and avoiding a burdensome and unprofitable Negro league schedule—was the team's only hope of staying afloat.

The predicament of the NNL was that organizational ingenuity alone couldn't salvage an entertainment enterprise that required so much overhead but generated so little money. During the relative prosperity of the early 1920s, black Americans as a group had little disposable income; they had considerably less by the middle of the decade, and, of course, virtually none at the height of the Depression. Given that racist hiring practices were the norm throughout the United States, the job prospects for a black man in 1931 were bleak. There were legions of unemployed white Americans willing to work for wages well below those that only blacks and other oppressed minorities had accepted a few years earlier. When every day is a struggle to stay alive, attending baseball games ceases to be a priority.

Many African-Americans from the period, including ballplayers, have averred that since black America was accustomed to a state of constant economic crisis, the onset of the Great Depression was not the sudden trauma that it was for white America. Indeed, some economists assert that the percentage drop in black income was roughly equal to, or even less than, the average drop in the cost of commodities (whereas the rate of decline in white wages exceeded the deflation rate). Nonetheless, the fact remains that during the early 1930s the subset of the black population that represented blackball's primary fan base—namely, adult black males in major northern cities—experienced a marked drop in earnings from already dismal levels, leading to a substantial decline in Negro league attendance. In other words, the forces that had effectively destroyed the Negro leagues were so pervasive that they were beyond the power of any one person to counter. Everybody in blackball tacitly accepted this by 1931, and so, with little fanfare, the NNL folded after the season ended. The Detroit franchise and the reigning champion St. Louis Stars' followed suit. Chicago's club survived, but was rechristened Cole's American Giants, for owner Robert A. Cole.

As the 1931 season came to a close it seemed Wilkinson was right, that the only viable strategy for a blackball franchise was to barnstorm. As impoverished as small-town white America was, there was still some discretionary income there that might very well be spent on a once-a-summer treat, to see some of the world's greatest practitioners of America's national pastime. Wilkinson spared no cost making sure that his brilliant band of ballplayers was on the cutting edge, that the Monarch experience would be topped by no one. With a tip of his characteristic wide-brimmed hat to the myth of American ingenuity, the cult of the inventor and innovator, and the language of the traveling medicine show, Wilkinson bet the house on developing night baseball. Having been one of the first baseball franchise owners to sponsor a game under the lights in early spring 1930, Wilkinson incorporated night baseball into his traveling show, touring with his own lighting equipment, including a huge generator. With these innovations, Wilkinson and his barnstorming Monarchs became the shining stars of the vast, baseball-crazy heartland.

The collapse of the NNL, the renewed emphasis on barnstorming, Cole's American Giants—it all must have made Rube Foster roll over in his grave. The father of the Negro leagues had died on December 9, 1930. Still not an old man physically during his period of decline, Foster was less than a shadow of his former

COMING! COMING! COMING!
KANSAS CITY MONARCHS NIGHT BASEBALL

We have successfully lighted every kind of a ball park in the country, including both Major Leagues, AND CAN REPEAT IN ALL OF THEM.

The Greatest Drawing Card Outside the Major Leagues

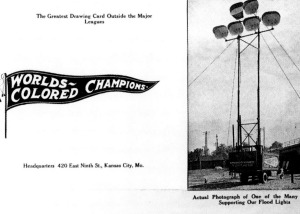

WORLDS~ COLORED CHAMPIONS·

Headquarters 420 East Ninth St., Kansas City, Mo.

Actual Photograph of One of the Many Towers Supporting Our Flood Lights

Actual Photograph of Trucks Used to Transport the Monarch Lighting Plant and Towers

✶ ✶ ✶ ✶

Like all Negro league teams, the Kansas City Monarchs had to struggle to survive the collapse of the NNL, an event directly tied to the ravages of the Great Depression. Visionary, innovative, entrepreneurial J.L. Wilkinson realized that his Monarchs would have to barnstorm to survive; in order to give the team that extra something that would distinguish its arrival in any town, Wilkinson developed a portable lighting system and blackball became the first official home of night baseball. And the Monarchs were able to stay in top form throughout those difficult years.

self. When his old compatriots made the pilgrimage out to the Illinois hospital that was his home in his final years to sit with him, he was irrational or absent, displaying only an occasional glimmer of sense.

Upon Foster's death, black Chicago wept. At that point the NNL was still breathing, so those with only superficial knowledge of the league's Sisyphian struggle didn't see Foster's efforts as entirely in vain. Of course, over the long run they were certainly not in vain. Thanks to Foster, organized blackball had expanded tremendously, though sponsorship of the game fell to members of the underworld (the only black men able to sponsor the game, heading into the Depression), which would have upset Foster greatly were he alive to witness it. Still, the players— the Satchel Paiges and Josh Gibsons, and, eventually, the Jackie Robinsons and Willie Mays—had Rube Foster to thank for nurturing blackball past its infancy into a sustainable maturity, where there were more than two or three professional teams and the black game was more than a novelty.

Foster's complete psychic and, finally, physical demise were tragic proof of the degree of the man's passion for his life's work. His body lay in state at a church in Chicago for days, like that of a fallen king. Thousands of mourners lined up outside in a gloomy drizzle, and filed past, offering their thanks. Per Foster's request, an old Negro spiritual played over loudspeakers. A dramatic wreath in the shape of a baseball, sent from the NNL offices, and a baseball diamond made of flowers sent by the American Giants Boosters Association stood out among thousands of bouquets. The captain had died, but his ship would sail on, even though he would have considered the men who took the wheel to be pirates.

4

THE GOLDEN AGE OF BLACKBALL

Perhaps no two adjacent decades in American history present such a stark contrast as the 1920s and 1930s—the boom-time of the decadent "jazz age" followed by the gloomy bust of the Great Depression. Thus, the collapse of Rube Foster's and Ed Bolden's Negro leagues around the cusp of the two decades would seem to offer a clear example of a financially vulnerable institution falling victim to the dire economic situation that engulfed the nation. However, as we've seen, even blackball's top teams were increasingly unable to turn a profit by the mid-1920s, reflecting the unique and constistently terrible economic realities of being African-American. Reflecting on the continuity of black experience in general, and the lives of black baseball players in particular during the 1920s and 1930s, one pundit noted: "The Great Depression? Well, I tell you, if you were black in America not much changed. We always had hard times."

Indeed, not much changed for most of black America or black ballplayers from roughly 1928 to 1932. Prospects were bleak in the late 1920s, poverty a virtual constant, and little changed in the early 1930s. Compared to the early 1920s, things

CRAWFORDS of 1932
3-18-32.

* * * *

OPPOSITE: *From 1937 to 1948, Hilton Smith was an essential part of the Monarchs' winning formula.*
His winning percentage over that period was .638 and included a 10–0 campaign in 1941.
ABOVE: *The mighty Pittsburgh Crawfords of 1932 featured (back row, from left) Jones, L.D. Livingston,*
Satchel Paige, Josh Gibson, R. Williams, Rev Cannady, William Perkins, Oscar Charleston; (front row, from left)
Sam Streeter, Chester Williams, Harry Williams, Harry Kincannon, Clyde Spearman, Jimmie Crutchfield,
Bobby Williams, and Ted Radcliffe.

looked especially grim if you were a black baseball star at the start of the new decade. Rube Foster was dead and with him had collapsed the Negro National League. Its counterpart, the Eastern Colored League, had suffered the same fate a couple of years earlier. Yet the 1930s would miraculously witness the renaissance of blackball, as touring teams kept the elite players razor-sharp thoughout the early years of the decade in the absence of organized top-flight leagues. This continuing abundance of exceptional blackball talent facilitated the emergence of two new "major" Negro leagues by mid-decade. From this fertile ground would emerge a spectacularly talented new generation of stars, a few of whom would eventually pass on their talents to both black and white counterparts in the major leagues following 1947, the year of Jackie Robinson's great breakthrough and the fruition of Rube Foster's dream.

How was blackball able to rebound so dramatically from its decline in the late 1920s? The revival of the 1930s was the product of a series of changes in the blackball landscape, which built upon the foundation laid by Rube Foster and his generation of pioneers. The four most conspicuous new elements in black baseball in the 1930s were: mob ownership of the top black teams; the establishment of the annual midsummer East-West All-Star Game at Comiskey Park as the premier single event in all of blackball; a renewed emphasis on barnstorming, especially throughout the region west of Chicago; and, finally, the emergence of a black superstar

* * * *

OPPOSITE: *The greatest pitcher of them all, Satchel Paige, warms up before a game. Paige was the central figure in the Negro leagues' resurgence in the 1930s.*
ABOVE: *Seen here in the K.C. dugout during a game in 1944 are (from left) Frank Forbes, heavyweight slugger Sugar Ray Robinson, Satchel Paige, and Pete Robinson.*

whose legend spread beyond black America and into mainstream white America—Satchel Paige.

It's hard to overemphasize the importance of Satchel Paige in the history of blackball; then again it's very hard to assess Paige at all. Somewhat in the manner of a court jester, who upon closer inspection happens to be king, Paige is one those magical historical figures who represents a carnivalesque inversion of the social order. A black pitcher mowing down a hometown team full of whites and receiving a standing ovation as he strolls leisurely off the mound to pocket the balance of the gate was an unusual sight in the heartland in the 1930s, yet such performances were Paige's staple.

Importantly, Paige was able to attain such celebrity throughout white and black America without being an "Uncle Tom." Paige certainly wasn't confrontational about race issues, and he had to understand that maintaining a nonthreatening persona was a precondition for his adoration among whites, but he never denied the blatant injustices of

segregated America, and his demeanor when dealing with white America was not conciliatory or subordinate. Instead, Paige had a congenial persona, was blessed with preternatural showmanship, and spoke in down-home, wisdom-laden quips that made him eminently quotable. On the mound and off, his clownishness was mixed with a warrior's hardened diffidence; he knew he was the attraction, the champion, and the conquerer.

Of course, the basis for all of the hype surrounding Leroy "Satchel" Paige was that he was, simply put, one of the greatest pitchers of all time. Baseball historian Bill James, in ranking the top major league pitchers ever, splits his analysis into two catagories: the pitcher at his peak, that is, during his best five years; and an assessment of the overall value of his career. Thus, Sandy Koufax, who was virtually unhittable for the Dodgers in the late 1950s through the mid-1960s, but then retired prematurely, places among the top five in terms of peak performance, but well down the list in terms of career value. Another southpaw, Warren Spahn, who anchored the Braves staffs for a seeming eternity from the 1940s to the 1960s, and compiled more victories than any left-hander in history, scores well in peak performance but ranks in the top-five all-time in terms of career value. Paige doesn't earn a place on Bill James' list because it's restricted to career major league pitchers, but it's safe to say that

by any standard Paige was that rarest of superstar pitchers who would rank among the top ten in both categories, and, in fact, whom one would be hard-pressed not to place at the very top of the career-value list. Indeed, as the years wore on, his longevity became a substantial part of the myth established during his peak years, roughly the first six or seven of the 1930s.

As noted in the last chapter, Paige burst upon the NNL scene in 1927 with an impressive showing with the Birmingham Black Barons, which helped lift the southerners to the second-half title. Already a legend in the South, the beanpole kid featured a blazing fastball, and as he matured throughout the end of the 1920s, increasingly pinpoint control.

❋ ❋ ❋ ❋

LEFT: *Before a game at Yankee Stadium on August 3, 1942, veteran Monarchs trainer Frank Floyd massages the pitching arm of Satchel Paige. Floyd credited himself with the rebirth of Paige's career in 1939.*

ABOVE: *Shown here after coming to the (Washington) Homestead Grays in 1942, shortstop and sometime outfielder Sam Bankhead was part of the mighty Pittsburgh Crawfords team of 1935, when he had one of his best seasons, batting an impressive .327.*

OPPOSITE: *The team that Rube built: the Chicago American Giants, circa early 1930s.*

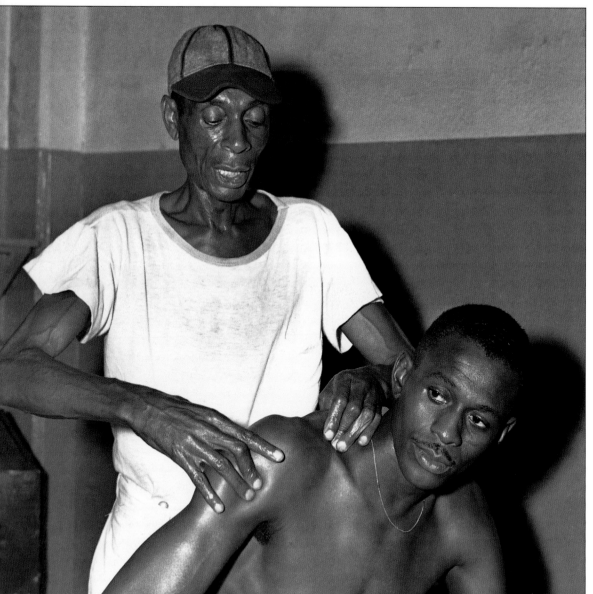

A key element of his effectiveness was his deceptive motion—it seemed impossible for a pitcher to have such a high, leisurely leg-kick and then release pitches as fast as bullets. As early as 1927, opponents were declaring that Paige was virtually unhittable if a batter didn't make serious adjustments at the plate, along the lines of shortening his swing. However, if a batter could manage to lay down a decent bunt against Satchel's heat, he had a fairly good chance of reaching first, because Paige finished his motion in rather poor fielding position. Furthermore, Paige's long motion made him extremely vulnerable to base stealers. In fact, Willie Powell, whose American Giants swept

the Black Barons in the 1927 NNL championship series, said the strategy against Satchel was "bunt and run, bunt and run, bunt and run; that's how you beat him."

During the late 1920s and early 1930s, Paige worked to correct these deficencies. He developed a set of stealthy pickoff moves, and learned to fire his blazing heat with a shorter motion when runners were on base and to use a vast array of different motions to fool both base runners and batters. He also improved his fielding. One thing Satchel didn't really develop throughout his prime years was a curveball, or any breaking pitches at all, though he would occasionally mix these in later in his career. As the

years passed, he relied more on change-ups, including his legendary hesitation pitch. Not technically a change-of-pace pitch, it dragged the batter into a house of mirrors: Paige would literally pause in mid-motion before zipping the ball by the tangled-up batter. But in his early days, Satch threw virtually nothing but blazing heat. While he would mix in an array of different movements, he primarily featured two pitches: a rising fastball that he called his "jumpball," in which he gripped the ball across the seams and released with backspin, causing it to rise; and his "bee ball," so called because batters only ever heard it zipping by them, in which Satch gripped only the smooth leather surface of the

ball and threw it straight as an arrow. Paige had uncanny control, perhaps unrivaled in the annals of the game, locating his pitches exactly where he wanted.

Following his successful debut in the NNL in the second half of 1927, Paige, a native of Mobile, Alabama, remained with the top black team from his home state for the balance of the next three seasons. However, Black Barons owner Bill Gatewood failed to re-sign some of his other stars from the 1927 club, most notably ace Sam Streeter, who skipped

off to the fast-rising Homestead Grays. The Barons suffered a drop in the standings, failing to challenge for the pennant over the next three seasons. The decline was no fault of Paige, who posted a 33–19 mark with the club, and set a Negro league mark with 184 strikeouts in 1929, including a record-setting seventeen Detroit Stars in one game. On the strength of such spectacular performances and spectacular gate appeal, Paige became the talk of the blackball world. The Barons' new owner, R.T. Jackson, who replaced Bill Gatewood before the

1929 season, took advantage of Paige's popularity by loaning him out to other teams for appearances, for which Jackson and Paige got a substantial cut of the gate, establishing a precedent for the remainder of Paige's unique career.

Paige had seemingly moved on from the Barons when he joined the mighty Baltimore Black Sox early in the 1930 season, following an impressive showing in the Cuban Winter League (Paige didn't enjoy his stay on the island and would never return to play in the popular, racially integrated league again).

Joining Baltimore represented Satchel's first extended appearance on the stage of big-time eastern blackball, and the young southerner did not receive a warm welcome from the more urbane Black Sox. Also, Paige was forced to take a back seat to Baltimore's resident flamethrowing phenom, Lamon Yokeley, who was as adored by local fans as Paige was throughout the South. After a slow start, Satch caught on, posting three impressive wins in a row. But after a June loss to the powerful Lincoln Giants, he decided he'd had enough and returned to R.T. Jackson's fold, where he finished out the season.

By the spring of 1931, the blackball world was reeling. The NNL was on its last legs as teams folded right and left, and top players floated around, hoping to land with a solvent team. The Lincoln Giants of New York, who had been stocked with blackball superstars in 1930, didn't even field a team in 1931—and the Lincolns had drawn huge crowds for the first blackball games ever played at Yankee Stadium during their unofficial eastern champi-

* * * *

OPPOSITE: *Perhaps the greatest single-season Negro league team ever, the 1935 Pittsburgh Crawfords pose for a photograph during spring training in Hot Springs, Arkansas. Seen here are (back row, from left) Olan Taylor, Judy Johnson, Leroy Matlock, unknown, Josh Gibson, trainer Hood Witter; (middle row, from left) Cool Papa Bell, Sam Bankhead, Oscar Charleston, Clarence Palm, Jimmie Crutchfield, Ernest Carter, Williams Perkins; (front row, from left) Timothy Bond, Howard, Bertram Hunter, Sam Streeter, Harry Kincannon, and Duro Davis.* **RIGHT:** *Umpires (from left) Vaughn, Bob Motley, and Frank Duncan meet with managers Buck O'Neil (far left) and Oscar Charleston (far right) before a game in 1949.*

onship series with the Homestead Grays. The Black Barons decided to cut operating expenses by retreating to the "minor" Negro Southern League. So Satchel signed on with the Nashville Elite Giants of the NNL, a former NSL team owned by Tom Wilson (a black businessman who had earned a sizable fortune by running the Nashville numbers racket). A few weeks into the season, the team relocated to Cleveland and rechristened itself the Cubs. Satchel was in the midst of another stellar year on another mediocre club when, in early August, he was enticed away from the Cubs to pitch for a team that was beginning to make waves in big-time blackball, the Pittsburgh Crawfords.

Up until the 1931 season, Paige's accomplishments in blackball included impressive victories over

top-flight teams like the St. Louis (as well as the Detroit) Stars, the Monarchs, and the American Giants. Though an ace by any standard and a bona fide sensation at the gate, until he anchored a championship club he would never achieve the legendary status of Smokey Joe Williams, Rube Foster, or Bill Foster. Satchel's journey down the path to immortality began in earnest in August 1931, when he took the ball for the upstart Pittsburgh Crawfords in a showdown for local bragging rights against the crosstown Homestead Grays, the reigning eastern blackball champions. The Crawfords had been trounced in two previous meetings that year, and fate seemed to have dealt them a cruel blow when Paige arrived late and missed the start. But the Craws, who had failed to score a single run in the

previous eighteen innings against the Grays, jumped to a 6–2 lead against a floundering Ted Radcliffe (who had joined the Grays from the St. Louis Stars before the 1931 season). The Craws stretched their lead with 2 more runs, but then Homestead stormed back with 5 runs in the fourth, cutting the lead to 8–7. All seemed lost for Pittsburgh when Satch finally arrived at the stadium and virtually walked straight to the mound to warm up.

Paige recalled the moment years later: "This was Pittsburgh's first look at me, but I didn't feel very nervous. I was young and I could throw like nobody else. When I kicked up my foot and threw that first one, the crowd screamed.... I kept kicking that foot up in the sky, twisting like a pretzel, pausing, and throwing."

Paige stifled Homestead the rest of the way, striking out six with no walks. Pittsburgh center fielder Harold Tinker said Paige was "throwing nothing but aspirin tablets." The Crawfords added 3 more runs for an 11–7 victory, and all due respect to the Pittsburgh bats, the day belonged to Satchel, whose performance was deemed "masterful and sensational" by the *Pittsburgh Courier*. Paige had most definitely arrived. The victory also marked the beginning of an internecine struggle between the two Pittsburgh clubs that would dominate eastern blackball through the mid-1930s. Gus Greenlee's Crawfords were upstarts, but Paige's performance instantly gave them legitimacy. Cum Posey's Homestead Grays had reached the pinnacle of eastern blackball only the previous season, following a steady rise during the mid- and late 1920s.

Cumberland Willis Posey Jr. had a rare pedigree for any American, let alone for a major power player in the increasingly shady subculture of blackball in the late 1920s and early 1930s. Born to one of Pittsburgh's leading black families in 1890, he attended college at Penn State and Pittsburgh before graduating with a degree in chemistry from Holy Ghost College (long since renamed Duquesne), while

excelling in basketball. He didn't hang up his sneakers following graduation, but played professionally, including with the Leondi team, considered the top pro club of the era, gaining recognition as one of the game's top players. Baseball was his second sport, and in 1911 he joined a year-old team composed of black steelworkers who played on the weekend, called the Homestead Grays. The team did well,

and in the summer of 1912, Posey took charge and actually arranged enough dates for the team to devote itself full-time to baseball. The club quickly became the top blackball franchise in the steel region, a status it maintained over the next decade.

Until challenged on his home turf, Posey hadn't sought to recruit any top blackball stars, but after fending off the Pittsburgh Keystones in 1922, he began to bring the Grays into the national blackball big time. Once the ECL was formed in 1923, the

Grays stood out conspicuously as the most profitable independent in the East. The club gained further notoriety in 1925 when Posey hired the ageless legend Smokey Joe Williams, who, it turned out, could still mow 'em down (and, amazingly, was still on the roster, at age forty-six, in 1931). Also in 1925, Posey acquired a fine slap-hitting left fielder in Vic Harris, previously with the American Giants, who became a fixture with the Grays, first as a player and then as a player-manager, into the mid-1940s. Posey turned some heads by signing the American Giants' starting shortstop, Bobby Williams, in 1926, and star pitcher Chippy Britt. But the talent upgrade really picked up in 1928 with the acquisition of top-flight star John Beckwith, former Birmingham ace Sam Streeter, and all-purpose Cuban superstar Martin Dihigo (who only stayed with the Grays for one season).

While the new and improved team failed to make an impressive showing in the fleeting ANL in 1929, despite the acquisition of star infielders Jake Stephens and George Scales, its participation in the league put it in a prime position to swallow up the talent set free by the decline, or collapse, of such clubs as Hilldale and the Bacharach Giants. By

✷ ✷ ✷ ✷

LEFT: *Shown here toward the end of his Negro league career, the last two years of which (1941 and 1942) he spent with the Chicago American Giants, outfielder Jimmie Crutchfield was a significant contributor to the awesome 1935 Pittsburgh Crawfords. Like many of his teammates, he personally had one of his best seasons that year, batting .326.*

OPPOSITE: *Crawfords owner Gus Greenlee (seated, left) had his fingers in many pies in mid-1930s Philadelphia. Here he witnesses a contract before a fight between light heavyweight champ John Henry Lewis (standing, left) and Tony Galento (standing, right).*

1930, the Homestead Grays roster were a truly elite blackball franchise, as Hall of Famers Oscar Charleston and Judy Johnson came over along with feisty outfielder Ted Page. Of course, the jewel in the crown was a muscle-bound backstop, only nineteen years old in 1930, named Josh Gibson.

Essentially a local product, Gibson had moved with his family from Georgia to Pittsburgh in 1927. The youngster had actually played a few games with the Grays in 1929, but wasn't with the team full-time until veteran starting catcher Buck Ewing broke a finger midway through the 1930 campaign. Nonetheless, Gibson was already a hero in the baseball-crazy region, renowned for his titanic home runs on the local semipro circuit. Still, he exceeded all expectations when he joined the Grays, hitting a stunning .441. He entered the realm of myth during the postseason showdown against New York's Lincoln Giants, when he hit a monstrous home run

in Yankee Stadium that some who were present claim traveled clear out of the ballpark. If true (and there are many naysayers), it would be the only time the feat was accomplished in the storied history of the most famous baseball stadium of them all. Certainly, if anyone could have accomplished such a feat it was Gibson, who was not a free-swinging slugger, but rather, like Henry Aaron, essentially a line-drive hitter who generated power with his wrists and strong grip (though he was much larger and stronger than Aaron, who was certainly no weakling). Also like Aaron, Gibson hit for a high average throughout his career. In 1931, Gibson's first full season with the Grays, he batted .367, and according to numerous sources, blasted a world-record 75 home runs.

Having won the 1930 eastern title, and with the greatest slugger blackball had ever produced coming of age on his club, Posey seemed poised to reign

supreme atop the otherwise decimated terrain of eastern blackball. In fact, his 1931 club was, if anything, even stronger than the year before: though Judy Johnson had departed, he was replaced with the even more potent bat of Jud "Boojum" Wilson; Ted "Double Duty" Radcliffe gave the club added depth; and the great Bill Foster moved to the head of the pitching staff. Across town, however, in a part of Pittsburgh that Posey had spent a lifetime avoiding, Gus Greenlee was plotting his downfall.

Officially, Greenlee was the wealthy proprietor of a couple of highly successful cabarets in Pittsburgh's Hill section. Unofficially, he was one of the top bosses, and the main front man, for Pittsburgh's black underworld. From North Carolina, Greenlee had resettled in Pittsburgh ten years earlier, after serving in World War I. He got a job driving a cab, and soon earned the nickname "Gasoline Gus," for all the bootlegged liquor he delivered around town. When the Chicago syndicate tried to invade Pittsburgh, Greenlee remained loyal to his hometown bosses. And when his actions helped the home team win out, he was duly rewarded with a nightclub and a cut of the local numbers racket.

"The numbers" were essentially a daily lottery that involved placing a bet and then selecting a three-digit number. The winning numbers were arbitrarily determined (usually the final three digits of the closing figure from the New York Stock Exchange). A large portion of every major black community in the North played the numbers on a daily basis. The key for those in charge of the game was to be able to pay out whenever the winning number happened to have a large amount on it. When a few of the men who shared the game in Pittsburgh were unable to cover their bets, Greenlee took over their turf, thus consolidating his position as the city's numbers king.

Greenlee, who was awash in cash, was a benevolent king: he helped out friends who lost their savings when banks collapsed during the Depression and bailed out the black newspaper, the *Pittsburgh Courier*, when it was about to fold. By the end of the 1920s, Greenlee had decided, looking with envy across town to the African-American community in the Pittsburgh suburb of Homestead, that he wanted to bring a big-time blackball team to his part of town.

Greenlee began to sponsor the team that played out of the Crawford recreation center, just down the street from his own Crawford Grill. A semipro team before Greenlee became involved in 1928, the Crawfords were fully professional by the top of 1930. By the following spring Greenlee began paying top dollar to attract such top-flight Negro league talent as shortstop/manager Bobby Williams, outfielder Jimmie Crutchfield, and second baseman J.H. Russell. A few months into the season, Greenlee lured two of Satchel Paige's teammates, pitcher Sam Streeter and backstop Bill Perkins, away from the Cleveland Cubs. Still, Greenlee understood that his team had to beat the Grays to gain legitimacy among Pittsburgh's black fans, and that the Crawfords were still no match for the mighty Grays. So, at midseason Greenlee began an all-out effort to entice the one man he felt could even things out. Satchel Paige arrived in Pittsburgh on August 9.

Paige didn't face the Grays again in 1931, but his acquisition did pay other dividends, as he attracted huge crowds and more press coverage than the Crawfords had yet known. Encouraged by the response, Greenlee took the unprecendented step of using his own money to build a brand new stadium in the Hill section, which opened to much civic fanfare in April 1932.

Homestead, for its part, rounded out another sterling campaign in 1931, claiming its second straight eastern championship (unofficial, but undisputed nonetheless). Unsatisfied with the club's earnings, Posey had a plan more ambitious than Greenlee Stadium—a new Negro league. It is ironic that Posey, who in retrospect had clearly benefited

from the restraint he had shown throughout the 1920s by keeping his club independent when the two leagues became the focus of blackball, would now singlehandedly spearhead the new East-West League. Like Rube Foster twelve years before, Posey even oversaw the personnel decisions of lesser clubs in Cleveland, Newark, and Washington. In an especially uncanny parallel to early days of the NNL, Posey actually built the new team in Detroit around players he sent over from the Grays. Also joining the association were more established franchises; the (midwestern) Cuban Stars, the Baltimore Black Sox, and Hilldale. Posey hoped, like Foster before him, not only to avoid the influence of illegal money in his league, but to sidestep the influence of white booking agents Nat Strong and Philadelphia's Eddie Gottlieb. Taking on way more than he could chew, Posey saw the East-West League crumble by June. And Gus Greenlee was waiting in the wings to ambush his staggering foe.

Greenlee had already demonstrated who the new boss in town was when he pilfered Josh Gibson on the eve of opening day, doubling the salary the slugger was receiving from the Grays. Overburdened by his responsibilities, Posey put up a fight, but to little avail. Black Pittsburgh marveled at the Crawfords' battery of Satchel Paige and Josh Gibson as a standing-room-plus crowd (including the mayor) inaugurated Greenlee Field on April 30, 1932. And Greenlee had only just begun his all-out raid on Posey's manpower, as he loosened his con-

* * * *

OPPOSITE: *Base-running wizard Cool Papa Bell and legendary player-manager Candy Jim Taylor confer during a game. In an era characterized by a mind-boggling amount of player swapping, Taylor managed to keep the core of one of the great western teams, the 1920s St. Louis Stars, almost exactly the same for several crucial years.*

siderable purse strings to lure frustrated players in the wake of the East-West League's demise. By July, the Crawfords roster was tantamount to the 1931 Grays, only more so. Greenlee nabbed Oscar Charleston, Jud Wilson, Jake Stephens, Ted Radcliffe, and Cool Papa Bell (who had joined the Grays at the top of the year) from Posey and snatched star right fielder Rap Dixon and the great Judy Johnson from the crumbling Hilldale Daisies.

As if that indignity were not enough, Greenlee further flaunted his ascendency over Posey when he organized a new league in the ensuing off-season. Though operating under the same name as Rube Foster's league, the new Negro National League was unabashedly made in Gus Greenlee's image: the clubs in Harlem, Philadelphia, and Newark were clearly funded by big-time racketeers, while Satchel Paige's former beneficiary, Tom Wilson, brought his Nashville club on board and functioned as Greenlee's righthand man. Also signing on were two of the older stable franchises, the Baltimore Black Sox and Chicago's Cole American Giants. Counter to expectations, the Crawfords not only did not run away with the crown, they were nipped in the first-half race by the rejuvenated American Giants, who were paced by the pitching of Bill Foster, the all-around brilliance of Willie Wells, and the bats of sluggers Turkey Stearns and Mule Suttles. Chicago's key victory came courtesy of Sug Cornelius, who pitched the game of his life to outduel Satchel Paige during a final series at Greenlee Field.

The race in the second half of the 1931 season ended in a dead heat between the Crawfords and Tom Wilson's Nashville Elite Giants, managed by the legendary Candy Jim Taylor and led by the young star outfielder Sam Bankhead. A best-of-three series ensued. Game one was a classic, as Nashville came back from the brink of defeat with 2 runs in the ninth to tie the game at 4; the score remained that way until the twelfth when Cool Papa Bell ripped a

ball between the outfielders and flew like the wind around the bases for a game-winning, inside-the-park home run. Game two followed immediately, and amidst a thickening fog the Crawfords triumphed 3–1 to take the flag for the second half of the NNL season. Then, to the dismay of American Giants owner Robert Cole, Greenlee declared the season officially over, without offering an explanation for the lack of the anticipated league championship playoff.

While the league wasn't a booming success, it had survived the difficult first-year hurdle. Also, Greenlee introduced a brilliant innovation that would become one of the high-water marks of blackball, the East-West All-Star Classic. The event was modeled after its major league equivalent, initiated that year as well, and was played in the same venue, Chicago's Comiskey Park. The inaugural black All-Star game was played on September 8, later than in future years. The late date caused considerable anticipation, which led to a sizable, if less than overwhelming, crowd of 20,000. As in the majors, the fans had voted to select the players via ballots in the black press. The resultant squads were loaded with blackball legends. Cool Papa Bell, Oscar Charleston, Biz Mackey, Josh Gibson, Jud Wilson, Judy Johnson, and Dick Lundy played for the East. The West featured top vote-getter (with 59,905) Turkey Stearns, Willie Wells, Mule Suttles (who was the star of the game, with two hits, including the only homer), and winning pitcher Willie Foster, who went the distance in a thrilling, if sloppy, 11–7 seesaw affair.

Conspicuously absent from Comiskey Park that afternoon was a certain Leroy Paige, who had been elected to the East squad but not as the top vote-getter among pitchers; as a result he chose to skip the event. Paige, by this time, was far away blackball's biggest star and drawing card, but he had been receiving increasingly bad press during the summer both for his squabbles with Gus Greenlee over money and for the growing resentment among his

peers over his preferential treatment. Paige had an arrangement with Greenlee in which he pitched every Sunday for the Crawfords and, with a few exceptions, was free to loan himself out to other teams the rest of the time. The problems arose because Greenlee would take full advantage of Paige's weekly appearances with the team, renting, and usually filling, the largest venues possible (including major league parks). But Paige merely collected his weekly salary from Greenlee, in contrast to the large cut of the gate that he received in his other appearances. As Paige noted: "Even though he advertised both Josh and me, Gus knew I was pulling the big crowds. When I was out there, there'd be a park full watching. But when Josh was there and somebody else was pitching, there'd be only about half or two-thirds as many."

Throughout the early part of the 1933 season Paige kept threatening to leave the Crawfords permanently, and at one point it looked like he had left for good when he joined fellow Mobile, Alabama, native Ted Radcliffe, who was staking new territory for an established blackball star by playing on an otherwise all-white semipro team in Wichita, Kansas. The occasion caused some of Paige's Pittsburgh teammates to fume in a manner they usually abstained from, because they knew Satchel helped pay their bills. The black media picked up the story, fueling the controversy all summer, which no doubt contributed to the lack of All-Star votes for

* * * *

OPPOSITE: *Manager Biz Mackey of the Newark Eagles and Frank Duncan of the Monarchs battle for home team advantage before the 1941 All-Star game at the Polo Grounds. Duncan won the advantage but lost the game to the East squad 8–3.*
RIGHT: *Willie Wells Sr. and Jr. share a lighthearted moment during the 1948 Memphis Red Sox campaign.*

Paige. Regardless, Satchel was in top form, dominating most games he appeared in while compiling a gaudy won-lost record (31–4, by some accounts). Ultimately, the controversy just added to his legend.

Paige remained with the Crawfords in 1934 in much the same capacity as before. The previous year's controversies aside, he was swept into the All-Star team with more votes than any other player in the East. Perhaps fearful that Satchel might skip the event, Greenlee named the redhot young ace of the Philadelphia Stars, Slim Jones, as the starter. Jones and the first man out of the pen, Crawford Harry Kincannon, kept the West scoreless through five. Meanwhile, the East's two pitchers, Amercian

Giant Ted Trent and Chet Brewer, the first Kansas City Monarch to appear in the East-West game, kept the East off the board. However, Kincannon gave up a double to Willie Wells to start the sixth. The call went out for Paige, who'd recall, "I'd been sunning myself in the bullpen." The lanky hurler grabbed his mitt and made his characteristic leisurely stroll to the mound in front of the 30,000 fans who packed Comiskey. Paige's performance inspired an article in the "white" *Chicago Times:*

He stoops to toy with the rosin bag—picks up the old apple. He mounts the bag, faces third—turns a sorrowful but burning eye toward the plate, nods a nod that Hitler would give his eye for—turns his gaze back to the runner on second—raises two bony arms high toward heaven, lets them sink slowly to his chest. Seconds pass like hours.

The batter fidgets in his box. Suddenly that long right arm shoots back and forward like a piston on a Century engine doing 90. All you can see is something like a thin line of pipe smoke. There's an explosion like a gun shot in the catcher's glove. 'Strike!' howls the dusky umpire.... Thereafter the great Satchel Paige had 'em striking out like a labor union leader.... The long, lean lanky Paige is truly the black Mathewson.

Paige fanned Alex Radcliffe, Turkey Stearns, and Mule Suttles, leaving Wells stranded at second. Willie Foster came in to pitch for the West, and after another scoreless frame, Cool Papa Bell led off the eighth with a single. He stole second, but remained there following two easy outs and a walk. Then Jud Wilson dribbled a ball past the pitcher's mound toward second, and with the infield playing back, Wilson was able to get down the line and beat the throw to first. By the time Mule Suttles got the ball he didn't have a chance of getting Bell, who hadn't

even thought of stopping at third on the play. It was the only run of the game, as Paige relinquished only one single the rest of the way.

The All-Star game was hardly the only memorable performance by Paige in 1934, as the lanky fireballer's myth grew. On July 4, in an inter-Pittsburgh showdown, Paige no-hit the rebuilding Grays. He relinquished a walk to rookie first baseman Buck Leonard in the first inning, but shut down every other man he faced, seventeen via strikeout.

Even more impressive was Satchel's midyear sabbatical to play for J.L. Wilkinson in a tournament of semipro and minor league teams in Denver that had become the biggest sporting event of the year in the Rocky Mountain region. The year 1934 marked the first that African-American teams participated and Wilkinson and his new co-owner, Tom Baird, wanted to boost their chances of winning, so they leased some of the top talent from the NNL. Turkey Stearns and Sam Bankhead played for the Monarchs (widely recognized as the top touring team, black or white, in the region), so Baird put Paige and the Crawfords' backup catcher Bill Perkins on the other Wilkinson/Baird club in the tourney, the all-bearded Black House of David. Paige donned a fake red beard and proceeded to singlehandedly blow away the competition, with victories including a 2–1 triumph over the stacked Monarchs in the finale.

✷ ✷ ✷ ✷

LEFT: *Two of baseball's greatest hurlers, Dizzy Dean (center) and Satchel Paige (right), together with Cecil Travis. Dean, who played many exhibition games against Negro leaguers, openly admired Paige's abilities and ranked the Monarch pitcher among the best in the game.* OPPOSITE: *Cleveland Buckeyes catcher Quincy Trouppe was one of the best in blackball. He was part of the 1945 squad that swept the Homestead Grays in the Colored World Series that year.*

The Crawfords did not take the NNL title, the blame for which shouldn't fall at the feet of the oft-absent Paige, who compiled a 10–1 league record in 1934. In fact, without their lanky ace, the mighty Craws managed only an 18–16 mark in league play, only good enough for back-to-back second-place finishes to the American Giants and the Philadelphia Stars, respectively. The Stars had been built up by none other than a revived Ed Bolden, who, with financial backing from Philadelphia's top booking agent, Ed Gottlieb, engaged in a few player raids and fielded a team that included not only Philly fixture Biz Mackey, but defensive stalwart Dick Seay at second, shortstop Jake Stephens, the incomparable Jud Wilson at third (who topped the league with a .355 clip), former Black Sox ace Lamon Yokeley, who had come back from an injury, and a twenty-one year old southpaw fireballer that Bolden lured away from the Baltimore Black Sox by the name of Stuart "Slim" Jones. The six-foot-six-inch lefty, who many saw as the mirror image of Paige, compiled a 32–4 mark.

Jones' most celebrated performance came against Satch, in the nightcap of a four-team double bill at Yankee Stadium that ended in a 1–1 tie—called after ten innings because of darkness, it became renowned as the greatest Negro league game of all time. Equally impressive was Jones' 2–0 victory over the American Giants in the seventh game of the best-of-seven league championship series that gave Ed Bolden and Philadelphia their first blackball title in nine years. Jones wasn't through yet. He capped off his dream season with a victory over Dizzy Dean, who had just pitched the St. Louis Cardinals to a World Series title, in a postseason exhibition. Sadly, in stark contrast to Paige's unparalleled longevity, Jones was a one-season wonder. Unable to control his drinking, he showed only occasional flashes of brilliance in 1935 and became even more erratic the following three seasons. He died in December 1938 at the age of twenty-five.

In 1935, Greenlee's Pittsburgh Crawfords finally put it all together, winning the first half of the NNL season with a stunning 26–6 mark, and then taking the league title with a postseason victory over the New York Cubans. The 1935 Crawfords are routinely referred to as the greatest team in Negro League history, the blackball analog to the 1927 New York Yankees. The canonization of the 1935 Crawfords,

however, is somewhat strange in light of the fact that Paige, the club's greatest star of the period, was hardly a part of the team at all, spending most of the season with his old pal Ted Radcliffe on a semipro team from Bismark, North Dakota. Historians who have called the 1935 Crawfords the best black team of all time invariably cite Paige as one of the team's top assets, a peculiar attribution since the scope of his Bismark tour is well documented.

While Radcliffe and a brilliant young black catcher named Quincy Trouppe were instumental in Bismark's success, and cameos by Monarch ace Chet Brewer and a fine young hurler named Hilton Smith also helped the team along, it was Paige who lifted the club to the national semipro championship, an acheivement that struck a notable blow for baseball's integration. Also notable along these lines was something Satchel had done the previous off-season, when the all-black Satchel Paige All-Stars had toured the Southwest. Meeting up with ace hurler Dizzy Dean's team six times, Satchel collected four victories, inspiring Dean's famous assesment: "Let 'em argue. The best pitcher I ever seen is ol' Satchel Paige. My fastball looks like a change of pace alongside the li'l pistol bullet Satch shoots up to the plate."

Of course, even without Satchel the 1935 Crawfords were an amazing team. Greenlee had acquired golden-gloved second baseman Dick Seay, who combined with sterling shortstop Chester Williams for one of the best double-play combinations in blackball history. Judy Johnson was a brilliant fixture at third and hit .367, while manager Oscar Charleston started at first and batted .304 (at age thirty-eight). Bill Perkins spelled Josh Gibson behind the plate on occasion, but the awesome slugger (who posted .440) rarely came out of the lineup, even if it meant starting him in the outfield. Not that Charleston had any need to sit any of his three regulars out there, as the lightning-fast Cool Papa Bell (.341) only kept getting better, Jimmy "Crutch in the Clutch" Crutchfield (.308) was a Pittsburgh institution in left, and recent acquisition Sam Bankhead (.354) had developed into an all-around superstar, especially noted for his "Howitzer" throwing arm. Lefty Leroy Matlock, a smart pitcher with an array of breaking balls and good control, assumed the position of staff ace in Paige's absence, and his 18–0 record says it all. Veteran southpaw Sam Streeter and righty Betram "Nat" Hunter helped round out the staff.

It's fair to say that with Paige, this team would probably deserve the preeminent place it has been accorded in blackball history, but at most he made only a few appearances with the club in 1935. The Craws' narrow four-games-to-three playoff victory over the New York Cubans—featuring Martin Dihigo, pitcher Luis Tiant (father of the Red Sox legend of the same name), and (oddly enough since the "Cuban" teams were almost exclusively made up of Cubans) Dick Lundy—further suggests that the 1935 Pittsburgh Crawfords may not have been the greatest of all Negro league teams.

The 1936 Crawfords, on the other hand, could probably have taken anyone, as Paige had returned to Pittsburgh and posted a 24–3 mark. The rest of Greenlee's gang returned, and the pitching staff even added an impressive rookie fireballer named Theolic Smith and veteran lefty Bill Foster. The players' offensive stats were comparable to the previous season (though pitcher Matlock fell to 19–9). Despite all this, the official NNL standings show these Crawfords struggling to a third-place finish in the first half, only one game above .500 (16–15). The Philadelphia Stars finished in front of them at 15–12, but it was Tom Wilson's Elite Giants, who had relocated to Washington, who took the first-half race at 14–10. The Elite Giants contributed six All-Stars to an East squad that trounced the West 10–2 that year in Chicago: ace spitballer Bill Byrd, third baseman Felton Snow, first baseman Jim West, speedy center fielder Bill Wright, cleanup right fielder Zollie Wright (no relation), and veteran receiver Biz Mackey (who posted two RBIs, as did Z. Wright).

The Crawfords, however, rebounded after the break, put all the pieces together and ran away from the competition with a 20–9 record. The Newark Eagles, who featured the two greatest shortstops of the past decade, Willie Wells and player/manager Dick Lundy, and the greatest third baseman of the

next, Ray Dandridge, came in a distant second at 15–11. The Elite Giants didn't get a chance to attempt an upset in a playoff, but given that the team had fallen to last place (7–14) in the second half perhaps it was for the better.

The 1936 half-pennant proved to be the last hurrah for the mighty Crawfords as the great team dispersed even faster than it had come together. The trouble started with the elections of 1936, in which a lot of entrenched local officials who had been cozy with Greenlee were unseated by a wave of pro–New Deal, anticorruption Democrats (Roosevelt, who had ended Prohibition, effectively killing the bootlegging industry, was no friend of organized syndicates of any stripe). With his numbers racket strangled, Greenlee was struggling to make ends meet by April. Desperate, he sold Josh Gibson back to—who else?—Cum Posey. The Homestead Grays had weathered the storm, and actually had joined

the NNL in 1936 (ironically, thanks in large part to the funding of another racketeer, R.T. Jackson). But before Posey could begin to stage his revenge, a lucrative offer appeared that neither Gibson nor Paige could refuse: to play in a new league on the island of Santo Domingo, on a team operated by the Dominican head of state, Rafael Leonidas Trujillo. Three other Crawford stars—Sam Bankhead, Leroy Matlock, and Cool Papa Bell—also headed to the Carribbean. In the blink of an eye, Greenlee's dynasty had disappeared.

The Dominican episode is one of the most bizarre in blackball history. The year 1937 was the first that the Carribbean countries had baseball leagues in the summer, and while the emissaries from these leagues knew they could not lure whites under contract in organized baseball, they felt it was open season on black players. Dictator Trujillo wanted Paige, and landed him for $6,000. He then got Satchel to entice the other aforementoined stars, offering each $3,000. Trujillo also collected top-flight talent from Puerto Rico (Petrucho Cepeda, Orlando's father), Cuba, and his homeland. Sparing no expense, Trujillo felt his team, Los Dragones, was particularly motivated to win because the other three clubs in the Dominican League were owned by potential political rivals. One of these teams, the Aguilas Cibaenas of Santiago, landed Chet Brewer (who tossed a no-hitter versus Los Dragones), Spoony Palm, and Betram Hunter,

* * * *

ABOVE: *Third baseman Ray Dandridge was one of several Negro leaguers who took advantage of the integrated atmosphere and higher salaries to be found South of the Border. Dandridge played in Mexico from 1939 to 1941 and again in 1943.*

OPPOSITE: *As this photograph of a 1942 game between the Chicago American Giants and New York Black Yankees shows, blackball thrived during the war years.*

among other black Americans, as well as superstar Cubans Luis Tiant and Martin Dihigo. A third team, from San Pedro de Macoris (hometown of Sammy Sosa), was predominantly Dominican (with only two lesser known Negro leaguers), which the team's backers hoped would make it the favorite among the country's fans.

The pennant race was close throughout, and it slowly dawned on Trujillo's players that failing to win the title might not be good for their health. Fortunately, Paige went 8–2, Gibson led the circuit with a blistering .453 average, and Los Dragones finished atop the standings. The best-of-seven championship playoff against the runners-up, Estrellas de Orientales (the team from San Pedro de Macoris), was a struggle. After six games the teams were knotted up. Satchel Paige took the mound for game seven. He recounted the experience a few years later when asked to describe his greatest day in baseball:

> *I bet no pitcher ever had more reason to bear down than I did that day.... All I know is that we were told we better win if we knew what was good for us. "What do you mean we better win?" I asked the manager. He says, "I mean just that. Take my advice and win."*
>
> *"Satchel, old boy," I say to myself, "if you ever pitched, it's now." But it ain't no cakewalk because that Estrellas de Oriente team is tough.... How them babies could hit that ball! I don't think I ever throwed harder but I wouldn't say I was relaxed. That was one day Paige was not free and easy.*

All I could hear from them fans was warnings about we better win. The more they yelled the harder I threw and I bet I never did have a better fastball; only I never see any better hitters than them guys. But in the seventh innings we score two runs and then I manage to shut them out the last two frames and we win, six to five.

No sooner was the game over than we was hustled back to our hotel and the next morning when we got up...there was a plane waiting for us...and we were glad to get on board. We never did see President

Trujillo again...you bet I ain't never going back there and so far as I am concerned President Trujillo and me is gonna stay as far apart as possible.

Sometimes I wonder where ol' Satchel would be if the other team had won that game. Yep, I guess so far as I'm concerned that was the biggest day of my baseball life although it's one I never want to live over again.

When the blackball expatriates returned stateside, the former Crawfords discovered that Gus Greenlee had banned them for life for skipping out

on him and wasn't ready to take them back or allow them to play elsewhere in the NNL. Josh Gibson didn't have such worries, as Cum Posey welcomed his prodigal slugger back to a Homestead team that had already won the first-half title. Gibson complemented the young nucleus—Buck Leonard at first, speedy Jerry Benjamin in center, crafty southpaw Edsell Walker and ace Ray Brown—of the rebuilt Grays. Homestead took its first NNL flag by repeating in the second-half race.

During this most turbulent of years, J.L. Wilkinson decided the time had come once again to form an association of midwestern and southern blackball teams. Thus was born the Negro American

League. For the previous six seasons, the Monarchs had been the the strongest team in a region through which busloads of barnstorming baseball clubs buzzed each summer, going from town to town, game to game. Many teams—though not KC's Royals so much—slept on buses or in fields as often as at houses. In fact, to call the Monarchs a barnstorming team belies its considerable civic identity, as the team regularly outdrew Kansas City's popular minor league team at Meuhelbach Stadium.

By the mid-1930s, Wilkinson was sponsoring other barnstorming teams, but the Monarchs were his pride and joy. The franchise was blessed with stars of phenomenal longevity, as Joe Rogan remained the club's player/manager (though his playing time was limited), Newt Allen its starting second baseman (though Newt Joseph had retired after 1935), and Chet Brewer its ace (though he spent the balance of the 1937 campaign in the Dominican Republic). Filling Brewer's shoes was another brilliant Monarch hurler, Hilton Smith, who was just at the beginning of his illustrious tenure. Smith not only compiled 20 victories in 1937, but also pitched a no-hitter. The team's other new stars included sharp hitter and first baseman Eldridge Mayweather, swift leadoff man Henry Milton, and the big man in the Monarchs order, outfielder Willard Brown.

✻ ✻ ✻ ✻

OPPOSITE: *Many of the Negro league teams traveled by bus or trailer, and among those perhaps none more than the barnstorming Kansas City Monarchs. The 1936 squad pictured here includes (standing, from left) Andy Cooper, Pat Patterson, unknown, Moocha Harris, Floyd Kransen, Henry Milton, Willard Brown; (seated, from left) Newt Allen, Leroy Taylor, Bullet Joe Rogan, Bob Madison, and Eddie Dwight.*

Wilkinson organized an eight-team league that included the Monarchs; the American Giants, who, significantly, hadn't played in the NNL in 1936; two long-standing southern franchises with stable ownership, the Birmingham Black Barons and the Memphis Red Sox; two old NNL stalwarts, the St. Louis Stars and the Detroit Stars; and two clubs with a degree of historical resonance, the Cincinnati Tigers and the Indianapolis Athletics. The season figured to be a contest between the Monarchs and the American Giants, who, in the absence of the great Bill Foster, were led by perennial All-Star third baseman Alex Radcliffe (Ted's younger brother) and two top pitchers, Ted Trent and Sug Cornelius. KC won the first half by a nose (19–8 to 18–8) and Chicago apparently took the second race (no final standings are extant), forcing a best-of-seven playoff. The Monarchs claimed the inaugural NAL title with a convincing four-games-to-one victory.

The Monarchs were favored to repeat in 1938, in spite of Chet Brewer's decision to take another sabbatical, this time in Mexico. And in most years, their 19–5 first-half record would have done the trick. But the upstart Memphis Red Sox, captained by Ted "Double Duty" Radcliffe (who as player/ manager/pitcher deserved to be upgraded to "Triple Duty"), posted a phenomenal 21–4 record to win the first half. Along with Radcliffe and star veteran backstop Larry Brown, the Red Sox featured youngsters like slick fielding Jelly Taylor at first and one of the top emerging all-around talents in blackball, slugger Neil Robinson. After the break the Monarchs failed to set up a showdown with Memphis, falling off to a 13–10 clip, which placed them behind the American Giants (17–7) and the longshot winners, the young Atlanta Black Crackers (12–4). The playoff was plagued by logistical bickering, and was called off after the Red Sox won the first two games.

Back east, Gus Greenlee agreed to pardon his players who had gone AWOL the previous season, though only Leroy Matlock and Sam Bankhead

returned to the no-longer-mighty Crawfords. Cool Papa Bell, like Chet Brewer, opted for the big money south of the border. Satchel Paige, meanwhile, was on the brink of signing with the Newark Eagles, who had purchased his rights from Greenlee, when his negotiations with owners Abe and Effa Manley hit a snag. Consequently, Satch darted down to Mexico to take the even bigger money offered to him. For their trouble, expatriates Bell and Paige were once again banned for life from the NNL.

The Homestead Grays flexed their muscles both on and off the field in 1938. On the field the Grays went 26–6, to run away from the Philadelphia Stars (20–11), the only other club to finish above .500. Led by Josh Gibson and Buck Leonard, dubbed the black Ruth and Gehrig, Homestead also topped the second stanza, to win its second straight NNL flag. Off the field, the Grays expanded their reach by playing many of their home games in Washington, D.C. In fact, Cum Posey and Sonnyboy Jackson's ambitious strategy was to play at Griffith Stadium in Washington on weekends when the Senators were on the road, and to rent Forbes Field in Pittsburgh on weekends when the Pirates were away from home.

Sadly, Gus Greenlee's club had come apart at the seams. The 1938 Crawfords had none of the drawing power they had had a couple of years before. Recognizing a hopeless situation, Greenlee sold the club before the 1939 campaign and it soon folded. The future of eastern blackball looked increasingly Gray. Indeed, the Gibson-Leonard, Posey-Jackson Grays won the next seven NNL pennants to give them a total of nine consecutive flags.

Meanwhile, out west a dynasty that paralleled the Grays' (at least for a few years) was in the making, though no one knew it at the time because the key ingredient was in deep trouble in Mexico. Satchel Paige blew his arm out late in the 1938 season. The doctors were not encouraging, saying he probably wouldn't be able to pitch effectively again. Paige's prospects looked grim (as grim, in fact, as they did every day for most black men in America). Paige tried to bank on his name, and luckily promoter Abe Saperstein thought the Satchel Paige All-Stars would still draw fans. Saperstein prevailed upon Wilkinson to put Satch in charge of one of the latter's second-tier barnstorming clubs. All Satch could do was stand in the first base coach's box, or maybe put in an inning or two at first base, but the crowds were good. Satchel, however, was growing frustrated, and in early summer 1939, he returned to the mound. Paige started slowly and felt no pain, so he picked up the pace and he still experienced no pain. The results were familiar—a lot of scoreless innings. Paige would never be the same after the injury, but he still had a wicked fastball that traveled down around the speed

of sound (instead of the speed of light). More significantly, Paige became even craftier on the mound, a trait that would serve him well in a career in pro baseball that wasn't yet halfway through. Satch reentered the big time as a Kansas City Monarch by the end of the season.

With the revitalized Paige, the Monarchs took the first of four consecutive NAL titles by posting a 17–7 first-half mark and then topping the second-half championship St. Louis Stars—led by outfielder Dan Wilson and pitching ace Theolic Smith—3 games to 2 in the playoffs. Over the next three seasons the Monarchs so dominated the NAL that they captured the 1940, 1941, and 1942 pennants without any post-season playoffs—they simply won both half-season races each year. These Kansas City teams were, as always, anchored by strong pitching, having two aces: the incomparable Paige had a peer in the great Hilton Smith. Smith, who played with the Monarchs from 1937 to 1948 and over that period had a .638 winning percentage, had his best year in 1940, going 10–0 in the regular season, with 3 saves. In 1939 he was also awesome, going 8–2 with 60 strikeouts and

1 shutout game. In the opinion of teammate Buck O'Neil, "From 1940 to 1946 Hilton Smith might have been the greatest pitcher in the world."

Complementing Paige and Smith in this era were a collection of fine Monarch hurlers, including George "Little" Walker and Frank Bradley, both of

whom were with KC through its four-year championship reign at the beginning of the 1940s; Baker McDaniels and Connie Johnson in 1941 and 1942; and the brilliant Chet Brewer in 1941. Meanwhile the Monarchs starting eight were no slouches themselves, led by star slugger Willard "Home Run" Brown in the outfield and anchored by ever-reliable veteran Newt Allen at second base. Joining Brown to create a lethal combination in the middle of the Monarch lineup in 1939 and 1940 was veteran superstar Turkey Stearns. Stearns retired in 1941, but his absence was nicely compensated for by the maturation of star first baseman and career Monarch Buck O'Neil, who had joined the Monarchs in 1938. Other standouts on Wilkinson's elite squad were third baseman/outfielder Ted Strong and stalwart shortstop Jesse Williams.

Meanwhile, back East, Cum Posey's Homestead Grays continued an even more impressive string of NNL pennants, beginning in 1937 and stretching the way though 1945. The one anamoly in this record occurred during the 1939 season. Though the 1939 NNL pennant did not ultimately belong to the Grays, Homestead did finish first in the regular-season standings (which in 1939 were not split into half-seasons), with an impressive 33–14 mark,

✦ ✦ ✦ ✦

LEFT: *Star first baseman Buck O'Neil of the Kansas City Monarchs joined the armed forces during World War II, serving with the U.S. Navy in 1944 and 1945. He is considered one of blackball's greatest managers.*
OPPOSITE: *Buck Leonard in the process of slapping an incoming pitch. Leonard played his entire career with the Homestead Grays, batting .328 over fifteen years and in general proving so valuable that he was elected to the Hall of Fame in 1972.*

outpacing perennial challengers the Newark Eagles (29–20) and the Baltimore Elite Giants (25–21). For the 1939 postseason, a playoff series among the league's top four teams was instituted to determine the proper league champion. The Grays handily dismissed fourth-place Philadelphia (31–32), while Baltimore managed to upset Newark. Then the Elite Giants stunned the prohibitive favorites, winning the best-of-3 championship series with 2 straight victories. Nonetheless, and perhaps due to the brevity of this series, it has remained customary to speak of Homestead's streak of 9 straight pennants.

This is not to suggest that the Eagles and Elite Giants were pushovers. Abe and Effa Manley's Newark squad was laden with superstar talent in the likes of Willie Wells, Mule Suttles, and Leon Day. Unfortunately for the Manleys, Wells and Day traveled South to find more lucrative contracts in Mexico in 1940. However, when both players completed their tropical sabbaticals, they returned initially to the Eagle fold. And though by 1942 the Eagles had landed another brilliant youngster in third baseman Monte Irvin, this team never succeeded in toppling the dynastic Grays. In contrast, the Elite Giants, who had managed to snatch the 1939 postseason from the Grays, had fewer top stars than the Eagles. But they were represented in the East-West classic in the late 1930s by the likes of outfielder Bill Wright, second baseman Sammy T. Hughs, hurlers Jonas Gaines and Bill Byrd, as well as a young catcher destined for major league superstardom named Roy Campanella, who studied under the great veteran Biz Mackey.

Oddly enough, in 1940 the Grays regained the undisputed NNL championship in spite of the fact that their greatest star, transcendent slugger Josh Gibson, took his bat and catcher's mitt down to Vera Cruz (Gibson remained South of the Border until 1942, when he rejoined Posey's roster). Nonetheless, the Grays won in each of those three years, as the Grays' other superstar, Buck Leonard, all-star third baseman Howard Easterling, as well as veteran fixtures Sam Bankeahd and Vic Harris, more than compensated for the loss of Gibson. Of course, it didn't hurt that the Grays had the strongest pitching staff in the East during this era, featuring Roy Partlow, Rayomond Brown, Terris McDuffie, and Roy Wellmaker.

At the end of the 1942 season, the powers that be in blackball arranged what looked to be the ultimate showdown, the first Colored World Series in fifteen years—between the great eastern dynasty, the Homestead Grays, and their western counterpart, the Kansas City Monarchs. This much-anticipated clash of the titans produced a series of 5 close games that resulted in a 4–0 sweep (with an asterisk) for the Monarchs. Kansas City won the first game on an 8–0 Satchel Paige, 2-hit gem; the second game behind a strong outing behind Hilton Smith; and the third another Paige victory. In game four, Paige was outpitched by the great Leon Day, and Homestead tallied 4 runs to the Monarchs' 1. But since Leon Day had spent the season on the roster of the Newark Eagles, Kansas City protested the game and their protest was upheld. This set the stage for game four (take two), in Philadelphia. Satchel Paige was scheduled to start, but was held up on his way to the stadium. "I was driving to that last game, must have been goin' pretty fast because a traffic cop stopped me. By the time I got to the ballpark it was the first of the third inning and the Monarchs is behind 0–5, and the Grays has got the bases filled with none out. I ain't got no time to warm up 'cept to throw a few while I'm walking to the mound, but I strike out the first two batters and makes the last one hit a pop-up. We finally win out, 9–5, and I don't give no hits." The Monarchs were again the undisputed champions of all of blackball.

Of course, by 1943 World War II had depleted the rosters of many Negro League teams as American males of every race and creed entered the military. However, while the war drained the pool of top black baseball players, it also sparked the ever-

anemic African-American economy with the unparalleled rise in heavy industry and manufacturing jobs that effectively ended the decade-long Great Depression. This rising trend in employment had become conspicuous by 1941, when the nation had

begun to prepare for the seemingly inevitable conflict. Soon thereafter the disposable income in the black community rose dramatically and with it attendance at Negro Leagues games.

Perhaps no single statistic better exemplifies both the success of the Negro Leagues by the 1940s and their relative significance to African-America during this era than the impressive, standing-room only crowd of 50,256 fans who flocked to the 1941 East-West All-Star Classic, more than twice the attendance of the previous year and 10,000 more than had witnessed any of the previous eight contests. The packed stands at Comiskey in 1941 were no doubt partially due to the return of the already legendary Satchel Paige to the game following a five-year absence but also clearly reflected the greater prosperity of black America.

To the dismay of western fans, Paige's presence could not prevent an 8–3 romp by the East. The following year produced a similar result as the East triumphed 5–2 in front of an only slightly less impressive 48,400 fans. In 1943, however, the West rebounded with a 2–1 victory; Satchel Paige took the decision in front of an astounding 51,723 (especially impressive since Comiskey's capacity was 50,000).

* * * *

LEFT: *Along with Satchel Paige, Hilton Smith anchored an awesome pitching staff for the Monarchs. In the landmark 1942 Colored World Series, the two men contributed performances that led to a 4–0 sweep of the Homestead Grays.*
OPPOSITE: *The great right-hander Leon Day pitched the 1942 season for the Newark Eagles, but agreed to come in to help the Grays out in the series against the Monarchs. He was the only pitcher to beat the Monarchs, but the win was disqualified. Day also spent two years in Mexico, in 1947 and 1948.*

Looking back in the aftermath of Jackie Robinson's integration of baseball only a few years later, many commentators felt these huge midsummer crowds at Comiskey had impressed upon major league owners that the exclusion of black players was effectively denying the major league teams a significant fan base.

At the time these record crowds were flocking to the midsummer classic in the 1940s, the immense popularity of the events was among the facts cited by a few white journalists (most notably Westbrook Pegler), and a larger group of superb black journalists (including Wendell Smith, Sam Lacy, Joe Bostic, and Fay Young), as a compelling argument for the integration of the majors. Also of note were the writers, mostly white, of the Communist paper *The Daily Worker*, who by the war years argued an organized protest against the unjust segregation of America's national pastime. And while Communism remained on the margins of American politics—even during World War II, when the United States was allied with the Soviet Union—these protests and polemics no doubt drew the attention of many white fans to the oft-forgotten world of blackball.

In contrast to the writings of Pegler and the general efforts of the Communists, black journalists no matter how exceptional—and men like Sam Lacy and Wendell Smith were among the great journalists of their day—rarely reached a white audience. Like the ballplayers whose cause they championed, these brilliant reporters were relegated to the lower-paying "shadow" world of black-only America. Yet this fact only stoked the energy and passion men like Smith and Lacy brought to their craft and crusade—as they served both as eloquent raconteurs of the black baseball season and responded and contributed to the ongoing, highly nuanced arguments concerning strategies for achieving the integration of major league baseball. Every angle was discussed and analyzed: Could blackball survive after integration? Were Satchel Paige's on- and off-field antics

(beloved by so many) good for the cause? Who was the right man to break the color barrier, or should a whole team serve that purpose? How did the Great Depression and then the war effort relate to baseball's segregation?

Besides begging the question, "If a black man can die for his country on foreign soil just like his white brethren, why can't he play the national game

alongside him back home?," the war produced some of the most stunning evidence that the top black ballplayers were at least on par with their white counterparts.

During the war enlisted men did not abandon their beloved national pastime, as, whenever and wherever the opportunity presented itself, troops

scratched out diamonds and played pick-up games and units fielded their best nine for officially sanctioned showdowns with other units. Soon a dynamic, and well-organized baseball subculture arose within the U.S. military, complete with showdowns between divisions for all-important bragging rights (and, undoubtedly, considerable wagers). No one wanted to let down their comrades in arms and, as such, these contests produced much passion and drama.

Of course, in a vast hierarchy like the military, trading for players wasn't exactly done on an equal footing, as generals could simply transfer the top stars into their units; and this was done to produce teams laden with major league ringers. Black troops, however, were segregated from white troops during the war; though the same logic applied in terms of ringers, as the 818th Amphibian battalion (which landed on Normandy six days after D-Day) featured Kansas City Monarch slugger extraordinaire Willard Brown and brilliant Newark Eagle ace Leon Day. This team rolled over most opponents, and in 1945 they advanced to the ETO (European Theater of Operations) championship against no less than General Patton's 3rd Army team, which featured numerous major league stars and a major league manager.

The title game took place at Hitler's favorite rally sight, the vast Nuremburg field (captured on film in Leni Riefenstahl's terrifying propaganda masterpiece *The Triumph Of The Will*), in front of more than 100,000 troops, making it one of the most dramatic scenes in baseball history. Leon Day was dominant and he took a 2–1 lead into the bottom of the ninth inning, but was met with a leadoff triple (only the fourth hit Day allowed all game). The St. Louis Cardinals' star outfielder, left-handed hitting Harry Walker, was next. "I pitched Walker high and tight," Day recalled years later. "All left-handers, I always went high and tight." Three pitches and three swings later, Walker had struck out. Next followed another ringer, Pittsburgh Pirate outfielder Johnny Wyrostek, another lefty. Three

more high and tight from Day, and Wyrostek was likewise retired on strikes. Patton's hopes rested on Cincinnati Reds second bagger Ben Zientara, a right-handed swinger; but he couldn't touch Day's offerings either. To the amazement of the vast crowd, Day struck out the side for the victory.

Next up for the newly crowned ETO champs were the MTO (Mediterranean Theater of Operations) winners, who also happened to be an all-black squad, the 29th "Buffalo" Division, featuring another Monarch star, catcher Joe Greene. Patton's team also made the trip down to Marseilles for a round-robin tourney of sorts, and when the 818th

actually faced the 29th for the official all-European championship, some of the white major leaguers, including Walker, played alongside Day and Brown for the ETO squad. ("You know how it is in the Army, they wangled their way on," Day noted.) This desegregated squad trounced the Buffaloes easily, but then Day and Brown joined the Buffaloes to face Patton's club, who sent major league ace Ewell Blackwell to the mound. But the game turned out to be not much of a contest as the all-black team crushed Patton's squad 8–0 behind two homers by Brown and more brilliance from the incomparable Leon Day.

Stateside, during the war years, many of the top Negro league stars were in the military (though this did not have an adverse affect on attendance, which actually increased due to the greater prosperity of the war years). No team was more affected by this talent drain than the formerly dynastic Monarchs. Besides superstar Willard Brown and catcher Joe Green, K.C. had to do without star right fielder Ted Strong. Stepping into the breach out West were the Birmingham Black Barons, who won their first NAL pennant in 1943 by winning the first-half title and then defeating a fine Chicago American Giants team led by a triumvirate of all-stars: outfielder Lloyd

Davenport; third baseman Alex Radcliffe; and Alex's older, even more brilliant brother, catcher-pitcher Ted "Double Duty" Radcliffe—in a closely fought playoff, three games to two. The Barons were a solid squad that featured three quality starting pitchers in Alfred Saylor, John Markham, and staff ace, southpaw Gread McKinnis. The starting lineup included two all-stars, sharp fielding second baseman Tommy Sampson and the team's top star, outfielder Lester Lockett. In 1944, Birmingham added "Double Duty" Radcliffe to this mix as well as brilliant young shortstop Art Wilson (who would eventually go on to play briefly in the majors). This group of Barons rolled decisively to their second straight NAL pennant, winning both half-season races.

The Barons' foe in both the 1943 and 1944 Colored World Series was, of course, the great Homestead Gray team led by the unparalleled duo of Josh Gibson and Buck Leonard. Surprisingly, the 1943 Barons gave these Grays a run for their money in a brilliant, see-saw seven-game series. Homestead finally prevailed with an 8–4 victory in the deciding game. Oddly, the 1944 Barons, though supplemented by Radcliffe and Wilson, were dismissed by the Grays in five games, as Homestead joined the 1926–27 Chicago American Giants as the only repeat winners of the Colored World Series.

The Grays were foiled in their attempt to "three-peat" in the NAL as the 1945 pennant was captured by a powerful Cleveland Buckeyes team led by veteran catcher Quincy Trouppe, who had returned to the Negro leagues after an accomplished six-year hiatus in the Mexican leagues, as a player-

* * * *

OPPOSITE: *As this 1942 photograph shows, Negro league baseball was not just a blue collar sport. It was also enormously popular with the growing African-American middle class, the beneficiaries of a surge in wartime employment opportunities.*

manager for the first time. The Buckeyes swept both halves of the NAL season with a squad that included four all-stars: Trouppe; brilliant fielding and fine-hitting first baseman Archie Ware, who hit .296 in 1945; lightning-fast outfielder and perennial all-star Lloyd Davenport, who batted .345; and crafty curveball artist Gene Bremmer, who posted an 8–4 mark. The best Buckeye of them all, a perennial all-star who just happened to skip the 1945 classic, was the great switch-hitting, speed demon outfielder Sam Jethroe, who led the NAL in both hitting and stolen bases in both 1944 and 1945 with .353 and .393 averages and 18 and 21 swipes, respectively. Jethroe, of course, would go on to win the 1950 National League Rookie of the Year honors when, at age twenty-eight, he hit .273 and led the league with 35 steals for the Boston Braves.

Meanwhile, Cum Posey's great Grays swept to another NNL pennant back East. But all was not well in Homestead, as transcendent superstar Josh Gibson was succumbing to substance abuse. Early in his career, drinking had not been a problem for Gibson, but this was not the case by the early 1940s; finally, the great slugger suffered a nervous breakdown and was hospitalized in January 1943. Gibson seemed to turn over a new leaf, recovering in time for the 1943 season, but he soon returned to drinking and philandering, and, according to some accounts, began taking a steady diet of illegal narcotics to counter his frequent, severe headaches (according to some the result of a brain tumor). Predictably, his play deteriorated. In 1943 he remained brilliant as ever at the plate, batting a whopping .474, but behind the plate his defense suffered conspicuously. By 1944, his offensive production also began to lag, and by that year's postseason he had been dropped to sixth in the Gray's batting order. In 1945, Vic Harris became the Gray's player-manager and he returned Gibson to fifth place in the lineup, where at least his legend could provide some protection for the still spectacular Buck Leonard, hitting in the cleanup

spot. Occasionally, Gibson could still launch a long ball, but on most days he was little more than a defensive liability and a singles hitter—and the drinking and headaches continued.

As it turned out, the Grays could have used vintage 1935 Josh Gibson in the 1945 Colored World Series, as the Cleveland Buckeyes pitching staff virtually shut down the once-vaunted Homestead attack. Through eight innings of game one, Cleveland's staff had held the Grays scoreless, and the Buckeyes led 2–0. But with one out in the top of the ninth, Homestead's Dave Hoskins and Buck Leonard reached base with back-to-back singles, setting the table for Gibson. Josh didn't homer, but he came through with his new specialty, a single, to drive in a run. However, with the tying run on second and the go-ahead run on first, hurler Willie Jefferson induced Sam Bankhead to hit into a game-ending double play. The following day, the contest was equally close, and once again the hero was a Cleveland hurler, Gene Bremmer, who not only pitched a complete game, but drove in the game-winning run in the bottom of the ninth for a 3–2 Buckeye victory. In game three, the Buckeyes' ace hurler in 1945, George Jefferson (Willie's younger brother), who had posted a brilliant 11–1 record and a spectacular 1.75 ERA that year, shut out the Grays, as Cleveland triumphed 4–0 to take a commanding 3–1 lead in the series. Game four seemed like a mere formality, as the Cleveland staff posted another shut-out; the Buckeyes won 5–0 to sweep the series, win the championship of colored baseball, and, as it turned out, effectively bring down the curtain on blackball's greatest dynasty, the 1937–1945 Homestead Grays. Indeed, by the following season a new eastern powerhouse, the Newark Eagles, had dethroned the Grays, thereby ending Homestead's nine-year reign over the NNL.

One of the most flamboyant and influential people in Negro league baseball by the mid-1940s was Effa Manley, wife of Newark owner Abe Manley.

Effa had been born at the turn of the century, to a white woman married to a black man in Philadelphia. But Effa was the result of an illicit affair her mother had had with a white man, making Effa an anomaly in the racially divided United States—a white person raised in black America. So while Effa was "genetically" white, she was culturally African-American. Effa grew up to be an intelligent and attractive woman. She met Abe Manley, a wealthy black racketeer, at the 1932 World Series at Yankee Stadium. The two fell in love and married, though he was twenty years her senior. They also shared a love for the national pastime. Abe fulfilled a lifelong dream in 1935 when he purchased the Newark blackball franchise. And while Abe focused on the task of scouting and on the quality of the players, he let his wife run the business side of the operation.

Effa became a vocal advocate for blackball. Just as she had used her position as the state treasurer for the New Jersey NAACP to spearhead numerous civil rights campaigns, Effa would always accompany her husband to the NNL ownership meetings, where she would often dominate the proceedings with her eloquence as well as the power of her ideas. Monte Irvin, who starred with the Newark Eagles before going on to a brilliant career in the majors remembered Effa Manley as "unique, effervescent, and knowledgeable. She ran the whole business end of the team. It's too bad the other owners didn't go along with her on many of her proposals. She wanted to create a lot of innovations. She thought they had to treat the ballplayers a little better—better schedule, better travel, better salaries."

By 1946 one thing the Manleys had succeeded in improving was their team. In fact, though by 1946 they had already lost one their top prospects, a young pitching sensation by the name of Don Newcombe, to Branch Rickey's scouts, the Eagles had talent to spare. Leon Day had returned to New Jersey following his dramatic conquest of Europe, joining a staff that included another sensational hurler in Max Manning, who posted an 11–1 record. Meanwhile the Newark everyday eight included two soon-to-be major league superstars, outfielder Monte Irvin, who hit .406 that year, and Larry Doby at second base, who hit a more modest .346 and two years later would become the first African-American to play in the AL. Alongside Irvin in the outfield were fleet-footed Jimmy Wilkes in center and one of Newark's "Big Four: bats, Johnny Davis, in right. Rounding out the team's quartet of sluggers (with Irvin, Doby, and Davis) was first baseman Lennie Pearson. A potent combination of pitching, power, and fundmanetals, these Eagles soared to the NNL flag by sweeping both halves of the season with equally impressive performances, going 25–9 in the first half and following it up with a 22–7 mark.

The Eagles' foe in the 1946 colored World Series was a revitalized Monarch club. The venerable J.L. Wilkinson's team had been energized by the return from Europe of superstar slugger Willard Brown, who hit .390 for the season. Young Hank Thompson, who would also soon have a stint in the majors, turned some heads as he replaced the departed Jackie Robinson in the infield, playing second base while veteran Jesse Williams returned to short. Veteran first baseman Buck O'Neil contributed perhaps his best season, winning the NAL batting title. And the staff was still anchored by the brilliance of Hilton Smith and the eternal Leroy "Satchel" Paige. These Monarchs reclaimed their rightful place as the rulers of the West by posting a 27–8 mark to take the first-half title. They ran away with the second-half title as well, matching the Eagles back East. The series was a classic, back-and-forth affair, with the Eagles edging the Monarchs 3–2 in the final game to win the series, four games to three.

A couple of events in the years 1946 and 1947 signaled a sea change in the Negro leagues and in black America as a whole. The most obvious was the integration of the majors, represented by the contract signed by Jackie Robinson to play for the Montreal Royals. The end of segregated baseball, which would influence countless aspects of life in the United States for years to come, was near. An event that occurred with somewhat less fanfare was the death of Josh Gibson, on January 20, 1947, just a few weeks after his thirty-fifth birthday and just a few months before Robinson signed with the Dodgers.

It is difficult to measure the importance of Gibson to the history of baseball; despite his dominance on the field, his influence on the game is hard to gauge because he wasn't a showy self-promoter like Paige or a civil rights champion (however reluctant) like Robinson. Certainly Gibson may have been the best hitter in Negro league history, and if he had played in the majors, in baseball history, period. Extrapolating from the available statistics, some feel he may have posted a batting average of close to .400 during his best years. There are also accounts that suggest he crushed a remarkable 75 home runs in one season and 89 in another, and that his longest home runs were well in excess of 500 feet (152m). While these numbers could be apocryphal, they are consistent with the legend of Gibson, which may be the most significant aspect of his legacy. His abilities were so prodigious that he was mythologized, his very name enough to inspire a pleasant thrill at the very thought that such a deity actually walked among us. In any event, his death came at a turning point in the history of baseball, a fitting juncture for one the game's greatest players ever.

* * * *

OPPOSITE: *Josh Gibson is out at home plate during the 1944 East-West All Star Game at Comiskey Park. Catcher Ted Radcliffe made the play. At this point, Gibson was still putting up great numbers, but he was nonetheless slipping away as his health steadily deteriorated.*

THE TRIUMPHANT DEMISE

Branch Rickey's successful orchestration of Jackie Robinson's entry into "organized" baseball with the minor league Montreal Royals in 1946, and Robinson's subsequent promotion to the majors in 1947, brought the era of Jim Crow baseball to a dramatic conclusion; the color barrier had been shattered. Before the 1947 season was out, two other major league organizations had signed African-American ballplayers, and within a few years it became evident that every franchise would soon be racially integrated. After all, the prominence of black superstars like Willie Mays and Henry Aaron (both of whom began their professional careers in the Negro leagues) made it abundantly clear that any club that did not tap into the wealth of black baseball talent would be left in the dust. Perhaps most importantly, a broad consensus emerged among baseball fans (at least in the northern cities that remained the sole domain of major league teams until 1958) that an exclusionary hiring policy based on race represented backward, pig-headed thinking.

The social significance of organized baseball was so pronounced in the United States at mid-century that once Robinson was signed by the Dodgers, even though he only signed a contract to play for a minor league club based

* * * *

OPPOSITE: *Outfielder Monte Irvin was one of the lucky ones: after ten years of Negro league, military, and Mexican baseball, Irvin was picked up by the New York Giants in 1949. He was inducted into the Hall of Fame in 1973.*
ABOVE: *Jackie Robinson (left) and Branch, two men whose resolve and guts changed the baseball landscape forever, come to terms on Robinson's 1950 Brooklyn Dodgers contract.*

in French-speaking Canada, he instantly became black America's greatest hero. Robinson successfully negotiated each challenge he faced throughout the 1946 season. Then, in 1947, as with increasing visability he broke new ground and passed each test during the spring, through the summer, and on into the fall classic, Robinson acquitted himself admirably, with quiet dignity, and his legions of fans grew increasingly ecstatic.

Lost in the euphoria were the Negro Leagues. Actually, 1946 had been a banner year for blackball, but by 1947, with summaries of every Brooklyn game being sent from coast to coast, African-American fans abandoned both the NNL and the ANL en masse and concentrated all their attention on Robinson and the Dodgers. For most black fans and players, the overriding concern was that the integration of organized ball progress successfully, while even non-fans recognized the integration of the national pastime as an important step in the opening up of major American institutions to blacks. If this meant that the Negro leagues were to be sacrificed, so be it.

Not all strategies for integrating organized ball were predicated on the notion that blackball would afterward be obsolete. Rube Foster had hoped that his Negro National League could facilitate the integration of the major leagues, if not the individual teams, by nurturing an all-black team (or two) so good it would be admitted, intact, into the majors. Foster felt it was significant that this model for integration would preserve the Negro league franchises, which were, after all, sizable black-owned organizations (a rarity in the United States). Furthermore, Foster felt that this paradigm also provided for the continuing operation of the Negro leagues as "official" minor leagues.

Foster's reasoning seemed somewhat informed by a nagging awareness of the inherent futility in founding institutions, whose purpose is to orchestrate their own destruction. Indeed, Foster was well aware

that the standard vision of baseball integration was to have each team fully integrated, and that many people criticized his proposal as maintaining partial segregation. In fact, long before Foster organized the NNL in 1920, and all the way through the late 1930s and early 1940s, when the black press led the push for baseball's integration, the vast majority of blacks who commented on the subject recognized that integration would signal the beginning of the end for blackball. And that is exactly what happened.

Branch Rickey signed Jackie Robinson to a contract with the Brooklyn Dodgers' organization in the fall of 1945. Robinson proceeded to have a brilliant 1946 campaign with the Montreal Royals of the International League, winning the batting title with a club-record .349 clip. He also led the league with 113 runs scored, stole 40 bases, and drove in 66 runs (even though he hit only three homers). Robinson also proved to the Dodgers' organization that he could play second base, a new position for

him in 1946, as he posted the top fielding percentage in the league among second baggers. It came as no surprise the following spring when Rickey promoted Robinson, who debuted with the Dodgers on April 15, 1947.

In the wake of these transformative events, Rickey and Robinson rightly gained immortality as the central figures who toppled baseball's color barrier. (Of course, Rickey and Robinson both enjoyed spectacular success at the major league level in their respective roles as general manager and player, which adds considerable luster to their legends, but it's safe to say that Rickey and Robinson's preeminent place in baseball history, as well as their status as national icons, stems primarily from their canonization as the co-integrators of the national pastime.) Nonetheless, the successful racial integration of organized baseball during the first two seasons following WWII, which effectively reversed the practice of seventy years of segregation, was not merely the product of two willful, talented, and courageous men, but of historical circumstances that set the stage for Rickey's and Robinson's initiative.

In the late 1930s and early 1940s, the black press had spearheaded an aggressive campaign

* * * *

ABOVE: *Hank Aaron of the Milwaukee Braves smiles in this 1965 view. Aaron never played in the Negro leagues, but his entry into the majors was made possible by countless men throughout the history of blackball in the United States, most directly Jackie Robinson.*

OPPOSITE: *Jazz was one of the cultural languages that bridged the divide between white and black America during the war years. Here, Ella Fitzgerald dines with a collection of Negro league superstars, including Joe Black (opposite her) and Don Newcombe (two to her left).*

calling for baseball's integration. Black writers, politicians, ballplayers, fans, and even a few whites argued persuasively for change, citing numerous reasons why the time had come for black men to play in the major leagues. And the effort wasn't entirely futile, as, at times, real progress seemed imminent. In 1942, Bill Veeck was set to purchase the lowly Philadelphia Phillies when he commented that he was planning to remake the team's roster in the im-

age of a Negro league All-Star team, at which point Commissioner Landis heard the rumor and blocked the sale of the team to Veeck. Meanwhile, black players were given tryouts with the Pirates, Dodgers, and Red Sox during the war years, yet no signings occurred.

So what changed? Why were Rickey and Robinson able to succeed where others before them had failed?

One significant factor was the death of Commissioner Landis, a staunch opponent of integration. As long as he was alive, the ancient judge's veto power was an insurmountable barrier. Landis was succeeded by former Kentucky governor Albert "Happy" Chandler. No sooner had Chandler assumed the office than he met the press and responded to a question about integration by saying, "I'm for the four freedoms. If a black boy can

123

make it on Okinawa in Guadalcanal, hell, he can make it in baseball." Strange as it may seem, a southern blueblood became an ally to black fans around the nation and singlehandedly countered stiff opposition to integration among the major league owners. Sportswriter Rick Roberts noted that "none of those people [Rickey et al.] could have done a doggone thing if they hadn't gotten a green light from the Commissioner. And he never got credit for it. I think he is long overdue for what he deserves."

Still, it took more than a cabal of three men to void the infamous gentlemen's agreement that had remained sacrosanct for sixty-nine years, functioning as if it were a de facto clause in the national pastime's charter. Indeed, it took nothing less than the evolution of American society itself. Shifting socioeconomic relations and slowly changing cultural attitudes, had, by the mid-1940s, created a context conducive to the desegregation of the national pastime. In short, American race relations were improving.

Whites in the industrial North had become familiar with the sizable black communities in their midst, and years of coexistence had greatly diminished racial tensions. It is particularly noteworthy that there had been relatively little racial violence during the hard times of the Depression. Then the war years lifted the economy out of its lull and mobilized the entire nation under a united cause like never before. The desegregation of the armed forces in early 1942 was not just symbolic; as a result, great numbers of black and white Americans lived and died side by side. This experience forged countless bonds across racial boundaries.

There were other factors, too. Jazz music, for instance, which all Americans recognized as an African-American creation, provided much of the soundtrack for the American war effort. Though the most popular big band and vocal group hits were mostly recordings by white performers, the product was still clearly jazz. And almost all of these white recording stars expressed reverence for such pioneering black jazz artists as Louis Armstrong, Duke Ellington, and Ella Fitzgerald, to name just three. At any rate, jazz was certainly an exhilarating reminder to millions of white and black soldiers that they were bonded as Americans.

* * * *

Commissioner Albert "Happy" Chandler throws out the first pitch before a Yankees-Phillies game in 1950. Chandler's progressive stance on the integration of the majors made it possible for Branch Rickey's "great experiment" to take place.

On a more somber note, the liberation of the Nazi death camps, and the discovery of the scope of the Jewish Holocaust, influenced many Americans' perspectives on racism. The horrible images from the genocide stunned the United States and the world, providing a graphic display of the evils of racist ideology. It also, no doubt, informed the adoption of antiracism as a central tenet of official American ideology in the postwar years. (It's a stance that many critics of the Eisenhower administration feel forced the U.S. president to intervene on behalf of civil rights demonstators when he would rather have not. Ike's main motivation, according to these pundits, was his fear that the Soviet Union would expose U.S. hypocrisy for tolerating abject racism at home.)

Nonetheless, while the significant black presence throughout the U.S. military did make a strong impression on many whites (witness Happy Chandler's comment at his inaugural press encounter), the tens of thousands of African-Americans who had fought in World War I a quarter of a century earlier had not enjoyed any postwar good will among the white mainstream. Twenty-six years after the United States had erupted in cataclysmic postwar race riots, World War II troops returned stateside protected and provided for by something novel in American history, the G.I. Bill of Rights. The G.I. Bill was probably inspired less by a sense of indebtedness to the soldiers than by a fear that a return to Depression-level unemployment would spark civic unrest. Such a scenario, even in the "evolved" context of 1945, could very well have spawned a brutal racist backlash, as so often had been the case throughout U.S. history. But the G.I. Bill provided unprecedented social and economic insurance to the returning troops. Better yet, it was colorblind and thus a boon to millions of returning black G.I.s.

Still, a look at the economic situation betrays the fact that the United States remained a racist society. Blacks were by far the poorest ethnic group in the multiethnic North, and down South they were both impoverished and without basic civil rights. It was in this context that Brooklyn Dodgers general manager Branch Rickey decided the time had come for baseball to integrate.

Branch Wesley Rickey was born on December 20, 1881, the son of a Methodist preacher, and was raised on the family farm in central Ohio. In between countless hours of book learning, chores, and Bible study, young Branch found time to pursue his true love, baseball, sometimes just by throwing a ball in the backyard with his mother.

When Branch went to college at Ohio Weslyan, he decided to earn some extra money by managing the baseball team. At the time, the team's star was also its only African-American player, Charlie Thomas. Rickey watched as the courageous Thomas was dealt one humiliation after another, if not from opposing players then from society at large.

Once, following a game against Notre Dame in South Bend, Indiana, the team's hotel refused to give Thomas a room. Rickey was able to persuade the hotel manager to let Thomas stay in his room. When he returned to the hotel later that evening, Branch found Thomas standing alone in a corner, attempting, in vain, to rub the skin off his body. With tears spilling down his face, Thomas uttered, "Black skin, black skin, if only I could make it white." Rickey tried to console Thomas but to no avail. The memory of that night stayed with Rickey his entire life.

Years later, after Jackie Robinson had successfully integrated baseball, Rickey would reflect on why it was that he took the course of action he did in bringing Robinson into the Dodgers organization. Sounding every bit the Methodist preacher, he said, "I could not face my God much longer knowing that his black creatures are held separate and distinct from his white creatures in the game that has given me all I own."

After college, Rickey pursued a career in professional baseball. He played on numerous professional clubs, and he broke into the major leagues at the end of the 1905 season, as a catcher with the St. Louis Browns. Rickey spent the next two seasons in the majors, collecting 82 hits in 343 at-bats for a .239 average.

He was out of the major leagues by 1908, and was soon headed to law school. However, he could not stay away from the game he loved for very long and soon returned as a scout. By 1913, he was managing the Browns, and in 1916, he moved across town to the St. Louis Cardinals.

Rickey became an advocate of what he called "scientific baseball," which ran counter to the prevailing theories of the day. Rickey's system was built around rigorous conditioning and practice regimens at spring training; in contrast, informed by the gospel that baseball was primarily a skill sport, the contemporary orthodoxy was to allow players to work at their own (usually quite leisurely) pace since only they knew how to refine the mysterious nuances of their baseball skills. While there were exceptions before Rickey, the rule was that managers, coaches, and veterans would actively teach and counsel youngsters, but rarely scrutinize the techniques of established players. As Rickey's system evolved, the organization's braintrust worked actively to improve every aspect of every player's game. Pitching and batting coaches in particular became year-long tutors who micromanaged their charges' skills. As Rickey's teams became more successful, this approach was adopted by other franchises and eventually spread throughout all of organized baseball.

The Cardinals club that Rickey inherited had been even less successful than the Browns, and the Redbirds remained a fixture of the National League's second division through the 1910s. But that all changed after World War I. In the process of rejuvenating the team, Rickey revolutionized baseball by developing the first elaborate farm system. Although other teams would follow suit, the Cardinals farm system remained the most extensive in all of baseball. It soon bore spectacular fruit. The Cards won their first NL pennant in 1926, and then upset Babe Ruth and the mighty New York Yankees in a thrilling seven-game World Series. The products of Rickey's farm system were merely part of the supporting cast in 1926, as the Cardinals were led by brilliant veterans like Grover Alexander and player-manager (and resident superstar) Rogers Hornsby.

The inflexible, hard-nosed Hornsby was soon gone, however, controversially sent to the Cubs for Frankie "the Fordham Flash" Frisch. A college product (a rarity in those days), Frisch was a second-tier star—nothing like the transcendent Hornsby. But unlike the Rajah, Frisch fit into Rickey's master plan, becoming the Cardinals' new player-manager on a squad culled from the cream of the franchise's vast farm system, which grew to include as many as fifty-five clubs. The result was the legendary Gas House Gang, which featured such stars as Pepper Martin, Ducky Medwick, and ace Dizzy Dean. The team's identification as a group was heightened by the players' colorful on- and off-field antics, but, more significantly (since the Gas House Gang's fame was predicated on their success), it reflected the fact that Rickey had built an extremely cohesive, complementary unit that played a distinctive, aggressive, and exciting brand of baseball.

If any further proof of the ingenuity and success of Rickey's farm system were necessary, he provided it in the late 1930s, by which time old age and injuries (most notably to Dean) had brought the curtain down on one era of Cardinal baseball. Rickey was able to make a rapid and relatively seamless transition, building another quintessential team by the early 1940s that captured four pennants and three World Series titles in four years, from 1942 through 1946. After the 1942 triumph, Rickey resigned because of a dispute with the Cardinal ownership and headed to Brooklyn.

Like the Cardinals franchise he had inherited a quarter of a century earlier, the Dodgers had never won a World Series when Rickey came to town. Brooklyn had won two pennants since the turn of the century, one in 1941 and one in 1920. Unfortunately, the nucleus of the 1941 team was either too old or too gimpy (as with Pete Reiser) by 1943, and certainly didn't represent much of a future. So Rickey turned his attention to developing talent in the farm system; in an era when almost every major league franchise cut back on scouting because of the pending war, Rickey emphasized recruiting.

The move from St. Louis to Brooklyn also gave Rickey cause to contemplate taking action about something that had haunted him since his days at Ohio Wesleyan with Charlie Thomas: the unjust segregation of the national pastime. St. Louis, after all, had a well-earned reputation as the most strictly segregated city in the majors (embodied by the separate seating section for coloreds at Sportsman Park). Brooklyn was a sharp contrast: already renowned as an ethnic menagerie dominated by huge Irish, Italian, and Jewish populations, the borough also had a sizable, and growing, black population. Also, in contrast to St. Louis at mid-century, Brooklyn was a hotbed of radical and progressive politics— fertile turf for striking a blow against institutionalized racism. Still, Rickey knew it was futile to sign a black player so long as Landis was commissioner of baseball. When the ancient judge died in 1944, Rickey's wheels started to spin.

The history of how Rickey proceeded toward signing Jackie Robinson will always remain somewhat shrouded in mystery. Like all great wheeler-dealers, Rickey was accustomed to functioning in extreme secrecy, complemented by a healthy dose of duplicity to further trip up his adversaries (and Rickey knew from the get-go that the integration of baseball was the most sensitive undertaking of his career). Shortly after Landis' death, Rickey had approached George McLaughlin, the head of the

Brooklyn Trust Company, the Dodgers' primary financiers, about the possibility of signing black players. After Rickey explained that there was no "official" policy banning African-Americans from organized ball, McLaughlin gave him the go-ahead. Rickey also sought, and won, the approval of his main rival within the Dodger organization, Walter O'Malley, a part-owner with designs on purchasing a controlling interest in the franchise. Rickey urged both men not to divulge his intentions to anyone.

Then, at a press conference in early 1945, Rickey made a stunning announcement: the Dodgers' organization was going to field an all-black team, the Brown Dodgers, that would play in Ebbets Field and be a charter member of the United States League, a new Negro league spearheaded by none other than Gus Greenlee, of Pittsburgh Crawford fame. Refusing to speculate too far into the future, Rickey deflected questions about whether the Brown Dodgers would function as a farm team, developing talent for the major league parent club. Rickey did assert that if the league functioned smoothly it could be recognized as an "official" minor league within a few years. By way of contrast, he denigrated the existing Negro leagues as disreputable, mob-run organizations (which begs the question of whether Rickey knew anything at all about Greenlee).

Debate over Rickey's intentions began almost immediately, and to this day historians remain divided over the issue. Some skeptics believe the Brooklyn general manager was primarily interested in generating revenue on the order of the $100,000 that the Yankees took in from renting out their stadium for Negro league games (though this fails to take into account that the reason this practice was so profitable for the Yankees is that they didn't have to share in the operating expenditures for the black teams). There were those in major league baseball who shuddered at the prospect of Rickey monopolizing a whole new branch of minor leagues. When they heard him say he hoped the USL could get official

sanction they had visions of Rickey having first pick of every blackball star. The prevailing theory is that the USL was merely a subterfuge that would allow the Dodgers organization to scout black players without attracting suspicion. Rickey had to denigrate the established Negro leagues because it was against the rules of organized baseball to recruit players already under contract.

While the historical record is surprisingly unclear, apparently a brief USL season was played among teams in eight cities. Included among these were the Brooklyn Brown Dodgers, managed by the legendary Oscar Charleston. The only other name blackball player involved in the league was Bingo DeMoss, who signed on to skipper the Chicago franchise. At any rate the league failed to catch on, and was all but forgotten by late summer, though it was never officially declared dead, which seems to support the theory that Rickey's intent all along was to use the league as a cover. In fact, when Roy

Campanella got word that Rickey wanted to talk with him, the star catcher assumed it was about the Brown Dodgers. The Kansas City Monarchs' rookie shortstop Jackie Robinson didn't know what to think when Dodger scout Clyde Sukeforth intercepted him in Chicago during a late August roadtrip and told him Branch Rickey wanted to visit with him in Brooklyn. Sukeforth didn't seem to know any more than that, but to Robinson that was enough. The shortstop grabbed his bags and joined Sukeforth at the station for a train ride into history.

Many sports pundits have commented that it's hard to imagine any man besides Jackie Robinson breaking baseball's color barrier, testifying, in effect, to how fully Robinson put his imprimatur on what has come to be called "baseball's great experiment." It suggests that Robinson, simply stated, stood out among men, that he was possessed of exceptional character. In the words of legendary sportscaster Howard Cosell: "Jackie Robinson can be best characterized, reflectively, in one word, unconquerable. Everything about Jackie Roosevelt Robinson was right. And when people ask me, 'Who was the greatest all-around athlete this nation has ever produced?' I say Jackie Robinson, also the greatest all-around man."

Jack Roosevelt Robinson, the son of sharecroppers and the grandson of a former slave, was born on January 31, 1919, in a cabin in Cairo, Georgia. Six months after Jackie's birth, his father left the family. Jackie's mother, Mallie, decided shortly thereafter that the land of Jim Crow was no place to raise her children. In the spring of 1920, the

✶ ✶ ✶ ✶

OPPOSITE: *The young Branch Rickey, circa 1925.* **RIGHT:** *The more seasoned version of the Dodgers general manager emerges from the club office wearing a strange expression on his face. He had just signed a five-year contract with the organization.*

Robinsons left Georgia for southern California. After a brief initial stay with relatives, Mallie got a job as a maid for a rich white family in Pasadena and the Robinsons settled into this rapidly expanding city adjacent to Los Angeles.

While antiblack prejudice was far from absent in California, race relations were, in the eyes of blacks, far better there than in Dixie, and even in the Northeast. In the 1920s, Pasadena, like Los Angeles, was just becoming a major population center. In essence, it was inventing itself. There was no precedent determining black-white race relations there. If nothing else, new race relations were being established according to the precepts of the 1920s, as opposed to the late-nineteenth-century, post–Civil War era (as in the Northeast) or the Colonial era (as in the South).

While antiblack racism was undeniably cruel in the 1920s, the nature of that racism was generally less brutal than previously in American history. Further mitigating antiblack sentiment, young southern California included large blocks of two other ethnic minorities: Asians and Mexicans. This meant that for the first time there were sizable ethnic groups in an American community besides blacks.

As of the 1920s, blacks were more assimilated into American culture than were the Mexicans or Chinese. In fact, there had been such a long history of brutal anti-Chinese racism and violence in California that whereas blacks were usually at the bottom of all racial and ethnic hierarchies (at least in the context of the South and the Northeast), this was not true in California. Like blacks or Native Americans in other parts of the country, Chinese-Americans had no reason to trust white Americans. The Spanish-speaking population's primary relationship to white America was likewise founded on suspicion.

Significantly, much of the white population that moved to California from the 1920s on recognized the need for a new paradigm of race relations, even though the emerging white power structure in south-

ern California sought to maintain black subservience. All in all, the subjugation of blacks was not as central a tenet of the community's belief system as it was in the South, or even in the ethnic hierarchy that so effectively divided the working class of the industrial North.

Blacks who came to California from the South like Mallie Robinson had no doubt heard that the West Coast was a land of improved race relations. While to a certain degree this was true, in the beautiful and (in the context of the Depression) prosperous town of Pasadena, blacks lived in a segregated neighborhood and sat in a separate section in the movie theaters. And the jobs most readily available to blacks were as domestic servants or gardeners.

Jackie Robinson's mother, however, was intent on bucking the system. Four years after arriving in Pasadena, she managed to rent a house at 121 Pepper Street in an otherwise exclusively white neighborhood. Soon a petition was circulated among the other residents of the area that called for the expulsion of the black family from their community. Mallie Robinson, whose strong moral convictions were grounded in a deep religious faith that she hoped to impart to her children, was not about to back down. Fortunately, the Robinsons' immediate neighbor had befriended the family (in particular Jackie's oldest brother, Edgar) and vocally condemned the organizers and signers of the petition, which soon after lost momentum. The Robinsons settled into their new home, which Mallie was able to purchase outright within a few years. The family became a cornerstone of the Pepper Street community.

With their mother working long hours at least five days a week, the Robinson children learned to

* * * *

OPPOSITE: *UCLA track sensation Jackie Robinson. Amazingly, he also excelled in three other sports: baseball, basketball, and football.*

fend for themselves. When the family's second child, Jackie's only sister, Willa Mae, was old enough to attend day school, she would take young Jackie along with her, leaving him in the playground when she was in the classroom. At recess time, Jackie would play along with the older children, and he proved precocious at sports, exhibiting athletic skills well beyond his years. But what was truly uncanny was the child's sense of gamesmanship, for regardless of the contest, whether it be checkers, marbles, Monopoly, or baseball, Jackie would readily comprehend the inner workings of the game and proceed to win. It was a seemingly innate skill that Jackie's teachers, friends, and family members marveled at throughout his childhood. Indeed, from the time he began school through his childhood and adolescence, Jackie, only a moderate-to-good student, was always the exceptional athlete of his year.

Jackie was not the first Robinson to excel at athletics. Willa Mae starred in three sports—soccer, basketball, and track—during high school. Jackie's two older brothers, Edgar and Frank, were largely unathletic, but the middle sibling, Mack, four and a half years older than Jackie, set some mighty lofty standards for the youngster to live up to. A fine all-around athlete who performed well at the three major team sports, Mack was blessed with blazing speed. Inspired by the 1932 Olympics, which were held in Los Angeles, Mack concentrated on track and field and four years later qualified for the 1936 U.S. Olympic team.

Ascending through the amateur ranks and winning trophies along the way in both the long jump and sprint, Mack's hard work paid off. In Berlin, he captured a silver medal in the 200 meters, finishing second to another African-American, the legendary Jessie Owens. Because Mack was not a legend like Owens, the following summer he found himself working for the city of Pasadena as a gardener.

Jackie drew inspiration from his brother's medal-winning performance, but at seventeen years

old (in 1936) the younger Robinson had long since established his commitment to athletic greatness. Jackie's childhood dominance on the playground carried over to the organized teams of early adolescence and onto his first interscholastic competitions in middle school. Regardless of the season, Jackie had a sport to excel at. In autumn he was the football hero. During winter he was the king of the basketball court. And in the spring and summer he took advantage of his free time by starring in baseball and track and even developing fine tennis and golf games.

In sharp contrast to the experiences of most young black athletes throughout the United States, Robinson's childhood and teenage athletic encounters took place almost exclusively in a racially integrated setting. In fact, the Pasadena public school teams were predominantly white, as were the majority of the high school and junior high school teams in greater Los Angeles that Robinson played against.

As the outstanding star of the teams he played for, Robinson was a conspicuous target for racial epithets and taunts from opposing players and hostile crowds. He knew that what he was hearing reflected real racist hatred and ignorance, but he was not so naive as to not recognize that the extreme vulgarity and violent threats were also ploys intended to affect the outcome of the contest by rattling him. Thus, Jackie rarely offered his adversaries the satisfaction of a response and maintained his focus on the contest at hand. Jackie understood that he was blessed with strength, speed, and agility, but he won games with his mind.

Jackie rarely displayed this mental acuity in the classroom, however. Although his teachers found him both proud and cordial, he also came across as somewhat aloof and not very engaged in his lessons. Around girls, his politeness and distance betrayed his shyness. But Jackie was anything but reserved when he was in his element, hanging out with his pals, a group that came to be known as the Pepper Street Gang.

By the time Jackie was in high school at John Muir Technical, the ethnic makeup of the part of Pasadena where his family resided had changed drastically from the time they first arrived. No longer predominantly white, the Robinsons' neighborhood was truly multiracial, with working-class whites, blacks, Asians, and Mexicans living side by side and, it should be noted, doing so in relative harmony. This ethnic diversity was reflected in the crowd of adolescents that Jackie spent much of his time with after school, on weekends, and during vacations.

While at the dawn of the twenty-first century, the idea of a group of urban male youths conjures up images of violence and antisocial behavior, the Pepper Street Gang did not represent any tangible threat to its community. While occasionally earning reprimands from cops, the gang never did anything more menacing than traditional boyish pranks, and in fact, the group primarily played sports. Not surprisingly, Jackie's domination of these games made him the group's natural leader.

After high school, Jackie attended Pasadena Junior College, where he continued to stand out as an athlete of uncommon skill, whatever the contest. By this point Jackie had become a large, powerful man (just shy of six feet [183cm], about 200 pounds [91kg]) who was also incredibly fast and graceful. More importantly, he was a smart player, capable of reading opponents and situations quickly and efficiently. And his talents did not go unnoticed. He was awarded an athletic scholarship at the University of California, Los Angeles, where he would eventually distinguish himself in four sports: track, baseball, basketball, and football. Of the four, ironically, baseball was probably his weakest (for example, in 1940 Robinson batted an anemic .097).

Robinson's junior year (his first at UCLA) was exceptional. He earned four varsity letters (becoming the first to do so in UCLA history), and in particular excelled at football. The star of the team at the time was senior Kenny Washington, but Robinson added his own special flair, setting the national record for punt returns in 1939. By his senior year, Robinson had truly come into his own, and was heralded as an All-American in football. Though he continued to shine on the gridiron, the team as a whole did not fare as well, winning only once all season. As always, there were other sports Jackie could fall back on—in this case, basketball, which he played exclusively in the second half of his senior year.

Of greater significance than all this, perhaps, Robinson met his soulmate during his tenure at UCLA. Nursing student Rachel Isum was the opposite of Jackie in her focus on academics, though perhaps his equal in commitment to excellence at her chosen field. Indeed, one of the things that Rachel recalled admiring most about Jackie was his pride in his heritage and in himself. No less could be said of Rachel herself, which Robinson respected deeply. Almost from the very start of their relationship until the end of their days together, she would prove to be the bedrock of Jackie's existence. At the end of the 1940 football season, Rachel was one of the primary reasons Jackie—who had decided not to go out for track and baseball, and in fact to leave UCLA altogether—decided to stick around for the back end of his senior year and play basketball. Displaying his usual skill, Jackie was superb on the court during the 1940-1941 season for UCLA, eventually winning the Pacific Coast Conference scoring title for the second year in a row.

Jackie did eventually leave school before the end of his senior year, to take a job as a physical education instructor for a National Youth Administration camp. Although Robinson eventually came to like the job, such New Deal holdovers as the NYA evaporated in the face of the mounting preparations for war that were under way in late 1941. With few job prospects, Jackie turned to football again, eventually winding up playing for the Los Angeles Bulldogs briefly, and then for the semi-pro Honolulu Bears during the 1941 season. The season started out bright, but Jackie reinjured his right ankle (the first time had been at Pasadena Junior College) and the team began to slump. On December 5, injured and frustrated, Jackie set out to return to Los Angeles. As his ship was crossing the Pacific Ocean, combined elements of the Imperial Japanese Navy and Air Force bombed the U.S. naval station at Pearl Harbor, bringing the United States into World War II. Upon his return, Robinson went to work as a truck driver for Lockheed, the beneficiary (like many other African Americans) of an abundance of jobs combined with a paucity of (white) labor.

Like many other young American men, Jackie Robinson was soon drafted into the U.S. Army, though he was ultimately unable to achieve fighting status due to his ankle. He was assigned to Fort Riley, Kansas, where he became fast friends with another of the most famous African-American sports heroes of the day, Joe Louis. On leave in 1943, he proposed to Rachel, who accepted, though the date for the wedding was put off indefinitely.

Life was rocky for such proud men as Robinson at the newly integrated Officer Candidate School, but he proved resilient and capable of effecting change within the largely racist military hierarchy; Jackie eventually became a second lieutenant. In 1944, Robinson and a number of other black officers received with mixed emotions the news that they were to be transferred to Camp Hood, Texas, so called in honor of Confederate Civil War officer John Bell Hood. They were on their way to the deep South. Justifying such apprehensions, an event occurred at Hood that foreshadowed Jackie's future as a warrior in the fight for civil rights, first on the baseball diamond and later as a citizen at large.

Getting onto a military bus headed for Camp Hood one evening, Robinson sat down in the front, next to a fair-skinned black woman of his acquaintance. After a while, the driver took exception to the fact that the dark-skinned Robinson was sitting next to a "white" woman and told Robinson to get to the back of the bus. Jackie refused, knowing full well that the army had recently ruled against segregated seating on U.S. military conveyances. After continued protests from the driver, a white woman joined in the threats to bring charges against Robinson, who still remained where he was. When the bus pulled into Camp Hood, Jackie was arrested by MPs and held for questioning, during which he firmly held his ground. He was summarily court-martialed for insubordination to the supervising officer at the scene. Not surprisingly, given his career and his history of impeccable personal conduct, Robinson was exonerated by the court. At first put on permanent leave, Robinson was finally honorably discharged on November 28, 1944, ostensibly for physical reasons related to his ankle.

Out of the army, Robinson kicked around searching for work. He was looking forward to a tryout the next spring with the Kansas City Monarchs that he had arranged earlier in 1944 (thanks to a timely run-in with ex-Monarchs pitcher Ted Alexander, stationed at Camp Breckinridge, Kentucky). He had reservations about the transient lifestyle of the average blackball player, including the physical discomforts of life on the road, the hostility of Jim Crow America, and infrequent paychecks of varying size—but he needed a prospect. To tide himself over in the interim, Jackie secured a position as physical education instructor at the all-black Samuel Huston Methodist University, in Austin, Texas.

Although he didn't shine at the tryouts for the Monarchs, Robinson was taken on as starting shortstop for the team, which at the time had a roster thinned by the draft. As usual, Robinson made the most of the opportunity, hitting .345 for the season, with ten doubles, five triples, and five home runs

(as always, an estimate based on the best available evidence). He was chosen as the starting shortstop for the West in the East-West All-Star Game.

From his experiences in multiracial Pasadena as a youth to his sports training in high school and college to his brush with institutionalized racism in the army to the time he spent with the Monarchs, every event in Robinson's life seems in retrospect to

* * * *

Officer Jack Roosevelt Robinson of the U.S. Army. His experiences fighting racism in the army helped prepare him for the sustained physical and mental effort it would take to integrate major league baseball.

have conspired to prepare him for his role as the integrator of major league baseball. A deeply religious man, Robinson would no doubt have attributed such steady guidance to God's hand. At any rate, the time for the integration of major league baseball—and the end of the Negro leagues—was not far off.

Shortly after he was taken on by the Monarchs, and just before the beginning of the major league season, Robinson and two other Negro league players, Sam Jethroe and Marvin Williams, had a tryout with the Boston Red Sox. The event had been organized by Boston councilman Isadore Muchnik, who in turn had been influenced by sportswriter Wendell Smith, an outspoken black journalist (for the black *Pittsburgh Courier*) who was part of a small but vocal group of writers and celebrities that condemned segregation, especially in sports. Nothing came of the tryout (even though Robinson was by all reports superb), but it was a dry run for events that would occur later in the year. On August 24, 1945, at a game against the Lincoln Giants in Comiskey Park, Chicago, Robinson was approached by Dodgers scout Clyde Sukeforth. Sukeforth would only—or could only—say that Dodgers general manager Branch Rickey wanted to talk to Robinson about playing for the Brown Dodgers. He also said (and this was as mysterious to Sukeforth as it was to Robinson) that if Jackie wouldn't go to Brooklyn, then Rickey would come to him. Jackie, who was tired of life as a Negro leaguer and intrigued by the overture, grabbed his things and headed for New York City with Sukeforth.

The August 28 meeting that took place between Rickey and Robinson is of such importance to the history of twentieth-century race relations that accounts of it tend to smack of the apocryphal. Although it is difficult to overestimate the significance of the encounter, it is also very easy to overdramatize what took place in that office on Montague Street in Brooklyn—not least because Rickey himself had a definite flair for the dramatic. Certainly both men would have been aware that something momentous might come of their collaboration, something beyond the realization of their personal ambitions.

Having spent the previous night in Harlem, Robinson was escorted by Sukeforth into Rickey's office. Robinson and Rickey sized each other up before Rickey asked if Robinson wanted a shot at playing for the Dodgers organization, first with the minor league Montreal Royals and, if all went well, ultimately with the Dodgers themselves. Robinson was floored. Yes, he wanted the chance. Rickey asked if Robinson had the guts to go through with what would be a torturous, painful journey toward integration. Robinson became defensive and asked if Rickey was wondering if he wasn't brave enough to fight back, to which Rickey responded that he wanted someone courageous enough to not fight back. His contention was that a combative player would set the cause back twenty years, whereas only a player who fought (and won) with just his glove and bat could integrate the majors. To illustrate what Robinson might face in the coming years, Rickey thundered up and down his office, pretending first to be a racist hotel clerk, then a hostile fan; now a prejudiced waiter, and now a southern ballplayer with hatred in his heart. Jackie was stunned, but by the time he left the office some two hours later he had signed an agreement saying he would play for the Royals. He had also agreed to keep the agreement under wraps.

Robinson returned to the Monarchs (who were not happy that he had mysteriously traipsed off to New York) with understandably little enthusiasm. Suspecting that Jackie was looking for another job, the Monarchs gave him an ultimatum: play the full season with the Monarchs or leave the team. With Rickey's ace up his sleeve, Robinson was only too happy to abandon ship, and

soon after he took off for California to join Rachel and his family. October found Robinson back in New York on a stopover on his way to Venezuela to fulfill a promise he had made to barnstorm in South America. Coincidentally (or providentially, depending on one's point of view), New York politics

* * * *

*On April 18, 1946, opening day of
International League play, rookie
Jackie Robinson of the Montreal Royals,
a farm team for the Brooklyn Dodgers,
poses for photographers.*

conspired to force Rickey's hand with Robinson in town. Mayor Fiorello La Guardia, wanting to secure the black vote for the upcoming election, began pressuring local franchises to make progressive changes with regard to the hiring of African-Americans. Rather than have his plan appear to be the result of such political machinations, Rickey preemptively announced that the Dodgers would be signing Jackie Robinson to the Royals. Not surprisingly, the brief press conference and ensuing coverage inspired much debate and commentary.

Predictably, the most stinging rebukes were delivered by whites, and for a variety of reasons. Some accused Rickey of using the "black race" for his own benefit while others derided him for picking the wrong player. J.L. Wilkinson raged, citing breach of contract and lack of compensation. But the black press by and large endorsed the signing, some going so far as to describe Rickey as a crusader for equal rights nonpareil. For his part, Rickey blasted back at the Monarchs patriarch by saying that he recognized no such formal body as the Negro leagues, and that any contracts or arrangements Robinson might have made with Kansas City were meaningless. While some revisionist historians have taken Rickey to task for his denigration of the Negro leagues and charge that in signing Robinson he was merely succumbing to politics, it is more accurate to view Rickey as one of the true champions of integration. For no matter what initial pressures Rickey encountered over the ensuing months, he stood strong against the unified opposition of every other major league owner and, enabled by his alliance with Commissioner Chandler, carefully put together and executed a plan for breaking down baseball's color barrier.

As an outspoken champion of equal rights—as well as a mentor to the new recruit on the diamond—Rickey earned Robinson's undying respect, particularly during the early days of Royals training camp in 1946. Playing exhibition games throughout southern Florida, the team faced innumerable difficulties because Robinson was on board. Frequently the team was barred from even taking the field against opponents due to the integrated roster; to his credit, Rickey canceled many games as a result, taking the loss in revenue rather than jeopardizing the fragile chemistry he was trying to foster. And while this must have generated resentment among the other players on the team, Rickey was careful to make sure at every step of the way that Robinson knew he was supported in full by his general manager. As Rachel was in his personal life, Rickey was his staff on the field.

Robinson was under the microscope wherever he went. Not only was he followed everywhere by Wendell Smith and photographer Billy Rowe (who together had an exclusive on one of the most important sports stories in American history), he was closely scrutinized by the media at large. Jackie's every mistake was magnified and every accomplishment diminished in the mainstream (white) press while he was lionized by the independent (black) press. Meanwhile, Rickey maintained a calm demeanor, never once giving a hint that he had any doubt that Robinson would perform. And when opening day arrived for the International League in Jersey City, New Jersey, all of Rickey's faith and careful planning—and all of Robinson's skills and moral strength—bore fruit. Robinson was exquisite, hitting safely in four out of five appearances at the plate (including a home run), causing numerous throwing errors with his daring base running, and fielding well (if not perfectly) at second, a position he had only just learned to handle during training camp. The Royals beat the Jersey City Giants 14–1 that April 18, and Robinson was the star. It was an indication of the success to come for the team, though there were to be many painful hurdles along the way for the rookie.

The next team the Royals played was the Baltimore Orioles, in Baltimore, which was essentially the South. There the reception was extremely hostile, and a rain of abuse showered down on Robinson from the stands. Rachel was frightened and dismayed as she was forced to listen to the din of the angry crowd around her, their voices hoarse from screaming unmentionable insults throughout the game. It was among the most trying of such experiences, but by no means was it an isolated event. Throughout the season Jackie would suffer the abuse of small-minded, racist, and hateful people on other teams, in public institutions, and in the stands.

Jackie felt the pressure, of course, taking great pleasure when he excelled and becoming deeply depressed at his mistakes—as he would all season, conscious as he was of the many African-Americans who were counting on him to win the fight for integration. When the team finally went to Montreal for its first home stand, the Robinsons were delighted to find themselves warmly welcomed both into the fans' hearts and into the community. It was a stark contrast to their recent experiences at the training camp in Florida and in Baltimore. Soon, Jackie would become a hero to the Royals faithful, who called him the "Colored Comet" (for his blazing speed around the base paths).

The Royals fans' adulation was warranted, for Jackie led the storied minor league team through its greatest season to date. Setting a team batting record, Jackie was undeniably the best player in the International League, a view that was held even by those who had been openly skeptical about his ability to play at the beginning of the season (including his own manager, Clay Hopper, a Mississippi plantation owner). Running away with their division, the Royals went through a grueling seven-game playoff on their way to face the Louisville Colonels in the Little World Series. The first three games, played in Louisville, mirrored the Baltimore experience in viciousness, ignominiously bracketing the season. The Royals went down in the series two games to one as Robinson slumped, his poor performance egging the Louisville crowd on to ever more wicked abuse. But when the series returned to Montreal, the Royals closed it out in seven behind the awesome play of Robinson. He was mobbed by the adoring Canadian fans on the field and again as he tried to leave the stadium, after having scored the last run in the last game, on October 4, 1946.

Jackie returned to California to join Rachel during the last stage of her pregnancy, hoping no doubt that the call to the majors would soon come from Rickey. The amazing 1946 season had shown he had the skills and the strength to integrate the majors, but his endurance was another matter altogether. As successful as Robinson had been on the field, the strain of keeping his cool and internalizing his reactions to the abuse he had suffered was exacting a terrible toll. Nonetheless, he was as determined as Rickey to complete the "noble experiment" they had begun. In the last game of a series of 1947 spring training exhibition games between the the Dodgers and Royals, the historic announcement was made: Jackie Robinson's contract had been bought by the Dodgers and he would be playing at first base (second base and shortstop were already manned by two stars, Eddie Stanky and Pee Wee Reese, respectively). The wall of segregation was crumbling.

Meanwhile, 1946 was a surprisingly good year for the Negro leagues. As fans continued to flock to NAL and NNL games, Negro league team owners and players ignored the writing on the wall. Many people even claimed that the Negro leagues would thrive next to the integrated majors, but that was wishful thinking. In another couple of years, the rosters of all Negro league teams would be severely depleted, and many teams—and the Negro National League itself—would disappear altogether. After

Robinson's breakthrough year with the Dodgers in 1947 (in which every Negro league team reported financial losses), all eyes in the United States, black and white, were on the majors. By 1949, when Robinson had his best individual year ever (he was voted MVP), the Negro American League—now split into two divisions to give some semblance of a rivalry in the vacuum left by the defunct NNL—was on its own. There was no Colored World Series for the first time since 1942, and there would never be another. Amazingly, the East-West All-Star Game had one of the highest attendances ever—48,112—but it was the event's swan song; in 1949, attendance was down to 26,697 and by 1951 the event was gone for good.

Of course, Jackie Robinson's major league career is now solidly part of American postwar mythology. After a slow start at the beginning of the 1947 season, he rebounded, hitting .297, winning the Rookie of the Year award, and carrying the Dodgers to the World Series (which they lost to the Yankees in seven games). Between 1947 and 1956, when Jackie retired, the Dodgers went to the October Classic six times, winning in 1955. Of course, racism and prejudice

✳ ✳ ✳ ✳

OPPOSITE: *Looking a little melancholy, the Cuban All Stars pose in front of empty grandstands sometime in 1942. Within a few short years of Jackie Robinson's entry into the major leagues, empty grandstands would become the norm at Negro league games. By the mid-1950s, the all-black game had just about disappeared.*
RIGHT: *It didn't take long for black players to establish themselves in the major league game—or to become heroes to all fans of baseball, black and white alike. Here superstars Willie Mays (left) and Ernie Banks pose in front of an adoring crowd of youngsters.*

followed him and the Dodgers everywhere, especially in 1947. There were two particularly vicious incidents that year, one in Philadelphia (where Phillies manager Ron Chapman incited the southern members of his team to hurl terrible abuse at Jackie) and the other in St. Louis (where the Cardinals nearly refused to play the Dodgers, thereby almost setting off a disaster within the National League). As per his agreement with Rickey, Robinson dealt with the on- and off-field

racism with great dignity, always appearing as a paragon of dignity, virtue, and courage.

With Robinson's great success in 1947, Negro league stars expected a rapid integration of the majors. As Monte Irvin put it, "There were ten, twenty, thirty guys who could just step right in." But rather than a steady flow, integration proceeded at a trickle. Through the 1950 season, only eleven black players besides Robinson made major league debuts: Dan Bankhead, Larry Doby, Willard Brown, and Hank Thompson in 1947; Roy Campanella and

that ageless wonder, Satchel Paige, in 1948; Luke Easter, Monte Irvin, Don Newcombe, and the first Latin African player, Orestes "Minnie" Minoso in 1949; and Sam Jethroe, the lone African-American rookie in 1950. Indeed, the wall of integration only really came down for good in 1951, when eight black rookies entered the major leagues, including the incomparable Willie Mays. Thirty-two more rookies of African descent would make the big show by 1954, including budding superstars Ernie Banks and Henry Aaron. By the end of the 1954 season, the Negro leagues were no longer a mandatory stepping stone for blacks on the path to the major leagues; by the same token, the few remaining Negro league teams could no longer cling to life by grooming young talent and selling them to the majors. By 1955, scouts for farm teams were actively recruiting African-American players.

For almost a quarter century following 1947, little credit was given to the Negro leagues for the role they played in integration. However, beginning with Robert Peterson's groundbreaking 1971 work *Only the Ball Was White*, it became clear to all who did not already know it that organzied blackball had set the table for integration, that there never would have been a Jackie Robinson without the likes of Josh Gibson, Oscar Charleston, and Rube Foster. Satchel Paige is not on the above list because his story was unique. A supremely talented athlete and showman with a personality perfectly suited to a life of carefully walking the race line without compromising his dignity or disowning his heritage, Paige was a figure whose greatness and agelessness probably would have secured his place in history even had integration not occurred in time for him to join the majors in the back stretch of his incredible career. When he was finally drafted, in 1948, it was the clap of doom for the Negro leagues. Even at his relatively advanced age, Paige was still the biggest draw in the Negro leagues. His departure caused the dike to burst once and for all.

Epilogue

In April 1997, an impressive group of luminaries—including major league officials, sportswriters, all-time great baseball players, the President of the United States, and Rachel Robinson—gathered at Shea Stadium in New York City to memorialize the fiftieth anniversary of Jackie Robinson's debut in major league baseball. "There are defining moments," President Clinton said, "in the life of a nation when a single individual can shape events for generations to come. For America, the spring of 1947 was such a moment, and Jackie Robinon was the man who made the difference." In a ceremony before that night's Mets–Dodgers game, presided over by acting Commisioner of Baseball Bud Selig, Major League Baseball took the unprecendented step of retiring a number—42, Robinson's number when he played for the Brooklyn Dodgers—for perpetuity for all major league teams. The event functioned both as a celebration of how far the nation has come in its struggle against the pernicious effects of racism, whether institutionalized or otherwise,

* * * *

OPPOSITE: *Hank Aaron breaks one of baseball's most cherished records, swatting his 715th career home run to relegate the Bambino to second place all-time. Symbolically, the feat had enormous resonance; Aaron received numerous racially motivated death threats against himself and his loved ones as he approached the milestone.*

ABOVE: *Overdue recognition is accorded to some of the greatest Negro league players at a reunion in 1991, including (back row, from left) Josh Johnson, Bobby Robinson, Double Duty Radcliffe, Ernie Banks, Napoleon Golley, Josh Gibson Jr., Bob Harvey, Monte Irvin, Willie Mays; (front row, from left) Marlin Carter, Jimmie Crutchfield, George Giles, Bubba Hyde, Armando Vazquez, Wild Bill Wright, Verdell Mathis, and Frank Evans.*

and also served notice for how far there is still
to go.

Indeed, there are several telling facts about the
relationship between African-Americans and the
national pastime that betray a continuing imbalance
in the United States—the legacy of the nation's long
history of racial inequality. For instance, at this writing there are no black general managers in the major
leagues. The trailblazing Bob Watson presided over
the New York Yankees 1996 World Championship
but was Steinbrennered (i.e., fired) a year later—
and there has never been black ownership of a major
league baseball franchise. This absence of black
ownership would have especially irked Rube Foster,
let alone such men as W.E.B. DuBois and Martin
Luther King, Jr., who recognized that economic
empowerment and self-determination was integral
to the struggle to overcome racism in any and every
industry, including baseball, and also throughout
American society at large.

Another symbol that all is not well with race
relations in baseball at the turn of the millennium
is the relative dearth of black American pitchers at
the major league level. The present generation of
baseball stars includes an abundance of African-
American talent—with such phenomenal players as
Barry Bonds, Ken Griffey, Jr., Frank Thomas, Derek
Jeter, Mo Vaughn, and incomparable veterans Tony
Gwynn and Ricky Henderson—but none of the
superstar pitchers is a black American. While there
is an abundance of Latin American pitchers who are
black, most notably superstar Pedro Martinez, there
are only a handful of African-American pitchers in
the majors, and there have been no top-flight stars
since Dwight Gooden's and Dave Stewart's heydays
in the late 1980s.

There is another aspect to the state of American
baseball that clearly highlights how far there is still
to go in the establishment of a truly equal society.
For almost as long as there has been organized
baseball, there has been little league baseball,

* * * *

OPPOSITE: *It is fitting that Satchel Paige became the first Negro league player elected to the Hall of Fame, in celebration of which this photograph was taken, February 9, 1971. It was a long time coming, however, and countless more stars of the Negro leagues have yet to be recognized for their immeasurable contributions to the game of baseball.*

ABOVE: *Buck O'Neil, circa 1994.*

RIGHT: *William "Judy" Johnson had one of the great Negro league careers. He played for eighteen years, almost exclusively in Pennsylvania, for several of the great teams of the ECL, including the Grays, Crawfords, and Daisies. He was inducted into the Hall of Fame in 1975.*

where small kids are cast in the mold of their adult counterparts. Unlike the major league game, however, little league baseball is predominantly played by whites. In part this is because, unlike basketball, for instance—where all you need to play is a ball and a hoop, which is often provided by municipal parks departments or schoolyards—baseball is an equipment-intensive sport that requires a well-kept playing field. Because many black youths grow up disadvantaged, it is harder for them to play organized baseball; put quite simply, in most instances, the African-American community cannot afford it. In affluent (white) suburbs, where families can afford uniforms and league fees and have one parent who has the time required to drive to little league games, the game flourishes but does not reflect the racial makeup of the country as a whole. And of course, the little league world series is lily-white.

On some level, the little league game reflects (albeit more visibly) the implicit racism that continues to inform the game on the major league level. It is ironic, for instance, that the old-boys network that owns and runs much of baseball today seems to be wedded to the project of preserving the all-white image of the game (in management and ownership, on the mound, and so on) when it could be argued that African-American involvement has insured baseball's survival, and perhaps even driven its phenomenal success. More ironic still is the fact that many of the greatest players in the modern history of the game have been African-Americans, from the prototypical baseball wunderkind Jackie Robinson (an All-American in several sports) to the current crop of black superstars.

Since its invention, baseball has been central in the American consciousness. A sport that's easy to learn and immediately rewarding to play—and has room to accommodate several different skill sets— it is an equal opportunity contest. It requires teamwork, but can also be a showcase for individual talent. In so many ways, therefore, baseball reflects the

structure of democracy. And yet, for the better part of baseball's existence as a professional sport, a huge percentage of the population was denied access to major league ball because they were not white. In this way, organized professional baseball has not lived up to its democratic promise, even now that many different ethnicities have risen to the highest levels of athletic achievement in the sport. The few enshrinements in the Hall of Fame aside, Major League Baseball, the media, and the nation at large have yet to take advantage of the leveling and elevating properties of baseball to open a progressive dialog on the issue of race in the United States. Until they do, though, at least baseball will continue to be open to all people, regardless of their color, creed, or religion—truly, a game for all races.

Bibliography

Bruce, Janet. *The Kansas City Monarchs: Champions of Black Baseball.* Lawrence, Kansas: University of Kansas Press, 1987.

Burns, Ken, and Geoffrey C. Ward, with S.A. Kramer. *Shadow Ball: The History of the Negro Leagues.* New York: Alfred A. Knopf, 1994.

Chadwick, Bruce. *When the Game Was Black and White: The Illustrated History of Baseball's Negro Leagues.* New York: Abbeville Press, 1992.

Craft, David. *The Negro Leagues.* New York: Crescent Books, 1993.

Dixon, Phil, with Patrick J. Hannigan. *The Negro Baseball Leagues: A Photographic History.* Mattituck, N.Y.: Amereon Press, 1992.

Dorinson, Joseph, and Joram Warmund, Eds. *Jackie Robinson: Race, Sports, and the American Dream.* Armonk, N.Y.: M.E. Sharpe, 1998.

Frommer, Harvey. *Rickey and Robinson: The Men Who Broke Baseball's Color Barrier.* New York: MacMillan, 1982.

Holway, John. *Black Diamonds: Life in the Negro Leagues from the Men Who Lived It.* New York: Stadium Books, 1991.

————, John. *Blackball Stars: Negro League Pioneers.* New York: Carroll & Graf, 1992.

————, John. *Voices from the Great Black Baseball Leagues.* New York: Dodd, Mead, & Co., 1975.

Humphrey, Kathryn Long. *Satchel Paige.* New York: Franklin Watts, 1988.

Leonard, Buck, with James A. Riley. *Buck Leonard: The Black Lou Gehrig.* New York: Carroll and Graf, 1995.

Moffi, Larry, and Jonathan Kronstadt. *Crossing the Line: Black Major Leaguers, 1947–1959.* Iowa City: University of Iowa Press, 1994.

O'Neil, Buck, with Steve Wulf and David Conrads. *I Was Right On Time.* New York: Simon and Schuster, 1996.

Peterson, Robert. *Only the Ball Was White.* New York: Oxford University Press, 1992.

Rampersad, Arnold. *Jackie Robinson: A Biography.* New York: Alfred A. Knopf, 1997.

Ribowsky, Mark. *A Complete History of the Negro Leagues.* New York: Birch Lane Press, 1995.

————. *Don't Look Back: Satchel Paige in the Shadows of Baseball.* New York: Simon and Schuster, 1994.

————. *The Power and the Darkness: The Life of Josh Gibson in the Shadows of the Game.* New York: Simon and Schuster, 1996.

Riley, James A. *The Biographical Encyclopedia of the Negro Leagues.* New York: Carroll & Graf, 1994.

Robinson, Jackie, as told to Alfred Duckett. *I Never Had it Made: An Autobiography.* Hopewell, N.J.: The Ecco Press, 1995.

Rogosin, Donn. *Invisible Men: Life in Baseball's Negro Leagues.* New York: Atheneum, 1983.

Rust, Art, Jr. *"Get that Nigger off the Field."* New York: Delacorte Press, 1976.

Sugar, Bert Randolph. *The 100 Greatest Boxers of All Time,* rev. ed. New York: Bonanza Books, 1989.

Tygiel, Jules. *Baseball's Great Experiment: Jackie Robinson and His Legacy.* New York: Oxford University Press, 1983.

————, Ed. *The Jackie Robinson Reader: Perspectives on an American Hero.* New York: Dutton, 1997.

Various, eds. *The Baseball Encyclopedia: The Complete and Definitive Record of Major League Baseball,* Ninth Edition. New York: Macmillan Publishing Co., 1993.

White, Sol. *Sol White's History of Colored Base Ball: With Other Documents on the Early Black Game, 1886–1936.* Lincoln: University of Nebraska Press, 1996.

Index

FIRST COLORED WORLD SERIES.
G GAME, OCT. 11, 1924.   KANSAS CITY, MO.

FOSTER   BOLDEN   SANTOP   WINTERS   CURRIE   LEE   CARR   C. JOHNSON   J. JOHNS